Windows System Policies

This book is dedicated to my soul mate, Janice

Contents

Preface

This book is an attempt to paint the broad and detailed picture of system policies and user profiles for NT networks (Windows NT 4.0 and the new version Windows 2000), as well as Windows 98 network clients. For most of us, even if we could install NT on every workstation, we probably have some Windows 98 systems still waiting to upgrade. Or not.

If you've read this far, and you primarily support Windows 95, fear not—the notes on Windows 98 apply to you, for the most part, as do the deployment, troubleshooting, and registry chapters. The book is divided into 16 chapters that can be read from cover to cover or used as a resource for system policies and user profiles.

The first chapter introduces you to the concept of a system policy and user profiles; the theories introduced in this chapter are used throughout the remainder of the book. The choices for system policies in the Microsoft world of systems and application software are also presented.

Chapter 2 deals with the NT user environment, details of the security levels that can be deployed from the user profile types available to security levels at the file and folder level, and how system policies are actually deployed.

Next, Chapter 3 details how to install the system policy editor for both NT and Windows 95/98 worlds. System policy templates for all platforms are introduced.

A detailed resource listing for Windows NT workstations and Windows 98 clients is detailed in Chapter 4. I find it's much easier to use this chapter for highlighting the choices I want to deploy and then going to the computer with a clear idea as to what settings to deploy.

Deploying system policies and user profiles may be a huge change in your company, and that's what Chapter 5 is for—to pose some questions you probably haven't thought of. Work through this chapter before deploying system policies. Internet Explorer has some nifty deployment tools of its own, as well as many system policy settings. Learn about the IEAK (the Internet Explorer administration kit) and how to create your own custom builds in Chapter 6.

All system policy settings are really registry settings. What happens when you check or uncheck a system policy setting and the results are not what you expected? It's then time to go under the hood into the Registry. Chapter 7 gives you a crash course in Registry settings and concepts as they apply to system policies.

Do you want to create your own system policy templates? Then Chapter 8 is for you. It's relatively easy to create your own custom templates once you know about the Registry and its structure. Using the Policy Template Editor software from *www.tools4nt.com/* turbocharges the process.

Don't you just love it when things go off the rails? When system policies and user profiles go bad, turn to Chapter 9 to help troubleshoot policy and profile problems. Office 97 has a wealth of system policy settings for both Windows 95/98 and NT clients. Get the highlighter out and start marking up Chapter 10.

Just when you get used to the Policy Editor, Microsoft goes and changes things. That's right—in Windows 2000, system policies get a facelift and morph into group policy. Chapter 11 is your primer for understanding Windows 2000 and group policy. Chapter 12 is a resource chapter on Windows 98 Second Edition and the additional system policy settings for the latest Windows 98 version.

If and when your company migrates to Office 2000, you'll be pleased to know that system policy templates are available that are much more powerful. Complete drop-down menus can now be disabled, and there are a plethora of new settings for you to consider in Chapter 13.

Chapter 14 introduces a different flavor of Windows NT called Terminal Server. This concept is important to be aware of because Terminal Server is also a network service in Windows 2000. User profiles and system policy settings take on a new focus when you are running all of your software from the server in "Terminal Mode."

NetWare users and administrators, take heart—I haven't forgotten you. Chapter 15 deals with the NetWare client and NetWare templates available for system policies.

And finally, Chapter 16 concludes the book with notes on ZAK. No, ZAK is not a Dr. Seuss character; it's the Zero Administration Kit from Microsoft. ZAK is another flavor of system policy settings and security for Windows 95/98 and NT clients for you to consider.

So enjoy, and it's my hope that you find this material useful and relevant for your users and network.

—Mark Wilkins
Mwilkins@sympatico.ca

Windows System Policies

Introduction

Hello and welcome to system policies for NT and Windows 2000. You hold in your hands a technical document that will be indispensable in aiding you in your successful design and rollout of system polices and user profiles for NT and Windows 2000.

In the Beginning...

The idea for this book came several years ago with the release of
Windows 95. Included in the initial version of Windows 95 was a
small utility called the *system policy editor* and a feature called
user profiles. At first glance, they didn't seem very useful, but in
those early days of supporting Windows 95 there was a lot of
new information to learn and use properly. See Figure 1-1.

A few months later it was evident that the system policy editor
was a valuable tool for editing the Registry and creating system
policies for securing our end users and workstations, and user
profiles could be valuable for computer systems shared by more
than one user.

However, the major problem with successfully deploying system policies was the lack of readable documentation—the
resource guide for Windows 95 had several errors and the system
policies themselves had several bugs.

Figure 1-1 *The system policy editor in Windows 95.*

When Windows NT 4.0 was released in 1996, the system policy editor and user profiles were included with NT Server but still with no documentation—a situation made even worse by the many bugs included with system policies and user profiles. But, by the time Service Pack 3 was released, system policies and user profiles actually began to show some promise.

So it was no wonder that when Microsoft surveyed its users to see how they were getting used to using the new Explorer desktop and other new features of the operating system, the results were discouraging to say the least. Only 20 percent of the people surveyed knew about and used system policies and user profiles. Even more amazing, only 40 percent knew about the right mouse button and its uses!

Microsoft has still not documented *in one location*, however, how system policies and user profiles actually work for the NT 4.0 world. You can get many technical articles on TechNet and at the Microsoft Web site on system policies and user profiles— hence, the bright idea to include as much information on system policies and user profiles in one resource.

This book has been written with the aim of completing the documentation cycle. I know you will find it useful regardless of the Windows platform you are currently supporting or migrating to.

So Many Window Flavors, So Little Time

Although the computer media covers the latest Windows versions with much hype, the fact is, the corporate world does not move to every new Windows release as fast as it might seem. For example, one of the largest Windows 3.1 site licenses was located in Hawaii at Kamehameha Schools Bishop Estate, where thousands of users are just now beginning to adopt Windows 95.

Windows 3.X users mostly upgraded to Windows 95 in 1995-1996, ignoring Windows NT 3.51. When Windows 98 was released, most Windows 95 users didn't choose to upgrade unless a new computer purchase was in the cards.

In 1996 when Windows NT 4.0 was released, about 15 percent of Windows 95 users migrated to NT and about 50 percent of

Windows 3.51 NT users migrated to Windows NT 4.0. However, there were still not a huge number of NT 4.0 users by the end of 1998; now, midway through 1999 the surge toward NT 4.0 is finally starting to happen, exactly at the time that Microsoft details its plans to release Windows 2000 (formally NT 5).

So when I talk to many corporate administrators I find the following server/client picture repeating itself over and over.

The New Corporate Computer User

The choice for Administrators when adding a new corporate computer user is usually the Windows NT 4.0 workstation, due to the fact it has a full-fledged security system and it is much more stable than either Windows 95 or Windows 98.

The New Home User

Home users and students are more likely to choose Windows 98 because it allows them to play computer games, period. NT is not even a consideration for the home user at this point due to the mix of older hardware and software.

Network File Servers

The network file servers in use today follow these general rules:

- New network installs are Windows NT Server 4.0
- File server upgrades are 60 percent NT Server, as NetWare is ousted altogether and 40 percent stay the course with NetWare 4 and 5
- If the existing platform is NetWare, then Windows NT usually appears in the organization as an application server

System Policies and Mixing and Matching

And now the good news: If your workstation client is Windows 95/98 or NT 4.0 and your server is either Windows NT 4.0, NetWare 3, 4, or 5, or any file server that understands and reads a

UNC network path (\\Server\path), then system policies can be used successfully. If you are using Windows 95/98 or NT clients with NT 4.0 Servers, then system policies and user profiles are fully supported.

What's a System Policy Anyway?

A *system policy* is first and foremost an extra level of security that you can deploy to control users, groups of users, and the computers your users work on, across your network. The security settings that you deploy through a system policy are numerous, and ever increasing. Choices are displayed through a *system policy template*, also called an *administrative template*, with an .ADM extension, that can be either checked off to enable the selected option, or cleared to disable the selected option. See Figure 1-2.

All system policy options are written to the Registry of the local workstation and user. The word *Registry* defines the master database, the "Yellow Pages" of your Windows 95/98, NT 4.0, and 2000 computer system. User, system, and software settings are all stored in the Registry. When a system policy is enabled and deployed, new Registry settings are written to the computer's Registry and to the user's own local Registry.

Note

A system policy is deployed from a POL file located on the network. For all flavors of NT 4.0, the POL file is NTCONFIG.POL; for Windows 95/98, the POL file is CONFIG.POL. For Windows 2000 there are two POL files, both called REGISTRY.POL; one deploys computer settings and one deploys user settings.

The system policy editor for Windows 95/98 and NT 4.0 is called POLEDIT.EXE and a version for each operating system is included on the operating system media. The correct version of POLEDIT.EXE must be used for each operating system or else it gets very interesting. For Internet Explorer 4 and 5, the policy editor changes form in the IEAK (Internet Explorer Administrative Kit) to the IEAK Profile Manager (see Figure 1-3). However, the same ADM templates can be used and supported by POLEDIT.

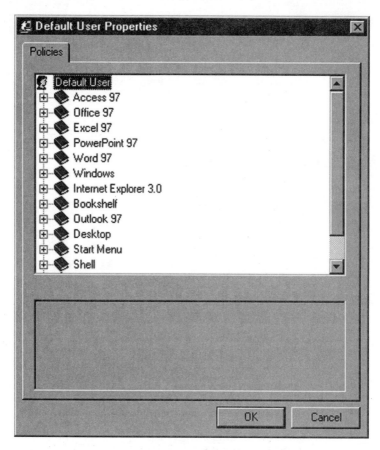

Figure 1-2 *System policy template options.*

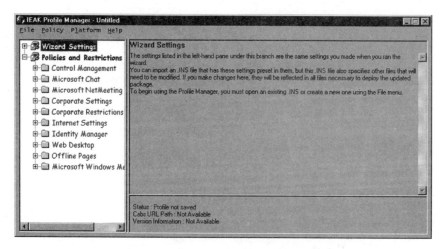

Figure 1-3 *The IEAK Profile Manager for Internet Explorer 5.*

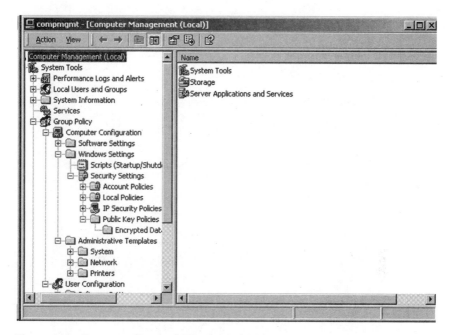

Figure 1-4 *Group policy and Windows 2000.*

Only with the release of Windows 2000 do we see the future for the system policy editor—it's gone! Don't panic; you can install it as an administrative tool for support of Windows 95/98 and NT 4.0 clients. But Windows 2000 clients do not support system policies using the system policy editor POLEDIT—the name of the game is now called *group policy*. See Figure 1-4.

The common thread holding all of the versions of system policies together is the ADM template although the templates for Windows 2000 have a slightly different design.

What's a User Profile?

A user profile is in force with every version of Windows since Windows 95. All of your own user settings, the color of your background, your screen saver, your file locations are called your *user profile*. Windows 95/98, NT 4.0, and 2000 clients can have their user settings automatically saved to a file server location and move with them around the network. See Figure 1-5.

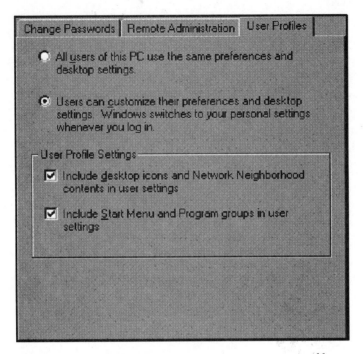

Figure 1-5 *Windows 98 can activate custom user profiles in the* Passwords *icon.*

If you have a home PC that you share with your family, the odds are that custom user profiles for each user are not turned on; however, you are all still sharing a user profile that defaults to every user. System policy settings overwrite user profile settings and computer settings.

Deployment of System Policies on Various Operating Systems

Let's overview the choices we have for deploying system policies. First we'll look at the client operating systems from Microsoft and see how user profiles and system policies apply.

Windows 95

Released in August 1995, Windows 95 had user profiles, the system policy editor, and NETSETUP. User profiles could be enabled through the `Passwords` icon in the Control Panel. Once custom user profiles were enabled, they became "roaming user profiles." If you had a NetWare or NT Server 4.0, there was a possibility of your user profile ending up on the file server in the home directory.

User profiles could be defined as local, roaming, or mandatory. System policies were deployed with POLEDIT and only one system policy template file was available: `ADMIN.ADM`.

A sampling of the user security settings that you could deploy through a system policy for Windows 95 Clients were:

- Require validation by the NetWare or NT network before Windows loaded
- Minimum Windows password length
- Restrict the Control Panel applets
- Disable the addition or deletion of printers
- Hide the device manager
- Disable any changes to virtual memory
- Disable the file and print sharing controls
- Disable the registry editor REGEDIT
- Disable the MS-DOS prompt and MS-DOS apps

These settings are still valid for Windows 95 and Windows 98 second edition. Windows 95 also provided support for deploying Windows 95 from the server. Since most PCs came with Windows 95, the NETSETUP utility was largely unused; however, it's interesting to examine to see how it applies to system policies.

It was not included and supported for Windows 95 version B and C, so it's only a point of interest about the early beginnings of system policies. The interesting part about NETSETUP is that it displayed choices using a system policy template called `NETSETUP.ADM`. See Figure 1-6.

If you had used NETSETUP for deploying Windows 95 it saved the settings in an `INF` or `Information` file. The choices we could deploy with NETSETUP were:

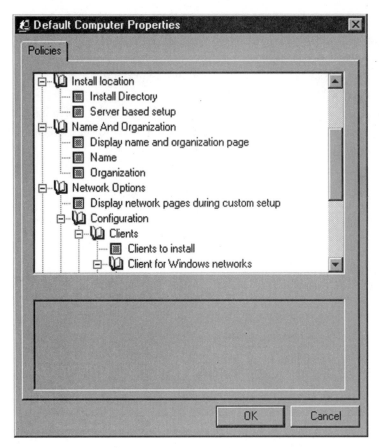

Figure 1-6 NETSETUP *options for network installation of Windows 95.*

- *Name and Organization.* This section could be used to update a user's registered name as well as the company name should some computers have to be moved around the company.

- *Most Recently Used Paths.* This section could be used for entering the most recently used paths for easy updating of new users with Windows 95 from the server.

Windows 98

Everything that was true for Windows 95 is true for Windows 98, except that NETSETUP is no longer with us. User profiles were the same and system polices had more ADM templates for

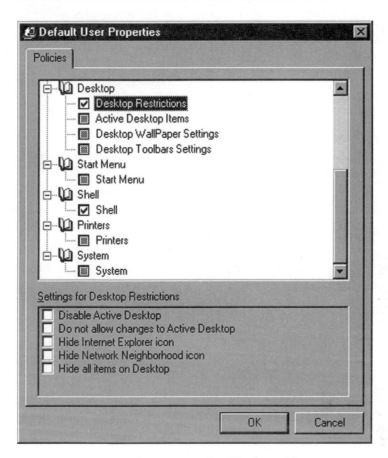

Figure 1-7 *New template settings for Windows 98.*

locking down the new Active Desktop plus Internet Explorer 4. A lot of the early bugs had been weeded out for user profiles and system policies. See Figure 1-7.

Windows 98 Second Edition

Ditto for Windows 98. The inclusion of a proxy server into this version of Windows 98 was all that is new. The plan is for Windows 98 to hang around for a few years yet. At this time of writing, Microsoft plans a new version of Windows 98 in the year 2000, called (drumroll please) *Millennium.* Then, the final version of "Windows 98" will occur in 2001. Yeah, right.

Windows NT Workstation 3.51

User profiles are present in NT 3.51 but are not the same as NT 4.0. The user profile is automatically updated the moment an NT 3.51 client logs onto an NT 4.0 server. System policies are not supported.

Windows NT 4.0

NT 4.0 was upgraded with the new Explorer shell and user profiles. User profiles could be local, roaming, or mandatory. System policies became more powerful with more choices. Settings common to Windows 98 and NT 4.0 were found in COMMON.ADM. Settings specific to NT 4.0 were found in WINNT.ADM.

The first versions of these templates were quite buggy—Service Pack 3 included bug-free versions of WINNT.ADM and COMMON.ADM, but forgot to update them when the service pack was applied. You have to do the update manually with the EXPAND command.

Windows NT 2000 Professional

This is the update for the NT 4.0 Workstation. User profiles are basically the same but with a few more options. System policies are the same concept but POLEDIT is not used for deploying system policy. The tool to use is called *group policy*, which allows you to deploy a wide variety of security, script, and policy settings. Group policy is not backward compatible with Windows NT 4.0 or Windows 98 at this time of writing.

Windows NT Server 4.0

System policies and user profiles for NT Workstation 4.0 are deployed from NT Server 4.0 Primary Domain Controllers. System policies can be defined for Global Groups and Users and Computer systems. Local Groups are not supported by system policies. At a minimum, Service Pack 3 should be installed, Service Pack 5 is the current offering. See Figure 1-8.

Windows NT 4.0 Enterprise Edition

A brief note on this version of NT. It was the first to allow the clustering of two NT Servers together for stability. Clustering has been rolled into Windows 2000 Advanced Server as a network

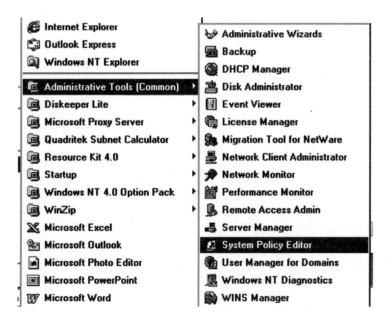

Figure 1-8 *The policy editor is installed on NT 4.0 servers.*

service called *IntelliMirror*. This service will provide offline storage, roaming folders, and data redundancy.

Windows Terminal Server

Terminal Server allows you to connect Network PCs or WYSE Terminals as NT clients. Terminal Server is NT Server 4.0 plus software licensed from Citrix that allows you to run all of your applications on the server but control them from a variety of network clients. Terminal Server also has system policy settings and its own Zero Administration Kit (ZAK).

Windows 2000 Server and Advanced Server

This is the next version of Windows NT. Many more Windows 2000 versions will be offered in the next few years. There will even be a 64-bit version of Windows NT 2000 called *Windows 2000 64*. Group policy controls all of the following features on Windows 2000 Professional clients. Sorry NT 4.0, you'd better upgrade—only limited support is provided.

- Groups of computers, groups, and users

- Registry-based policy settings

- Security settings

- Software installation

- Scripts—logon, logoff, startup, and shutdown

- Folder Redirection

Note

> The most important concept to understand about group policy is that it is deployed by default in Windows 2000, so you can't choose to ignore group policy. You have to deal with the security levels it sets in place after installation.

NetWare

NetWare 3.X and 4.X support system policies for users and computers but not groups of users. Windows 95 and 98 clients can have roaming or mandatory user profiles stored on NetWare servers but not NT 4.0 clients. ADM templates have been provided with the Windows 95, 98, and NT 4.0 IntraNetWare Client from NetWare. NetWare 5.0 has practically every feature of Windows 2000. See Figure 1-9.

Microsoft Software Applications

Other than the NetWare templates, Microsoft has the most system policy templates available. If you have any version of Internet Explorer, and any version of Office, you can control the software settings with system policies. With Internet Explorer, the menu item Tools | Internet Options allows you to set the majority of software settings for the operation of Internet Explorer. The system policy templates provided by Microsoft allow you to control the Tools | Internet Options settings from the network. There are many other options as well that deal with security, proxy settings, and Outlook Express options.

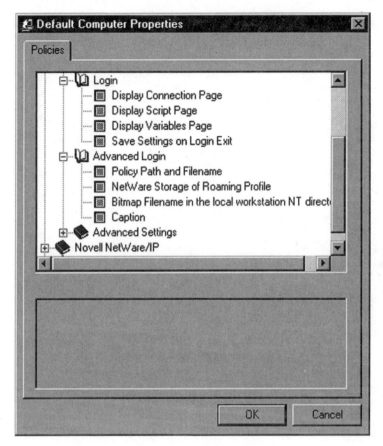

Figure 1-9 *NetWare template choices for NT clients.*

Office 95

Office 95 ADM template choices allowed you to control Word, Excel, and PowerPoint from a system policy for both users and computer.

Office 97

Office 97 ADM template choices allowed you to control Word, Excel, Access, and PowerPoint from a system policy for both users and computer. Clients could be either Windows NT 4.0 Workstation or Windows 95 or 98 clients. See Figure 1-10.

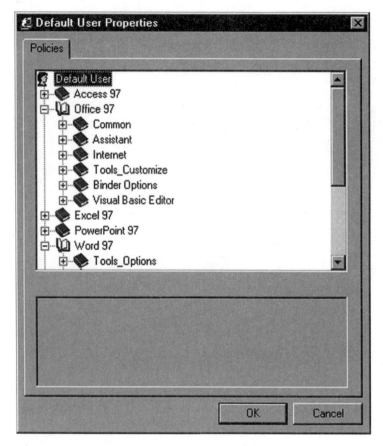

Figure 1-10 *Template choices for Office 97 users.*

Office 2000

The newest version of Office is designed for Windows 2000. It
will work on NT 4.0, but some of the system policy settings will
not work. The software applications that are now considered
Office 2000 worthy are Word, PowerPoint, Excel, Access, and
Outlook plus Publisher, Front Page, and Clip Art Gallery. There
are lots of new settings for controlling what menu items (File |
Edit | View | Insert | Format | Tools) can be removed or
shown (see Figure 1-11).

Internet Explorer 5

The latest version of Internet Explorer (IE5) has several ADM
templates to choose from. The templates for IE5 also show up in

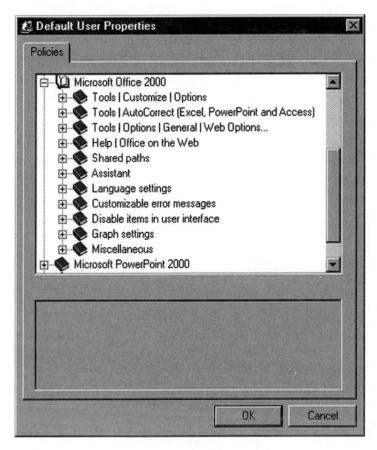

Figure 1-11 *Template choices for Office 2000 users.*

Windows 2000 as IE5 is built in. For the details on Internet Explorer 5 and the Internet Explorer Administrator Kit see Chapters 5 and 6.

A Quick Tour

A quick walk through this book will show you where to start. The book does not have to be read sequentially one chapter after the other; however, I suggest you first read Chapters 2 through 5 for the basics of user profiles and system policies.

Chapter 2: The NT User Environment Find out all about the NT security system and how user profiles and system polices are actually deployed.

Chapter 3: Installing and Using the System Policy Editor
Installing and using the system policy editor are explained in
detail along with explanations for computers, users, and
groups.

Chapter 4: Policy Templates in Windows NT 4.0   Find out
about the template choices for NT 4.0 users and computers.

Chapter 5: Deploying System Policies and User Profiles
Probably the most important chapter, the deployment of system policies and user profiles is a huge task. Lots of questions
and suggestions for the rollout.

Chapter 6: Internet Explorer 5 and Policy Settings   Tips on
using the IEAK to deploy custom packages of IE5. Full discus-
sion of ADM template choices.

Chapter 7: System Policies and the Registry   Detail on the
Registry and where system policies are stored in the Registry.
A must read if you are interested in creating custom ADM
templates.

Chapter 8: Creating Custom System Policy Templates   Programming requires lots of coffee and patience. Learn how to
create ADM templates and also troubleshoot template structure.

Chapter 9: Troubleshooting System Policies   Well, where do
you turn to when policies and profiles don't work—this chapter, of course. Lots of questions and answers plus details on
Service Packs 3, 4, and 5.

Chapter 10: Creating System Policies for Office 97   Template
details for Office 97 are discussed and detailed here.

Chapter 11: Creating System Policies for Windows 2000
Learn about Windows 2000 and group policy settings.

Chapter 12: System Policies for Windows 98   Windows 98
and Windows 98 second edition template settings are discussed.

Chapter 13: System Policies for Office 2000   Remember this
chapter when you are migrating to Office 2000. Full details on
the template choices are available.

Chapter 14: System Policies for Terminal Server   If you are
using Terminal Server or migrating to Windows 2000, this

chapter explains the concept of Terminal Server and its system policies.

Chapter 15: Mixed NetWare and NT Environments   If you are still supporting NetWare servers and/or NetWare Client software the details are here in this chapter.

Chapter 16: Rolling Out Zero Administration   Ever heard of Zero Administration? Although ZAK is now part of Windows 2000, it is still viable for NT 4.0 and Windows 98 clients.

The NT User Environment

This chapter acquaints you with the NT security system inherent in the operating system. You will learn:

- How user profiles are deployed for NT and Windows 98

- The difference between local, roaming, and mandatory user profiles

- How system policies are actually deployed

- The types of permissions we can deploy: directory and file

The NT operating system was designed and built with the security system involved with every operating system decision and process. When you sit down at your workstation or server and log in to access files and folders, the NT security system is always accessed; the users or group requesting consent for the task at hand must have the required permission or permissions to successfully continue. The pieces that make up NT security together provide a complete security environment.

System Logon

To actually use any NT computer system you will have to first log onto NT Workstation or Server and have your login name and password verified by the security system. You are then assigned an *access token*, which defines all the user groups to which you belong, plus the permissions that are enabled and disabled for the resources that are on the workstation or domain you are accessing.

- *User Profile.* You must have your own user profile with your name on it. No unknown users can access NT.

Login Script

A user *login script* that defines one or more startup conditions can be applied to each user. Login scripts can be applied to multiple users by using the %USERNAME% variable in the naming of the login script.

A System Policy

A *system policy* is a collection of registry settings that overwrite any current settings in your local Registry.

Permissions for Shares, Folders, and Files

In order to access any resource on your computer—files, folders, drives, printers—you must have been given the appropriate security permissions. (*Note*: I'm assuming that you are using the NT file system NTFS, which provides file and folder security.)

Understanding User Profiles

When you sit down at a Windows NT 4.0 or Windows 98 desktop and are presented with the Start Button and system icons, you are viewing and using your user profile. Your *user profile* is a section of the system database, called the *Registry*, that controls much of what goes on inside your computer.

The Registry is divided into three distinct sections of information: user profile settings, system settings, and system policy information.

- Desktop settings—like application preferences or screen colors—update the *user hive* portion of the Registry.

- Most of the network, hardware, and security access permissions and security parameters update the *system hive* portions of the Registry.

- System policy information is stored in specific policy folders in either the user or system hives of the Registry.

Note

Now before we go any further I must explain the word *hive*, a term used by Microsoft to describe the Registry database contained in NT. For some reason the hive word seems confusing to a lot of us. The real reason the word *hive* was adopted was because of an early system developer's insistence that a printed copy of the Registry database bore a striking resemblance to the inside of a bee hive. There now, not so scary is it? Just a word we have to get used to. My favorite Microsoft terms are *forests* and *trees*, which are used when describing clusters of NT Servers using the Active Directory Services. Can't see the forest for the trees? Oh well.

User profiles can be stored in two locations: locally in the WINNT \ PROFILES location or in a network location. The user profile can be further defined by the method in which it is used:

- As a local profile for a specific user
- As a roaming profile for a specific user
- As a roaming profile for a group of users

- As a mandatory profile for a specific user

- As a mandatory profile for a group of users

First, let's deal with the local user profile. If you're wondering why all the fuss about user profiles in a system policy book, the answer is simple: User profile settings can be controlled by system policy settings. Further, a system policy can overrule many user profile settings, providing that extra level of security.

NT 4.0 Local User Profiles

Each user must have a defined user profile combined with an active user account to be able to use any NT computer system. There is no option to cancel the login process and use the default user profile settings as we can do in Windows 98. A user profile is built from a Windows NT registry hive plus a set of profile template directories. The user profile registry hive is called NTUSER.DAT and is mapped immediately to the HKEY_CURRENT_USER section of the Registry once the user has successfully logged on. The folders that make up each user's template profile on an NT Workstation or Primary Domain Controller are stored under the path WINNT \ PROFILES.

This directory also stores the shortcut links, desktop icons, and startup applications for each new local user under two folders: ALL USERS and DEFAULT USER. See Figure 2-1.

All Users

The ALL USERS folder contains the "common" settings for the Desktop and Start menu. These settings are always available on an NT computer or server regardless of who is logged in. The quick way to view the All Users settings is by right-clicking on the Start menu and selecting Explore All Users. Only the defined Administrator can create, make changes to, or delete the common program groups.

Default User

The DEFAULT USER folder contains the default user hive NTUSER.DAT and the shortcuts to the installed Accessories found off the Start menu. See Figure 2-2.

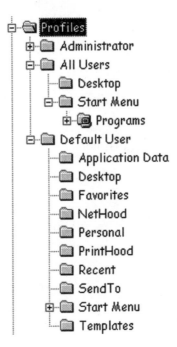

Figure 2-1 *The* Profiles *directory found on every NT computer.*

Windows NT Explorer settings	All settings changed from the default explorer settings plus persistent network settings
Taskbar	Personal program groups, program items, plus all taskbar settings
Printer settings	Network printer settings
Control Panel	User settings created in Control Panel
Accessories	User application settings including Calculator, Clock, Notepad, Paint, and others
Help bookmarks	Bookmarks created in Help

Figure 2-2 *Settings stored in the* NTUSER.DAT *hive.*

Settings	
Desktop	Desktop items including files, folders, and shortcuts
Favorites	Shortcuts to programs and Internet Explorer favorites
NetHood	Shortcuts to Network Neighborhood locations
Personal	The default storage folder for the user's documents
PrintHood	Shortcuts to printers
Recent	Shortcuts to the most recently used files also found on the `Start Menu	Documents`
SendTo	Shortcuts to storage media locations
Start Menu	Shortcuts to system and software items
Templates	Shortcuts to template items

Figure 2-3 *Settings stored in the* `WINNT \ Profiles \ Default Users` *directory.*

Settings Stored in the Default User's Folder

The `PROFILES \ DEFAULT USER` folder under `%SYSTEM ROOT%` contains the following additional folders. (Note that the `%SYSTEM ROOT%` is where the NT operating system has been installed, usually `\WINNT`.) See Figure 2-3.

Creating a New User Profile

As mentioned earlier, you must have a valid user account to access a computer system running NT. A user account must first be created using the administrative tool User Manager (for NT Workstations) or User Manager for Domains (for Primary Domain Controllers). Then the logon process actually begins when the user profile is created by the operating system, depending on several conditions that the administrator may have defined. See Figure 2-4.

New User

Username:	Mark		OK
Full Name:	Mark Wilkins		Cancel
Description:			Help
Password:	✕✕✕✕✕✕		
Confirm Password:	✕✕✕✕✕✕		

☑ User Must Change Password at Next Logon
☐ User Cannot Change Password
☐ Password Never Expires
☐ Account Disabled

Groups   Profile   Dialin

Figure 2-4 *Creating a new user with User Manager.*

Keep in mind that creating the user through this process does not create the user profile, but the action of logging in does.

Note

Steps in the Creation of a New Local User Profile

When a new user first logs onto an NT system, the default user shortcuts and folders located in the \WINNT\PROFILES\Default User folder, the default user's NTUSER.DAT hive file, and the short-cuts and folders located in \WINNT\PROFILES\ALL USERS are all copied into the newly created Users Profile folder creating the new user profile. See Figure 2-5.

UserData	SendTo	All Users	Start Menu	NetHood	PrintHood	Templates

Recent	Cookies	Personal	Desktop	Favorites	Application Data

History	Temporary Internet ...	ntuser.dat...	NTUSER....

Figure 2-5 *A new local user profile.*

From now on, whenever the user logs onto his or her NT computer system their individual user profile will be loaded for their use. As they install software and make changes to their system, the user profile accepts and stores the changes. This profile is accessible only on this computer. This example is the standard out-of-the-box process for user profile creation.

NT systems, however, can take advantage of two other types of user profiles called roaming and mandatory user profiles. Let's see how they are created and deployed.

Supporting User Profiles Through the Control Panel

The User Profiles tab in the System applet in the Control Panel is where maintenance of user profiles is performed. From this location you can examine the listing of current user profiles the computer system knows about. The only profiles that will be listed are of users who have logged onto this local PC. Users who do not have administrative rights, however, will see only their user profile, whereas the Administrator will see all of the profiles stored on this computer. This listing will match the user profiles viewed under \WINNT\PROFILES. However, copying of any user profile must be done using the Copy to software tool rather than at the Explorer shell because the Registry knows only about changes made through the Control Panel. See Figure 2-6.

Tasks include copying, renaming, deleting, and changing permissions on user profiles.

Copying User Profiles

The Copy to button is used to copy any existing user profiles from the local PC to another local profile location or to a shared network location. The word *local* can get confusing, as it applies to the computer system—either workstation or server—that we are doing the work at. Clicking the Copy to button opens the Copy to dialog box and presents us with two options (see Figure 2-7):

- *Copy profile to*: Enter the path to copy the user profile to. The Browse button allows us to quickly browse for the preferred path to copy to.

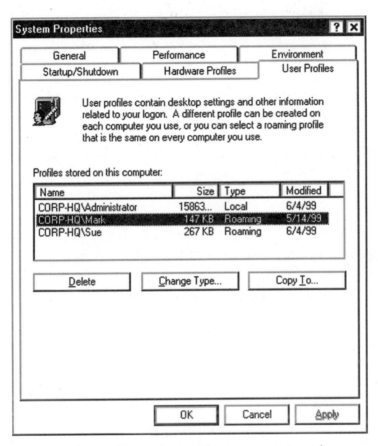

Figure 2-6 *System Properties and the* User Profiles *tab.*

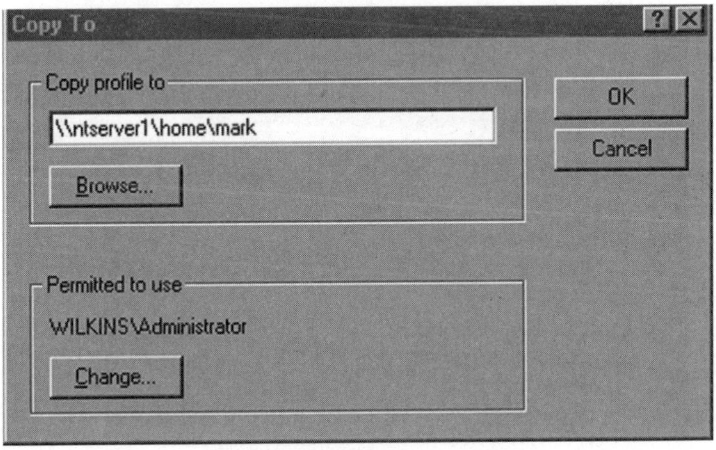

Figure 2-7 *The* Copy to *dialog box and choices.*

- *Permitted to use*: Select the user or group account to use the selected user profile.

To copy an existing user's profile to another user:

1. Log on as Administrator to the Windows NT system holding the user profile to be copied.

2. Open the Control Panel and select System. On the User Profiles tab select the user profile to be copied and use the Copy to function to enter the path of the user's system and profile directory that is to receive the user profile.

3. Click the Change button and change the permissions to allow the new user access to the user profile. Click OK to accept the changes and OK to copy the user profile.

Changing the Profile Type

The Change Type option allows you to specify which copy of your user profile is read when you log on to the PC. The choices are local or roaming; however, if roaming user profiles have not been initialized then local is your only choice. See Figure 2-8.

Local User Profile

The *local user profile* is stored and maintained by the local computer. The roaming user profile is stored at a specified net-

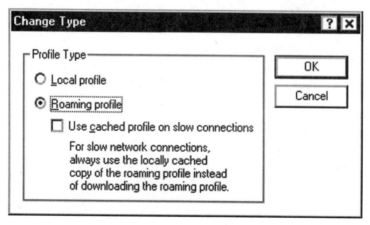

Figure 2-8 *Options with the* Change Type *option.*

work location. Selecting this option can force the system to make the roaming profile now local to this PC. The network copy of the user profile will be copied to the local profile location and be used from now on; however, if the current user profile is set by the Administrator as mandatory, then no changes are allowed.

Roaming Profile

If the roaming user profile is selected, when the user first logs in, NT will resolve whether the local or server profile copy is newer. If the local copy is newer, the user is prompted as to which user profile to use for this session; however, if the current user profile is set by the Administrator as Mandatory, then no changes are allowed.

Roaming Profile Option

Selection of the `Use cached profile on slow connections` option results in the locally cached copy of the user profile in `WINNT \ PROFILES \ USERNAME`. The operating system may also decide to use the local profile if the user logging on is a remote user and the connection is slow.

Deleting Profiles

Any user with Administrative rights can use the `Delete` button to delete unused profiles that still exist on a local computer. Selecting a user profile and clicking the `Delete` button removes the user profile but does not remove the user account that was created through User Manager or User Manager for Domains.

Roaming Profiles

A *roaming profile* is a user profile that is stored on a network share on a server rather than locally. The reasoning from Microsoft is that this is a handy way to back up your user profiles to a central location, which of course it is.

In addition, any user who has a roaming profile path configured can log onto any computer that has access to the network share where the roaming profile is stored, and download that user profile from the network to the PC where they are logging in. In reality, you may not want to enable this feature depending on how you install software and whether or not you want or need your users to roam. Here's how roaming profiles actually work:

Scenario 1. Roaming User Profiles Not Enabled

When users log onto their computer system and are authenticated by a domain controller, their user account is checked to see if a specific path has been defined pointing to the network location of the user profile to use for each individual user. If no network path has been specified for a user profile, the local path `\WINNT\PROFILES\USERNAME` folder is checked for a user profile matching each user who is logging in. If a user profile is found locally, it is loaded and used. When the user logs off, the user settings are saved locally.

Scenario 2. Roaming User Profiles Enabled

When users log onto their computer system and are authenticated by a domain controller, their user account is checked to see if a specific path has been defined pointing to the network location of the user profile to use for each individual user. If a user profile path has been specified, the user profile in this network location is compared with the local path `\WINNT\PROFILES\USERNAME` folder to see if a local user profile is also present for each user who is logging in.

If no user profile is found locally, the network user profile is loaded and used. When the user logs off, the user profile is stored locally in `WINNT\PROFILES` as *the locally cached copy* and also stored back on the server in the defined user profile path.

The next time the user logs in, both the local and network copies of the user profile will be checked. If one is more recent than the other, the user will be presented choices in the form of a confusing dialog box that says in effect, "Do you wish to use the newer user profile or the older version?" *Whenever users opt to use an older version of their user profile stored on the server, the older settings will overwrite the locally cached copy and any new work could be lost.* When the user logs off, the network location will be updated with the new settings.

Scenario 3. Roaming Around the Network

When a user logs onto somebody else's computer system, the domain user account is checked to see if a specific path has been defined pointing to the network location of the user profile to use for that user. If a user profile path has been specified, the user profile in this network location is compared with the local path \WINNT\PROFILES\USERNAME folder to see if a local user profile is also present for the user who is logging in. Since this computer system is not the user's, we will assume no user profile is found locally, so the network user profile is loaded and used.

When users log off their user profiles are stored locally in WINNT\PROFILES as *the locally cached copy* and also stored on the server in the defined user profile path. If the user comes back to this PC in a few weeks and logs in again, the user profile will be still stored locally, but it will be older than the most recent copy stored on the server. The user will be prompted as to which user profile to use: the newer network copy or the older local copy.

Enabling Roaming User Profiles for
Windows NT Clients

The following steps detail how to enable roaming user profiles for NT clients:

1. If a profile location has not already been established on the Primary Domain Controller, first create a directory on the server and then establish a network share to this new directory.

2. Permissions of Add, Read, Change, and Write must be given to each user or group that will use the shared directory.

3. Next create a user account for the new user using User Manager for Domains.

4. Enter the user profile path where the user profile will be stored in the format \\server\share\username.

5. If the user profile is to be stored within the user's home directory, use the format \\servername\usersshare\usershomedir\ profile.

6. If you wish the user to use a specific profile, go to the computer where the desired profile settings are stored. Next copy the complete contents of the local `Profile` folder to the shared network folder using the `Control Panel | System | User Profiles` tab and the `Copy to` command.

Mandatory User Profiles

A *mandatory profile* is a user profile that does not change. It is actually a preconfigured roaming profile that cannot be changed by the user. Upon logout, any changes made by the user during the logon session are *not* saved back to the original profile.

Creating a Mandatory Profile: Windows NT Clients

The steps to create and deploy a new mandatory user profile are as follows:

1. First decide where you are going to store the mandatory user profile on the server. Next create the folder on the server and make sure that you establish a network share to this folder. The only permission required for users using mandatory user profiles is Read. It is highly recommended that you don't use the same network location for both roaming and mandatory user profiles.

2. For a new domain user, use User Manager for Domains to create the user account.

3. Open the `Profile` button for the newly created user and enter the user profile path, which can be one of two locations:

Note

For the *shared network location* where the user profile will be stored, the path format is `\\Servername\sharename\ mandatoryuserprofiles`.

For the *local folder* location where the user profile will be stored, the path format would then be `C:\WINNT\PROFILES\ USERNAME\`.

4. If you want the user to use only the mandatory user profile from the server and no server access will be granted unless the

mandatory user profile is used, add the name .MAN to the user profile name as follows:

- **Network Path:** \\Servername\sharename\ mandatoryuserprofiles\domainuser.man
- **Local Path:** C:\WINNT\PROFILES\USERNAME\NTUSER.MAN

5. Log on to the workstation that the user will be using as that user and make sure that the user's settings are properly defined and usable. Then log out and log in as Administrator.

6. Open the Control Panel and open the System applet. Selecting the User Profiles tab, highlight the user profile to be made mandatory and select the Copy To button.

7. Enter the path that you entered in step 4, either a network path or a local path, including the user profile with a .MAN extension.

8. Click the Change button to change the permissions allowing the user (or group) to access this mandatory user profile.

9. Click OK and the complete user profile including the NTUSER.DAT and supporting folders will be written to the specified location.

Creating a Default User Profile Using NETLOGON

NT can also use a network location for storing a default user profile as the starting point for all new NT workstation users rather than the default local user profile.

1. First create a folder called DEFAULT USER in the NETLOGON share on the Primary Domain Controller. If you are using a collection of PDC and BDC systems, remember that both the PDC and the BDC perform authenticating of users. In this situation all primary and backup servers require a DEFAULT USER folder in the NETLOGON folder. Directory replication of the NETLOGON share can be accomplished by enabling directory replication in order to automatically export these and other settings to all participating servers. The Server applet is where directory replication is enabled. More details on setting up this feature

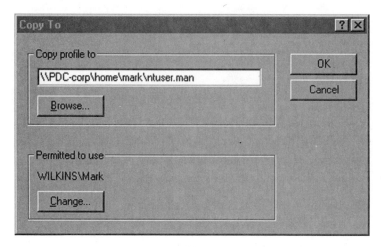

Figure 2-9 *Copying a user profile to the* NETLOGON *share.*

are presented in Chapter 9, "Troubleshooting System
Policies."

2. Copy the desired user profile from the local NT workstation to
   the default user location using the User Profiles applet found in
   the Control Panel under the System icon. See Figure 2-9.

3. When the new user first logs on, the NETLOGON share will be
   checked for a user profile in a folder called DEFAULT USER. If
   the default user profile exists in this location, the new user will
   receive these settings for the starting settings rather than the
   local default user profile template settings. Once the user logs
   out, these settings will remain in the user's PROFILE \ USERNAME
   folder to be used the next time the user logs in.

Note

> The Login Process:
> 1. The Current Settings in the Local Registry are read and
>   deployed.
> 2. The Login script settings (if present) are read and performed.
> 3. If a user profile is active, its settings are written to the Local
>   Registry and deployed.
> 4. If a system policy is active, it is deployed, overwriting all other
>   previous settings in the Local Registry.

Windows 98 Local User Profiles

A default user profile is always enabled for a Windows 98 session. When starting a Windows session, even if you are not prompted to log on to the Windows 98 PC, you are using the default user profile.

You actually may be prompted to log on to a standalone Windows 98 PC because you have enabled a desktop password; however, the default user profile is still being used. The default user profile file for Windows 98 is called USER.DAT; the folders under the WINDOWS folder hold the default user's shortcuts and other settings (see Figure 2-10). There is no PROFILES directory until user profiles have been enabled on the Windows 98 PC through the Passwords icon in the Control Panel. Once multiple user profiles have been enabled, you will then have a PROFILES folder under WINDOWS that stores all of your user-specific settings and your user portion (USER.DAT) of the Registry. The name of the user portion of the Registry will be USER.DAT regardless of the user.

Folders	
Desktop	The contents of "The desktop"
Recent	Recent documents that were opened
NetHood	Shortcuts that appear in Network Neighborhood
History	Internet history
Start Menu	Programs and shortcuts
Programs	User program shortcuts
Temporary Internet Files	Temporary Internet files
Send To	Right-click options for files and folders

Figure 2-10 *Folders that make up the Windows 98 user profile.*

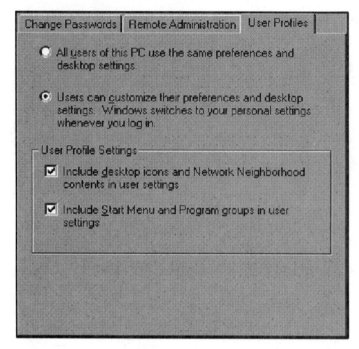

Figure 2-11 *Enabling user profiles for Windows 98.*

Enabling User Profiles for Windows 98 Clients

Enabling user profiles for Windows 98 starts in the Control
Panel with the `Passwords` icon. Clicking `Users can customize their`
`preferences and desktop settings` enables custom user profiles on
this local PC. Settings at the bottom of the `User Profiles` tab allow
you to specify what is included in the user profile. See Figure 2-11.

You will be prompted to reboot your system. Next time you log
on to your Windows 98 PC, a dialog box will welcome you to the
PC and ask you if you want to save your settings for the next time
you log in. Selecting `Yes` creates your user profile. If you have a network connection you may also have enabled roaming user profiles.

Roaming User Profiles and Windows 98

Every time that a user logs onto a Windows 98 computer that has
user profiles enabled, the Registry is queried under the key
`HKEY_LOCAL_MACHINE\SOFTWARE \ Microsoft \ Windows \ Current`
`Version \ Profile list` to see if the user has a local profile; if so,

then Windows 98 will check for the presence of a user profile on the user's home directory on the file server if a home directory exists. If the user profile located on the file server is the most current, it is copied to the local PC for use in the current session. If no profile is found either locally or on the server, a question will be posed to the new user, "Would you like Windows to save your user settings to be used the next time you login?"

Clicking Yes, a user profile is created from the default settings stored in the \WINDOWS folder. Clicking No means use the default user profile.

Windows 98 users who belong to 3.11 or 3.12 Novell NetWare networks will find their roaming profiles in the user-assigned mail directory on the NetWare network in the path \\preferred_server\sys\mail\user_id.	**Note**

In NetWare version 4.X and 5.X, the bindery has been replaced with NetWare Directory Services. The MAIL directory exists only if bindery emulation is running. If bindery emulation is not enabled, administrators of NDS environments must specify the path for the USER.DAT file in the Home Directory attribute of the NDS user profile. This can be done through NWADMIN by choosing a user, choosing the Environment tab, and then entering a Home Directory for the user.

Once the user finishes his or her session and logs off, the network and local copies of the user profile are updated if changes have been made. If a user is logged onto more than one computer system at the same time, then the last user to log out will update the network copy of the user profile.

Another potential situation you should be aware of: When Windows 98 users are logging into their PC and, rather than logging on the usual way with their name and password, they press the <ESC> key. This action tells the system to load the default user profile instead of the user's profile. We can stop this behavior through a system policy setting that forces all users of a particular PC to properly log on before the Windows 98 desktop is loaded.	**Note**

Enabling Roaming User Profiles for
Windows 98 Clients

The following steps enable roaming user profiles for Windows 98 users:

1. First make sure that user profiles have been enabled through the `Passwords` applet in Control Panel.

2. On the NT Primary domain controller create a shared network folder that will hold the Windows 98 roaming user profiles.

Note

> If you have a collection of both Windows 98 and Windows NT users, make sure that you don't use the same shared network location. Interesting problems can occur in companies with users of the same name using a common location for different operating systems.

3. Use `User Manager for Domains` to create the user account. Selecting `Profiles` for the users profile directory, enter the location where the User Profile will be stored using a UNC path in the format `\\server\share\username`. The full path including the user's home directory must be entered. The NT environment variable `%USERNAME%` cannot be used with Windows 98 clients.

4. If you wish the user to use a specific profile, go to the Windows 98 computer where the desired user profile settings are stored and copy the complete contents of the local `Profile` folder to the shared network folder for Windows 98 user profiles from the Explorer shell. If you wish the user to use a default profile, no action is required. Windows 98 will move the contents of the user's profile to the server automatically when the user logs out.

Windows 98 Clients and Mandatory Profiles

The following steps will enable mandatory user profiles for Windows 98 clients:

1. From the Windows 98 PC where the mandatory profile is to be used, copy the complete contents of the local profile folder that pertains to the end user, to the user's home directory, or share on the file server.

2. Then rename the USER.DAT to USER.MAN.

3. Next time that the user logs onto the network and downloads the mandatory profile it will be cached locally in RAM. Once the user logs off no changes will be written back to the server.

NT 4.0 and Windows 98 User Profiles Compared

User profiles as we know them were first seen in Windows 95 and then Windows NT 4.0. They will continue to evolve as you or your users upgrade to Windows 2000 and Office 2000. For now let's compare the two most popular Microsoft platforms—NT 4.0 and Windows 98—and how user profiles stack up.

- The Windows NT 4.0 user profile file is a binary file called NTUSER.DAT; the Windows 98 user profile is a binary file called USER.DAT.

- In Windows NT, an NTUSER.LOG file is used as a transaction log file. This allows the user profile to be recovered if there are problems after a reboot; in Windows 98, every normal boot USER.DAT is backed up into a CAB file.

- Windows 98 users can log on to their PCs using the local default user profile; each NT user must have a defined local user profile before logging in.

- NT users have their user profile created from the common group ALL USERS; Windows 98 does not support common groups.

- Windows 98 does not support a Default User Profile stored in the NETLOGON share on a Primary or Backup Domain Controller.

Using Logon Scripts

The use of *logon scripts* allows you to enforce user security on the local PC as well as automate other security options. For NT, the

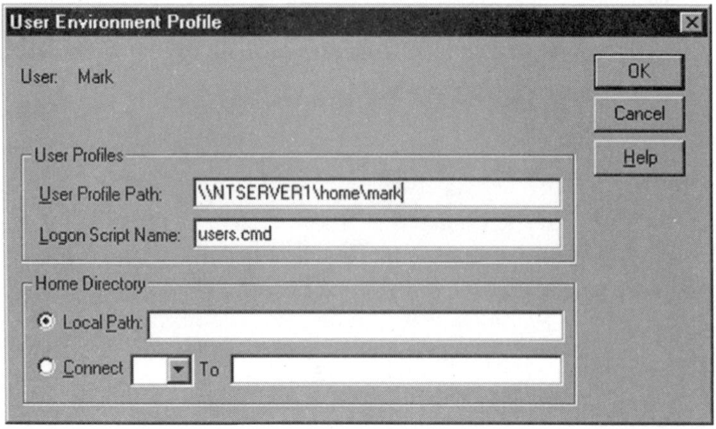

Figure 2-12 *Login scripts defined in the user's profile settings.*

file is a text-based file with either `.BAT` or `.CMD` as the extension. Any executable file can be used in logon scripts including the `NET` command line parameters.

The logon script is stored in the `NETLOGON` share by default (the path for `NETLOGON` is `WINNT\SYSTEM32\REPL\IMPORT\SCRIPTS`) and is enabled through the User Manager for Domains utility. The login script location should remain the `NETLOGON` share so that directory replication between PDC and any BDCs will include the logon scripts. See Figure 2-12.

The commands that can be included in a login script include:

- Environment variables for NT Workstations

- Any command line you wish to execute

- Any command line–based `NET` command

For example, if you wished to synchronize the workstation's time with that of the domain, delete all system policy template files and remove `Regedit`. Then the following batch file would do the job.

```
@echo off
net time \\Kingston /set /yes
del c:\*.adm > null
del c:\regedit.* > null
```

System Policies

System policies are the saving grace for Windows 95/98 and NT
Workstations attached to a validating NT server. Complete control of computer resources can be achieved and maintained by
the system administrator for the individual, or group of like
users, through the creation of one small policy file usually
located on the server. I say "usually," because a system policy
can also be deployed on a notebook or local PC if your intent is
to control a standalone computer system running NT 4.0 or
Windows 98.

The defined settings in the system policy overwrite the default
local Registry settings when the user logs on to the network.

System policies are changes that can be made to either the user
or machine portion of the Registry. These can be categorized as:

1. *User restrictions.* User profiles, remote access, control panel
   restrictions

2. *Networkwide standards and restrictions.* Global security settings for the network security

3. *Groupwide standards and restrictions.* Global groups of users

4. *Computer restrictions.* Specific computer settings that apply to
   all users that log onto NT

A number of the settings that can be deployed through a system policy are:

- Require validation by network for windows access (95/98
  Clients only)

- Set a minimum Windows password length

- Restrict certain Control Panel applets

- Disable the addition or deletion of printers

- Hide the Device Manager (95/98 Clients only)

- Disable any changes to virtual memory

- Disable all file and print sharing controls

- Disable the registry-editing tools

- Disable the MS-DOS prompt and all applications

- Disable dial-in access

How System Policies Are Deployed for NT Clients

1. When a user logs onto the network using Windows NT, the system checks in the local Registry for the presence of a system policy file called NTCONFIG.POL, either on the server in the NETLOGON share or in some other defined location.

2. If system policies have been enabled and the system policy file is found, it is opened and a match is attempted between the user's workstation name. If no defined computer policy has been defined, the default computer policy settings are applied.

3. Next a match is attempted between the user's logon name and any defined user or group policy contained in NTCONFIG.POL. If no specific user policy has been defined, the default user policy file is applied, modifying the local Registry settings.

How System Policies Are Deployed for Windows 98 Clients

1. When a user logs onto a NT network using Windows 98 as the client, the system checks in the local Registry to see if user profiles have been enabled. Second, the current location of where the system policy file called CONFIG.POL is read, either on the validating server in the NETLOGON share or in some other defined location.

2. If system policies have been enabled and the system policy file is found, it is opened and a match is attempted between the user's workstation name. If no defined computer policy has been defined, the default computer policy settings are applied, modifying the local Registry settings.

3. Next a match is attempted between the user's logon name and either the defined user or group policy contained in CONFIG.POL. If no specific user policy file has been defined, the default user policy settings are applied, modifying the local Registry settings. See Figure 2-13.

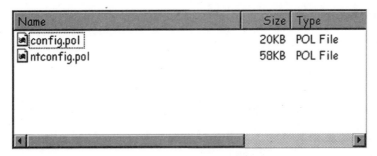

Name	Size	Type
config.pol	20KB	POL File
ntconfig.pol	58KB	POL File

Figure 2-13 *The* NETLOGON *share with system policies for both Windows 98 and NT 4.0.*

Policies for Computers

The *system policy editor* creates two policies by default. One of these is a policy for the default computer. A system policy can be set for all computers or for individual computer systems. If your computer system has not been named in the system policy, your computer system will get the settings set inside the default computer policy. A policy setting for a computer named in the system policy will not affect another computer system.

However, the default computer policy could affect the named computer policy if settings in the default computer are activated and not taken into consideration.

Policies for Users

System policies can be set for all users by specifying settings in the Default User icon. The default user settings can be thought of as settings that apply to all users; like the defined global group, Everyone does. System policies can also be set for individual users by adding the name of the user to the system policy.

Any users that we add to the policy must already exist on the Primary Domain Controllers list of active users on the network.

> When a system policy is applied, the default user settings will always be applied to all users; next, all defined users in the system policy will be applied.   **Note**

Policies for Groups

Policies for groups of users can also be set with the system policy editor. Keep in mind that the type of group is important.

Note   Only global groups will work with system policies.

Local groups and groups defined in a NetWare environment are not supported. In most cases it is much easier to manage by groups.

The groups that we add to the policy must already exist on the Primary Domain Controllers list of defined groups on the network.

Remember that the first policy that always gets loaded is the default user policy. Next the group policies are loaded in order of priority if there is more than one group. The priority level of defined groups listed in the system policy is very critical in deciding what group policy setting gets applied last. Priority levels as applied to system policy groups are a bit strange at first glance; the first group that is initially created has the highest priority, then the second group created, and so on. See Figure 2-14.

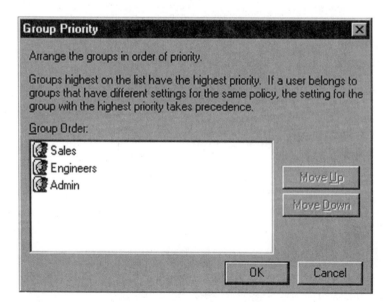

Figure 2-14 *Setting group priorities for system policies.*

> The system policy editor sets priority in the order of the creation of the groups in the system policy. **Note**

Policies for Networks Other Than NT Server and NetWare

The major focus for this book is the Microsoft Clients, Windows 95/98 and NT 4.0, working in the two favorite network environments, NT Server and NetWare. However, other networks can fully participate in system policies—the key is if the Registry of the local PC knows where to find the system policy file.

Since the clients of choice are Windows 95/98 and NT Workstation, the local registry can be manually edited to tell the local operating system where to search for its system policy settings.

The conditions for using system policies are having either a Windows 95 or NT 32-bit software client for your server environment, such as SUN or Banyan Vines. Then all you have to do is tell the local Registry location where the system policy file is to be loaded from.

NT File Security

NT File security is set through the Explorer applet. File and folder security can be enabled only when the file partition chosen is NTFS (the NT file system). The FAT16 (File allocation table) file system has no real security and should not be used for NT systems if a secure environment is needed. Windows 98 can use either FAT16 or FAT32, but there is no security advantage by using either choice. See Figure 2-15.

Setting Directory and File Permissions on NTFS Partitions

The choices for setting file permissions are varied and must be set correctly for a secure network. Usually this is the weak point of most networks. Don't make the mistake of assigning too many permissions before you test them out in the real world. The more permissions you assign, the higher the level of administration on a

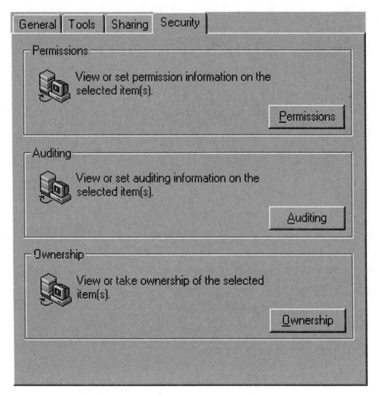

Figure 2-15 *The security tab is available only with NTFS.*

daily basis. Make sure your company can support this hidden cost.

Directory Permissions for NTFS

Directory permissions are cumulative—they build on previous rights from a higher directory level. Permissions should not be assigned at the root level for files unless the user is an Administrator. Directory permissions actually apply to the named directories and the files in these directories. See Figure 2-16.

No Access   The user has no access.

List   The user can view all files and subdirectories
                and can change to shown subdirectories.

Read   The user can read all files shown in the direc-
                tory and can run the shown applications.

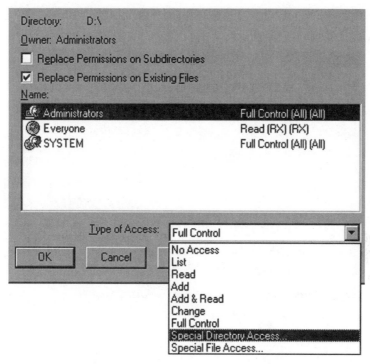

Figure 2-16 *Directory permissions for NTFS partitions.*

Add	The user can add files to the directory but cannot read or change the shown files in the directory.
Add & Read	The user has add and change permissions for the directory.
Change	The user has read and add permissions; in addition, the user can change the contents of files and also delete files.
Full Control	The user has Add, Read, and Change permissions and can also change file permissions and take ownership of files.

File Permissions for NTFS

File permissions are to be applied sparingly, if at all. These permissions apply to actual files within a directory. See Figure 2-17.

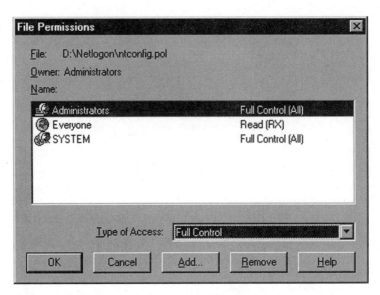

Figure 2-17 *File permissions for NTFS partitions.*

Read	The user can read all files shown in the directory and can run the shown applications.
Change	The user has read and add permissions; in addition, the user can change the contents of files and also delete files.
Full Control	The user has Add, Read, and Change permissions and can also change file permissions and take ownership of files.

Users and Groups for NT Domains

User profiles and system polices are designed to function in a Primary and Backup Domain environment; however, both users and groups are defined for both local and global environments.

Local Groups

NT uses groups to define users and groups that can be granted permissions to resources such as printers, files, and folders. Local groups are created in both NT domains and on NT Workstations. The confusion begins! The bottom line is that local groups are not used in creating system policies—so no big explanation of these groups is needed here.

Global Groups

Global groups are the only types of group for which system policies can be created. A global group contains users that have user accounts in the domain where the global group was created. If you have trusts linking your primary domain controllers, then global groups from the other linked domains can be included in a system policy.

Installing and Using the
System Policy Editor

In this chapter you will learn:

- How to install the system policy editor on your NT or Windows 98 workstation

- How to make sure that the correct template is loaded

- How to operate the system policy editor in both Registry and Policy mode

- How to load multiple template files

- How to deploy system policies for Windows 2000

Installing the System Policy Editor

The system policy editor (POLEDIT.EXE) has been with us since the initial release of Windows 95. From 1995 to 1998, there have been three versions of the policy editor released by Microsoft that correspond with the version of Windows that you were using, or planning to deploy: either NT 4.0, Windows 98, or Windows 95. See Figure 3-1.

Installing the System Policy Editor for Windows NT 4.0

You have at least three options for installing the system policy editor when working in the NT camp.

Option 1. From a Functioning NT Server

1. First copy the system policy executable, POLEDIT.EXE file from \WINNT\SYSTEM directory on the Windows NT Server 4.0 to the \\WINNT directory of the Windows NT Workstation machine.

2. Second, copy both of the needed NT system policy template files: COMMON.ADM and WINDOWS.ADM from the \\WINNT\INF directory on the Windows NT 4.0 server to the \\WINNT\INF directory of the Windows NT Workstation machine.

3. Finally, create a shortcut to the system policy editor executable (Poledit.exe) either on your Start menu or on your desktop.

System Policy Editor Version POLEDIT.EXE	Released with
4.00.950	Windows 95
4.00.950	Office 95
4.00	Windows NT 4.0
4.00	Office 97
4.00	Windows 98
5.00.1849.1	Windows 2000

Figure 3-1 *System policy versions available.*

Figure 3-2 *Domain software tools for NT Administrators.*

Option 2. From the NT Server Resource Kit CD

1. Run NTCSETUP.EXE file from the Windows NT 4.0 CD-ROM located in the CLIENTS\SVRTOOLS\WINNT directory. This will install the Client-Based Server Tools that are normally found on the Administrator menu off the Start menu onto your NT Workstation Start menu (see Figure 3-2). It's a little confusing at first to have two similar sets of tools showing up, so I like to rename the shortcut for the Client Based Tools to Domain Admin.

Option 3. From the NT Server CD

1. Run the SETUP.BAT file from the Windows NT 4.0 CD-ROM \CLIENTS\SRVTOOLS\WINNT directory. This will install the Client-Based Server Tools that are normally found on the Administrator menu off the Start menu on an NT Server onto your Start menu.

Installing the System Policy Editor for Windows 98

For Windows 98 systems you install the system policy editor from the TOOLS\APPTOOLS\POLEDIT directory located on the Windows 98 CD.

1. Open the Control Panel and select the Add/Remove programs applet.

2. Click the Windows Setup tab and then click the Have Disk button.

3. Click the Browse button and then enter TOOLS\APPTOOLS\POLEDIT for the browse path; then click OK.

4. Respond to the dialog box with OK and then select the System

`Policy Editor` and `Group Policy Support` by checking the corresponding checkboxes and then click `Install`.

The system policy editor is now installed on your `Start` menu under `Start | Programs | Accessories | System Tools`.

Note

Installing the System Policy Editor for Windows 95: If you are using Windows 95 as your client base and have no immediate plans to upgrade for now, the Windows 95 installation is presented in summary format.

Use the `Add/Remove Programs` icon located in the Control Panel to install the Windows 95 version of the system policy editor. This installation procedure applies to you if your client base is any of the Windows 95 versions of: 4.00.950.0000, 4.00.950.0000.A, 4.00.950.0000.B, or 4.00.950.0000.C.

1. Select the `Windows Setup` tab.
2. Next click the `Have Disk` button
3. Install from the Windows 95 CD-ROM by locating the directory `\ADMIN\APPTOOLS\POLEDIT`.
4. Accept the installation script file `POLEDIT.INF` that is highlighted in the dialog box (`GROUPPOL.INF` is automatically selected as well) and click `OK`.
5. Now click `OK` again to start the installation process.
6. You have two choices: Install the system policy editor and/or group policies. Select both and click `OK`. See Figure 3-3.

The system policy editor is now installed on your `Start` menu under `Start | Programs | Accessories | System Tools`.

Install Notes to the Wise

Now you may be thinking to yourself, "Why bother installing the policy editor; it seemed to run just fine by double-clicking the `POLEDIT.EXE` filename?" And you're right—you don't have to install the policy editor in order to create some system policy types, but you should; otherwise, you will always start off with errors if the install is not completed because the policy editor expects to find its template files in the `%SYSTEM ROOT%\INF` directory. If the install has not been performed when you run the policy editor, it then will report that it can't find its template files

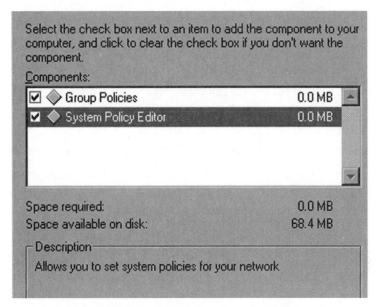

Select the check box next to an item to add the component to your
computer, and click to clear the check box if you don't want the
component.

Components:

☑ ◇ Group Policies	0.0 MB	▲
☑ ◇ System Policy Editor	0.0 MB	

Space required: 0.0 MB
Space available on disk: 68.4 MB

┌ Description ────────────────────────
  Allows you to set system policies for your network

Figure 3-3 *System policy and group policy selections.*

and leave you in a bind. That is why I recommend that you
always do the install.

The second reason to perform the install is to activate support
for group policies. The power of deploying system policies is
through global groups. No activation of group policy support
during the install means that group policies won't work on your
PC; since you will most likely be doing the testing and deploying
on your PC to start with, remember to perform this step.

Your users may also perform the install, however, by reading
the appropriate resource kit or other documentation available just
about anywhere on the Internet.

So you want to be aware of the default locations where the
executable file and template files can be found if you have a
"power user" who is on the loose.

You may even want to "search and remove" through a logon script   **Note**
to ensure that any installed copies of the policy editor and relevant policy templates can be removed from a user's workstation
every network login.

Also note that the system policy editor is preinstalled on all versions of NT Server 4.0; note, however, that the worst possible location for creating and testing system policies is on a production NT server. One slip and you could lock everyone out—including you, the administrator. Do your testing and planning on a workstation that matches the group or client for which you are creating a system policy—that is, Windows 95 for 95 clients, Windows 98 for 98 clients, and NT Workstation for NT clients.

Office Administrator Options for Installing the System Policy Editor

Talk about confusing! How many options do we need for installing the policy editor? Since the system policy editor is bundled with both the Office 95 and Office 97 Resource Kits, Microsoft has seen it necessary to include yet another installation program called POLSETUP.EXE that can be run from Windows Explorer. In turn, it will call the associated INF files to execute the install.

The install also places the .ADM system policy template files in the INF directory. From the Explorer Shell, locate the policy editor installation file POLSETUP.EXE and double-click to perform the install. The system policy editor is now installed on your Start menu under Start | Programs | Accessories | System Tools, whether you have Windows 95, 98, or Windows NT as your operating system. See Figure 3-4.

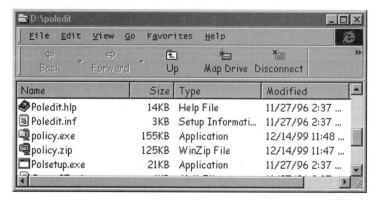

Figure 3-4 *Run* POLSETUP *to install the system policy editor bundled with Office 97.*

System Policy Templates

Now that we have installed the system policy editor we are ready
to create system policies. Or are we? To use the policy editor to
create system policies we must first ensure that we have a template loaded and, also, we must make sure that the *correct* system
policy template is loaded. The right template must match the version of Windows or software for which you want to create system
policies. First, let me describe what a template is and does—that
is, who, what, when, where, and why of the matter.

The system policy editor uses a file type classified by Microsoft
as an "administrative" file, hence the extension (.ADM). However,
Notepad or any text editor can also open and view these template
files, as they are in plain ASCII text.

They are actually a script file that displays the Registry settings
available to be added, changed, or removed when using the system policy editor in registry mode or policy mode. System policy
template files (as previously mentioned) are by default stored in
the \WINNT\INF folder. Most of the template files available (at this
time of writing) are created and provided by Microsoft (no surprise there); choices are grouped below in Figure 3-5 so you can
quickly see what's available and what particular template to use
for a given situation on a particular operating system. These are
just the pure operating system choices; Microsoft applications
have templates for your use as well, such as Office 95, 97, and

Windows Version	System Policy Templates Available	What They Are Used For
Windows 95	ADMIN.ADM	Windows 95 computer and user settings
Windows NT 4.0	WINNT.ADM COMMON.ADM	NT Security Settings common to Windows 95 and NT
	WINDOWS.ADM	Windows 95 computer and user settings

Figure 3-5 *System policy templates.*

Windows Version	System Policy Templates Available	What They Are Used For
Windows 98	WINDOWS.ADM	Windows 98 computer and user settings
	SHELL.ADM	Active desktop settings
	CHAT.ADM	Chat settings
	CONF.ADM	Net Meeting settings
	INETRES.ADM	Internet security and Active Desktop
	INETSET.ADM	Internet environment
	SUBS.ADM	Subscription content
	OE.ADM, PWS.ADM	Mail and news settings Computer Internet settings
Internet Explorer 3	IEAK.ADM	Proxy server settings
Internet Explorer 4	CHAT.ADM	Chat settings
	CONF.ADM	Net Meeting settings
	INETRES.ADM	Internet security and Active Desktop
	INETSET.ADM	Internet environment
	OE.ADM	Mail and news settings
	SHELL.ADM	Active Desktop
	SUBS.ADM	Subscription Content
Windows 2000	CHAT.ADM	Chat Settings
	WINNT.ADM	Windows 2000 security
	WINDOWS.ADM	Windows 2000 user and computer settings
	SUBS.ADM	Subscription content
	SHELL.ADM	Active Desktop settings
	OE.ADM	Mail and new settings
	INETSET.ADM	Internet security and Active Desktop
	INETRES.ADM	Internet environment
	CONF.ADM	Net Meeting settings
	COMMON.ADM	Setting common to Windows 98 and 2000

Figure 3-5 *Continued.*

Internet Explorer 3, 4, and 5. We will cover more details on these templates in the later chapters.

Loading the Wrong ADM Template

The matching templates for Windows 98, Windows NT 4.0, and Windows 2000 are bundled with the different versions of the policy editor; however, you can initially load any template you wish without receiving any error messages when you start. So it is easy to load the wrong template by mistake. Consequently, the first task you want to perform when first opening POLEDIT is to check what template file has been loaded, if any. We do this by selecting the drop-down menu Options and then selecting the Policy Template option. See Figure 3-6.

In order to add initial or additional templates you select the Add button and then Browse if needed to locate further templates. To remove an existing template, first highlight the template to remove and then click Remove.

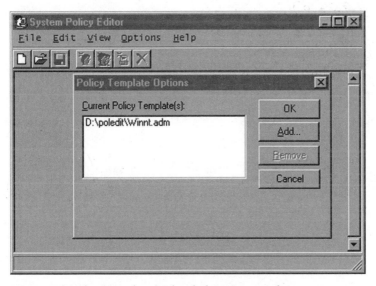

Figure 3-6 *Checking for the loaded ADM templates.*

In order to add or remove templates you must first close your current session with the policy editor. The Add and Remove buttons will remain grayed out during a current system policy session.

Loading Multiple System Policy Template Files

One major change made to the system policy editor from the initial Windows 95 version is how it handles the loading of .ADM template files. The original Windows 95 version had the ability to open only one template at a time; however, Windows 98, Windows NT 4.0, and Windows 2000 versions of the policy editor have the ability to load multiple templates at the same time. This allows us to create a "master template" with many more options available. For example, if we want to control the NT operating system, Office 97, and Internet Explorer, this can be done in one

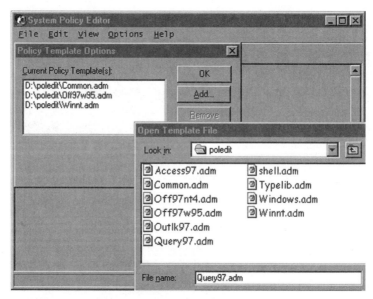

Figure 3-7 *Loading multiple templates.*

system policy session. Using the first version of the system policy editor would have required us to individually load each desired template one at a time, saving our changes as we unloaded, and then load the needed templates. Be careful though. There is no internal check performed by the policy editor if you should load the same template twice. See Figure 3-7.

Using the System Policy Editor

By executing POLEDIT from the Start menu, or a shortcut on the desktop, we can open the system policy editor. See Figure 3-8.

Initial startup of the system policy editor is less than exciting. For this very reason, the busy Administrator has not made use of this powerful utility as it initially shows none of its promise until you select a mode of operation. The system policy editor is designed to operate in two different modes: Registry mode and System Policy mode. Both of these choices are found on the File drop-down menu. See Figure 3-9.

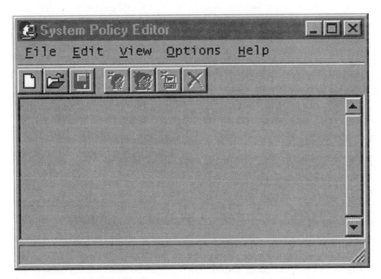

Figure 3-8 *The initial system policy editor.*

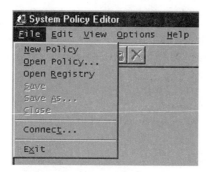

Figure 3-9 `File` menu options.

Registry Mode

Both modes of `POLEDIT` will display different icons. When operating in `Registry` mode, `Local Computer` and `Local User` icons appear. `Local Computer` choices are the computer-specific registry/system policy settings that apply to the user logged on. `Local User` choices are the current logged-on users' current registry/system policy settings. In order to see a different user's settings you must log in to the PC again as that user.

In `Registry` mode you actually have two choices: the first choice is directly editing the Registry of the computer system that you are currently using. Registry settings that are currently in effect on your machine that correspond to the template or templates that are loaded will be viewable and able to be changed or modified.

Think of the `Registry` mode as a window into the current Registry settings on a particular machine, where we can view and make changes in real time. Any changes are applied instantly; in most cases, you will not have to reboot in order for any new changes to take effect. The rule that is followed is that if the system policy editor changed a setting that would normally require a reboot, then you must reboot to see the change implemented.

For example, Figure 3-10 shows that the `Run` box on the `Start` menu is disabled and if we check, we see that this is the case. By simply checking or unchecking the options available, the active template file makes the requested changes to the local Registry once we save our work.

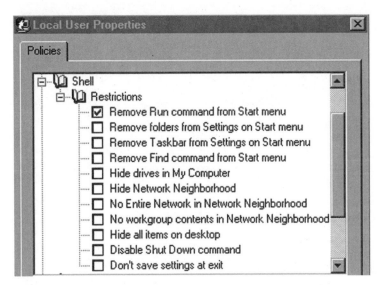

Figure 3-10 *Current system policy settings viewed in the* Registry *mode.*

In Registry mode there are only two obvious choices: a checked box is selecting an option or enabling a choice; an unchecked box is an option that is not currently enabled (until it is checked, that is).

You can also remotely view and change current Registry settings on a remote computer if you have enough rights to perform this task. The local and remote computer systems must be the same OS platform: NT to NT or Windows 98 to Windows 98, not a mix of the two. Remote services are installed by default on NT as its complete client-server design for administrative tools includes remote procedure calls. For Windows 98 you have to enable this service. Here's how.

Remote Registry Services for Windows 98

There are several conditions that must be met on each workstation in order for remote registry services to work with Windows 98 clients.

● All workstations must be members of the same domain.

- All workstations must be using a 32-bit Microsoft network client.

- All workstations must be using a common network protocol such as TCP/IP, IPX/SPX, or NetBEUI.

- Microsoft Remote Registry Services must be installed on each workstation.

- User-level security must be enabled. You also must have a dedicated server such as NT Server or NetWare to authenticate security. Share-level security is not supported.

Installing Remote Registry Services

1. Open the Control Panel | Network icon. Use the Add button to select Service. This will lead to Select Network Service.

2. Click the Have Disk button. Enter the path to the remote registry tools folder on the Windows 98 CD: ADMIN\NETADMIN\REMOTREG. Click OK and then make sure that Microsoft Remote Registry is highlighted and click OK. Reboot your computer when it prompts you to.

3. Next Remote Registration must be enabled. Open the Control Panel | Passwords icon and select the Remote Administration property-sheet. Check the box to enable remote registration of this machine. Finally, click the Add button and add the administrators that will be using this service on this particular machine. The key to understanding this screen is realizing that the administrators must be added to all computer systems where remote registry services are to be performed, not just on the administrators' PCs. Remote administration is enabled automatically for the Domain Administrator's groups on a Windows NT domain. For NetWare, either Supervisor (for 3.X) or Admin (for 4.X) is also enabled as well. See Figures 3-11 and 3-12.

Making the connection to the remote computer is simple. From the File drop-down menu, select Connect and type in the name of the remote computer to which you want to connect and administer. The computer name is the same as the network identi-

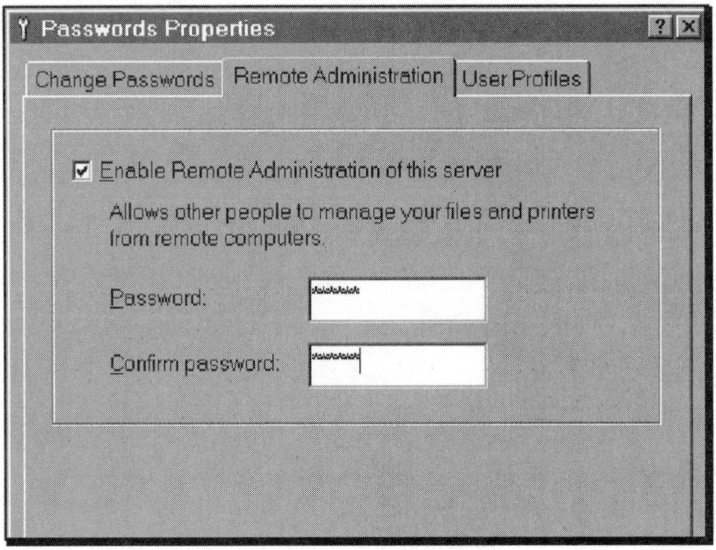

Figure 3-11 *Enabling remote registry services.*

fier that is entered on the Identification tab in the Network icon in Control Panel. See Figure 3-13.

The title bar of the system policy editor indicates whether you are connecting to the local PC or to a remote computer system. Editing, browsing, and making changes are exactly the same as on the local PC; however, speed might be a factor across a busy network. I like to use this remote mode only as a "lookup" ser-

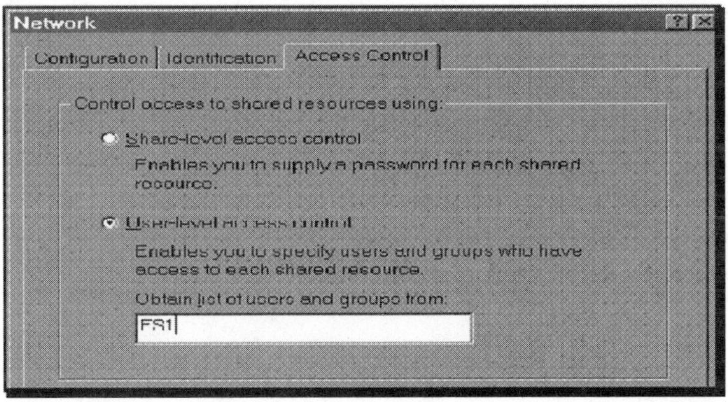

Figure 3-12 *Enabling user level security.*

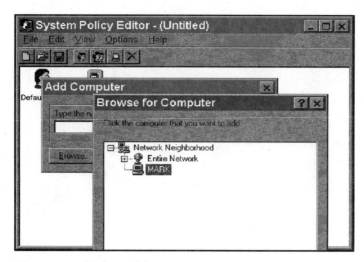

Figure 3-13 *Making the remote connection.*

vice in most cases. We can't control the remote user's ability to turn off the darn PC just when we want to remotely control it from afar. So be careful.

System Policy Mode

System policy mode is selected by choosing `File > New Policy`. Note that the icons have changed from `Local Computer` and `Local User` to `Default Computer` and `Default User`. The title bar shows the mode that the policy editor is currently operating in. See Figure 3-14.

In this mode of operation we are allowed to create settings only for future use, because we are not editing the local Registry.

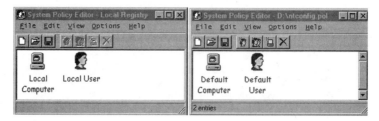

Figure 3-14 *System policy mode versus Registry mode.*

The choices we select will be saved in a system policy file with a
.POL extension. The automatic choices are NTCONFIG.POL for NT
Clients and CONFIG.POL for Windows 95/98 clients. System policies can be created for users, global groups of users, and also for
specific computers. The settings will be activated only when the
user logs in to a machine and network where system policies are
enabled.

In Registry mode we had two checkbox choices: Enable (on)
or Disable (off). However, in system policy mode we have three
choices: Enable, Disable, or Ignore. These choices are sometimes
confusing, so reread the following section several times if it first
doesn't make sense.

Understanding the logon process is essential to understanding
the system policy checkbox configuration options. A system policy is usually deployed from a system policy file usually located
on a dedicated file server, but the policy file can be located anywhere, even locally. When a Windows NT 4.0 or Windows 98
user logs onto his or her PC, the local Registry is checked during
the boot process to see if system policies have been enabled, and,
if so where the current policy file is located.

Assuming that system policies are enabled, the Windows operating system opens the policy file and applies the relevant system
policy settings from the opened policy file to the logging on the
user's local Registry. (Since the recommended procedure is to have
the system policy file located on the file server away from the
user, I will focus at this point in the book on this method; however, the standalone or notebook method of applying system policies will be covered as well.)

The reality on your network is that network traffic is usually
at a premium during logon hours. If it were necessary to check
every system policy template checkbox for every single user during a network logon against the current local Registry value, it
would take forever to log on.

Consequently, we have the default starting option of Ignore
displayed when we are in system policy mode. Ignore is a checkbox that is grayed out. In this situation, when the policy file is
next applied, the corresponding Registry setting on the user's
local machine will not be modified by the system policy. This set-

ting helps streamline the applying of system policies, as only
checked or cleared checkboxes are applied.

Windows 2000 and System Policies

Windows 2000 has completely changed the interface for deploying system policies and administrative tasks. Tools and "snap-
ins" have replaced the system policy editor that was familiar to
NT 4.0. At this time of writing (summer 1998) Microsoft is holding true to its claim that support for Windows NT 4.0 and Windows 98 through Windows 2000 management/administrative
utilities *will not be offered*. I expect this may change as Microsoft
is increasing the life for Windows 98 by releasing two new versions; however, I could be wrong as Microsoft sometimes changes
its mind very quickly.

Windows 2000 uses several older features found in the current
NT 4.0 user profile camp—group policy and roaming user profiles—and adds in some new features under Active Directory Services and Offline Folders, all tidied up together under the heading
of *Group Policy*.

Features of the new group management arrangement are:

- *Software Policies*. Similar to the existing system policies of NT
  4.0 plus some new settings to control system services, the look
  and feel of the new active desktop, and new versions of
  Microsoft applications (Office 2000).

- *Software Installation*. The capacity to *dispense* or *publish* a
  standard application or Web-based document from a distribution server/share.

- *Security Settings*. Registry settings for the Local Computer,
  Domain, and Network.

- *File Deployment*. Specifies files to be placed on the Start menu,
  or in a desktop folder.

- *Folder Redirection*. The ability to redirect particular folders
  such as My Documents to a specified location on the network.

- *Scripts*. New-style Windows Scripting Host (WSH) scripts that replace the old standard batch file for controlling computer startup and shutdown and user logon and logoff.

- They may be written in Java or VB Script, or by `.bat` and `.cmd` files.

As administrator you will use the *group policy editor* (GPE) to manage both the old and new policy settings. For Windows 2000, *policy* refers to all of the features on the list. The feature list can be added to by third-party programmers, who can create and extend the existing or new system policy template files (`ADM`).

All of the policy settings that are created by the GPE are now stored in a *group policy object* (GPO), and these GPOs are replicated to all domain controllers within a single domain that will receive these objects through automatic replication services.

In order to maintain support for Windows 95, 98, and NT 4.0 workstations the Windows 2000 Optional Administrative Tools must be installed. This will provide the system policy editor (`POLEDIT.EXE`) and the administrative files (`ADM`).

Using the Microsoft Management Console

Depending on your use of Microsoft software you may have seen the early versions of a software tool called the *Microsoft Management Console* (MMC). It appeared first in the Internet Explorer Administration Kits (IEAK) and also in Internet Information Server (IIS) 3.0. (You and I are beta laboratory testers for all of Microsoft's new ideas, whether we like it or not.) Using the MMC you can build a customized set of administrative tools that meet your needs. The idea is that you and third-party software utilities will take advantage of this design and develop tools for Windows 2000; Symantec, for example, is already doing this.

By creating MMC console files (`.MSC`) we can create custom sets of specific administrative tasks to assign to users or groups through system policies. The process is to start with either a new or existing console and customize it to meet your needs.

Adding the Group Policy Editor to a Custom Management Console

If you wish to set up a custom management console for creating group policies for your Windows 2000 server or workstation, execute the following steps.

To configure the console:

1. Log on to your server as an Administrator.

2. Now click the `Start` button and select the `Run` dialog box.

3. In the text box of the `Run` dialog type `mmc` and click `OK`. See Figure 3-15.

4. Click the `MMC console` menu item and click `Add/Remove Snap-in`. See Figure 3-16.

5. In the `Add/Remove Snap-in` dialog box, click on `Add`.

6. In the `Available Stand-alone Snap-ins` list box, click `Active Directory Manager` and click `Add`.

7. Click `Active Directory Sites` and `Services Manager`, then click `Add`.

8. Now click `Computer Management`.

9. When prompted, ensure that the `Computer Management` snap-in has the `Local Computer` selected and click `Finish`.

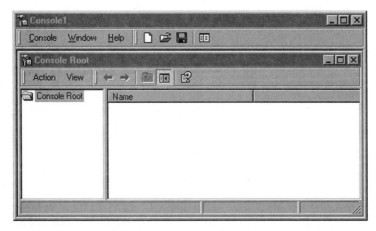

Figure 3-15 *The default MMC console.*

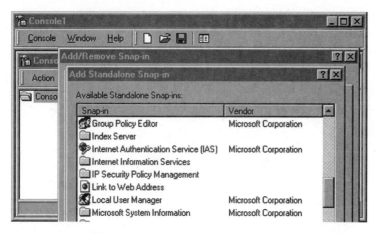

Figure 3-16 *Adding a snap-in to the MMC.*

10. Click Add, and then click Close.

11. Next click the Extensions tab.

12. Make sure that the Add all extensions checkbox is checked.
    (Figure 3-17 shows the finished product.)

13. Now you can check on the Start Menu | Programs | My
    Administrative Tools to see the newly created set of system
    policy tools.

Keep in mind while using the group policy tools for Windows
2000 that the creation of group policies is also linked to the
active directory structure and the associated global objects. The
group policy editor (GPE) is accessed through the Microsoft
Management Console (MMC). We create and set system policy
through the MMC for either the local computer (Windows 2000
Workstation) or the complete active directory world (Windows
2000 servers).

By accessing the Active Directory Manager or the Active Directory Sites and Services Manager you can set group policy for
organizational units (OU), domains, or entire sites. These two
software tools are located in the Administrative Tools software
group; however, you can create a custom suite of administrative
tools with the MMC for your specific needs.

Using the Management Console to Set
System Policy

Opening up the group policy editor from My Administrative
Tools we are presented with an Explorer-like shell interface.
Maximizing the choices available for setting computer and user
settings shows the template choices available for the Windows
2000 environment. See Figure 3-17.

For standalone workstations that do not belong to a domain, a
policy can be enabled and applied to the local machine. Both
local and remote local machines can benefit from a group policy.
Local group policy is set for the following file extensions:

• File Deployment

• Login Scripts

• Software Policy

• Security Settings

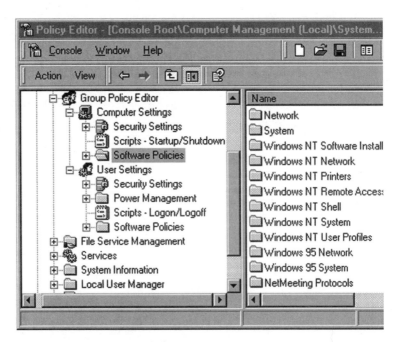

Figure 3-17 *Computer and user settings.*

Policy Templates in Windows NT 4.0

In this chapter you will learn:

- What user and computer settings does the `WINNT.ADM` template control for NT clients.

- What user and computer settings does the `COMMON.ADM` template deploy for NT clients.

- What computer and user settings are deployed through `WINDOWS.ADM` for Windows 95 and 98 clients.

Choosing a System Policy Template to Use

Three system policy templates are included with NT 4.0: WINNT.ADM, COMMON.ADM, and WINDOWS.ADM.

- WINNT.ADM   Used for NT security-specific settings

- COMMON.ADM   Settings common to Windows NT and Windows 98

- WINDOWS.ADM   Settings specific to Windows 95 and Windows 98 only

The reasoning behind providing these three templates is that most NT networks support a collection of Windows 95, Windows 98, and NT 4.0 workstation users. This template is provided so that you can deploy system policy settings for Windows 95 and Windows 98 users from the NT Primary Domain Controller.

Both WINNT.ADM and COMMON.ADM are usually loaded at the same time so we will deal with the default computer settings first, and then deal with user settings. The most current WINNT.ADM and COMMON.ADM templates are found in Service Pack 4; each ADM file has a file date of October 15, 1998. Service Pack 4 also includes several important settings with regards to user profiles.

The WINDOWS.ADM template is found in two locations: on the Windows NT and Windows 98 CD. This book deals with the newest version for Windows 98 users. The settings that are common to both Windows 95 and Windows 98 will be noted.

The COMMON.ADM Template: Computer Policies

Computer \ Network \ System Policies Update \ Remote Update

The path entered under Remote Update tells the local NT Workstation where to search for the system policy file (NTCONFIG.POL) once system policies have been deployed. The default path is called Automatic, which is one of two locations: either the NETLOGON share on your Primary Domain Controller

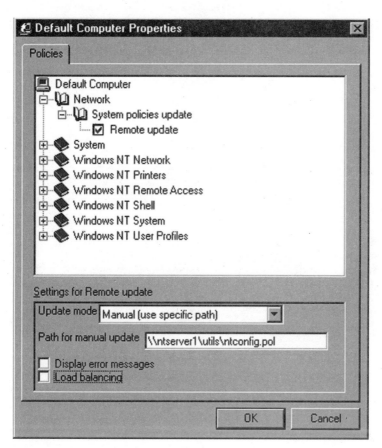

Figure 4-1 *Remote update options.*

(PDC) if your server mix is NT or, if you are using NetWare servers, the default path is SYS:PUBLIC. When you first look at this setting no path will appear to be set; you have to first check this value to see the choices. Even though it looks like no choice has been set, the Automatic mode is in effect until you select Manual mode. See Figure 4-1.

You may enter a local path if you wish to enforce a system policy running on the local machine, which may be handy for mobile users. If you wish to change the network location from NETLOGON to another shared network location, you may also do so, but make sure that your path is a UNC path as follows:

`\\Server\Share\NTCONFIG.POL.` The filename `NTCONFIG.POL` must be included for the manual path to work. The other choices are `Display error messages` and `Load balancing`.

- *Display error messages.* Checking `Display error messages` will produce an error message if the system policy file is not available.
- *Load balancing.* Checking `Load balancing` allows the workstation to read its policy file from a Backup Domain Controller (BDC) if users are logging into a BDC. This setting is for Windows NT and Windows 98 users only; Windows 95 users will look for their policy file setting only on a PDC.

Computer \ System \ SNMP

If you are using SNMP (Simple Network Management Protocol) for remote administration and communication, you can add your settings to a system policy. See Figure 4-2.

There are three settings for enforcing your SNMP environment:

1. *Communities.* Adds in one or more groups that query to SNMP agent.

2. *Permitted managers.* When checked, this setting lists the only IP or NWLink addresses permitted to receive information from an SNMP agent. Unchecked means any SNMP agent can in turn query the SNMP agent.

3. *Traps for Public community.* Lists the trap destinations in your SNMP community.

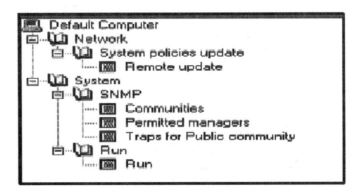

Figure 4-2 *Default Computer options for NT.*

Computer \ Run

This option specifies software utilities or applications that are to be run every time the named computer system is booted. This could be used to automate software installations when the user logs onto the network; however, this policy setting would have to be cleared after the software installation executed or it would reexecute every time the user logged in. A better use of this setting would be a virus checker or other utility that you want to run every time the user logs onto the network.

The WINNT.ADM Template: Computer Policies

Computer \ Windows NT Network \ Sharing \ Create Hidden Drive Shares (Workstation or Server)

Inside NT, the operating system creates hidden shares for all hard drives on NT systems by default. These shares are accessible by the Administrator without a password on the computer system that he or she is currently logged into. This setting allows the Administrator to control the creation of these shares. Other users would need to know the Administrator password when mapping network drives to access the hard drive(s) from the root. There are settings for NT Workstation or Server. See Figure 4-3.

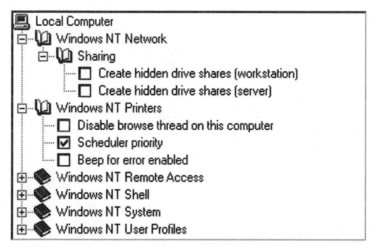

Figure 4-3 *Default Windows NT Network and Printer options.*

Computer \ Windows NT Printers

This selection deals with printer security, something usually not a high priority in a company. We have three choices:

1. *Disable browse thread on this computer.* By selecting this option on a particular computer system, the printers set on this PC would not show up in any browse list. You could still connect to the printer but the correct name of the printer would have to be entered.

2. *Scheduler priority.* Enabling this setting sets the printer priority to high; disabling this setting reduces the printer priority to below normal. The same setting can be set on the `Scheduler` tab under your printer properties.

3. *Beep for error enabled.* Generates a "beep" error every 10 seconds when a remote print job has problems on a print server.

Computer \ Windows NT Remote Access

- *Max number of unsuccessful authentication retries.* We can specify the number of retries to retype the RAS password. This would be set only on systems that have RAS access enabled.

- *Max time limit for authentication.* Sets the maximum time the user has to enter their password in seconds.

- *Wait interval for callback.* Defines the time duration for a callback from the RAS server to a user who is requesting a connection on a RAS server.

- *Auto Disconnect.* Specifies how long the RAS session should be before automatically disconnecting the user. See Figure 4-4.

Computer \ Windows NT Shell \ Custom Shared Folders

- *Shared Program folders.* UNC path to custom `Programs` folder.

- *Shared desktop icons.* UNC path to shared icons and folders.

- *Shared Start menu.* UNC path to custom `Start` menu.

- *Shared Startup folder.* UNC path to a shared `Startup` folder.

These options set up the user's common desktop items that you

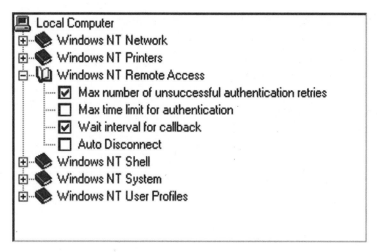

Figure 4-4 *Remote Access options.*

wish to share from a network location. This is a powerful option that allows you to control the following options regardless of the user that is logged onto a particular PC. Remember they are `Local Computer` settings so they define the users that share the computer, not the specific user.

If you decide to use one or all of these options, remember that if you ever switch back to the default settings you will have to reenter the default path in order to actually get the default settings back—for example, if you were to create a custom shared programs folder on the network and then after a few months decide to go back to the default settings. If you merely disable this setting the next time this PC is used, the Programs option on the `Start` menu will be empty until you reenter the default local path again under shared program folders in the system policy. See Figure 4-5.

Computer \ Windows NT System \ Logon

- *Logon Banner*. This enables the creation of a text logon banner that appears to all users that log onto this workstation or server.

- *Enable Shutdown from Dialog Box*. This displays a `Shutdown` button on the `Logon` dialog box.

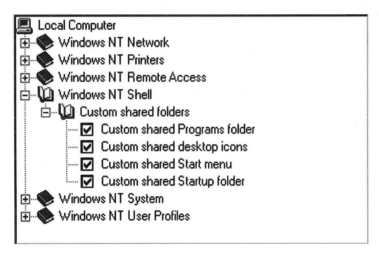

Figure 4-5 *Custom shared folders for the computer.*

- *Do not Display Last Logged on User Name.* Stops the last logged on user from showing up in the `Logon` dialog box.

- *Run Logon Scripts Synchronously.* This setting runs the complete login script before the Explorer shell is started on the PC that has this setting.

Computer \ Windows NT System \ File System

- *Do not Create 8.3 Filenames for Long Filenames.* When enabled, this setting can improve performance because the OS does not have to make duplicate filenames that are most used. This does not affect Windows 3.X or DOS apps, as they cannot make long filenames anyway.

- *Allow Extended Characters in 8.3 Filenames.* This allows you to extended characters with 8.3 filenames.

- *Do not Update last Access Time.* All files have information sheets that record the last time that the file was accessed. Turning this update off speeds up file performance when accessing read-only files.

Windows NT System \ File System \ Windows NT User Profiles

- *Delete cached copies of roaming profiles.* When a roaming user moves around the network he or she receives a roaming profile from the server. This user profile will be used if the server cannot be accessed. This setting deletes the cached profile from the local location once the roaming user logs out. In spite of this action the user profile is still copied back to the server.

- *Automatically detect slow network connections.* This setting is enabled by default. A slow network connection means a remote connection.

- *Slow network connection timeout.* The default is set at 2000 ms. You could increase the timeout for slower modem or X.25 connections.

- *Slow network default profile operation.* New to Service Pack 4, this setting allows you to specify the use of either the local user profile or a remote connection to save time logging onto the remote server. The user profile could be megabytes in size.

- *Choose profile default operation.* This setting allows you to define what user profile the users at this PC will use. If you don't want your users to use a user profile stored on the server, then choose Use local profile. If you want to enforce roaming profiles from the server, then choose Download profile. If the server is not available, then the user on this PC will not be able to log into the PC.

- *Timeout for dialog boxes.* This setting sets the time that a dialog box will warn you about a condition on the system before it disappears. See Figure 4-6.

The COMMON.ADM Template User Policies

This template holds the user or group settings that are "common" to both Windows 98 and Windows NT 4.0.

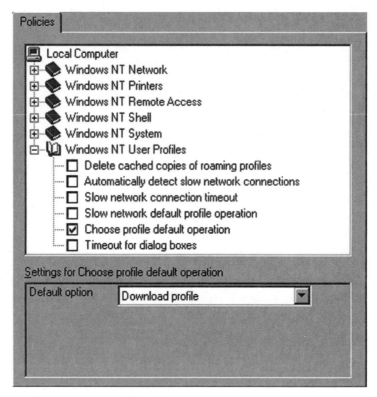

Figure 4-6 *User profile settings.*

COMMON.ADM **User Settings**

User \ Control Panel \ Display

This section is useful for disabling the entire Display icon
found in Control Panel. Users always seem to change the
Settings tab that can be accessed through the Control Panel |
Display icon or by right-clicking on the Desktop. The user can be
denied access to change the monitor, adapter, or resolution settings. You can also restrict the user's ability to change colors,
backgrounds, or screen savers.

User \ Desktop

- *Wallpaper.* Set the desktop wallpaper.
- *Color Scheme.* Set the color scheme to be used.

User \ Restrictions

This is a list of on/off settings that cover the Start menu, My Computer, and Network Neighborhood. Some are trickier than they first seem. See Figure 4-7.

- *Remove Run command from Start menu*

- *Remove folders from Settings on Start menu*

- *Remove Taskbar from Settings on Start menu*

- *Remove Find command from Start menu*

- *Hide drives in My Computer.* This means no drives from A to Z.

- *Hide Network Neighborhood.* The user can't see any servers.

- *No Entire Network in Network Neighborhood.* This setting can be handy in restricting the servers that users see in their work area.

- *No workgroup contents in Network Neighborhood*

- *Hide all items on desktop.* This means all desktop items, files, folders, and icons are gone.

- *Remove Shut Down command from Start menu*

- *Don't save settings at exit*

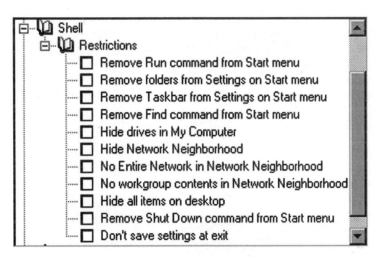

Figure 4-7 *User restrictions for the desktop.*

User \ System

- *Disable Registry editing tools.* Regedt32, Regedit, and Tweak UI are disabled when this option is checked.

- *Run only allowed Windows applications.* This selection allows you to enter all the Windows 32-bit applications that you wish your users to run. Unfortunately you must include every EXE file that the user needs, such as Systray.exe, Explorer.exe, and Clock.exe. So it has some drawbacks. If you select this option the user can execute only the applications that were added to the list. See Figure 4-8.

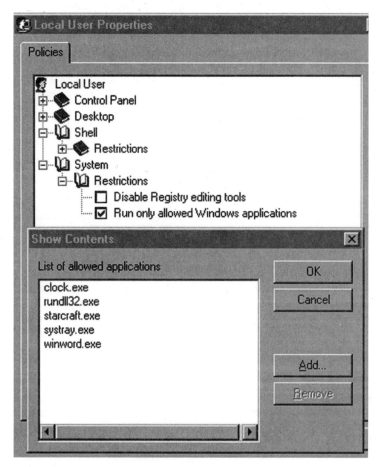

Figure 4-8 *Run only these applications.*

The WINNT.ADM **Template: User Profiles**

Windows NT Shell \ Custom User Interface

This setting allows you to define that the user will use a custom user interface rather than the Explorer shell. This is a setting used in the Zero Administration Kit (ZAK). Details on ZAK are presented later in the book.

Windows NT Shell \ Custom Folders

Keep in mind that these settings apply to the users and groups and not the named computer system.

- *Custom Programs Folder.* These settings are most useful for setting common desktop icons, folders, and shortcuts to groups.

- *Custom Desktop Icons.* The distribution of desktop shortcuts (icons) is a powerful option.

- *Hide Start Menu Subfolders.* This removes the standard Programs subfolders on the Start menu.

- *Custom Startup Folder.* This setting allows you to assign a custom startup folder to users or groups.

- *Custom Network Neighborhood.* You can specify what servers and shared folders are available across the network.

- *Custom Start Menu.* This setting allows you to assign a custom Start menu to users or groups.

Windows NT Shell \ Restrictions

- *Only use Approved Shell Restrictions.* This allows only registered file types to be accessed and opened. The standard way of looking at this list is to open the Explorer and View | Folder options.

The following toggle options remove or enable Explorer options. See Figure 4-9.

- *Remove View Folder Option menu from Explorer.* Enabling this setting stops the user from changing file associations and extensions. You can initially set up the user's Explorer shell settings and then enforce them with this setting.

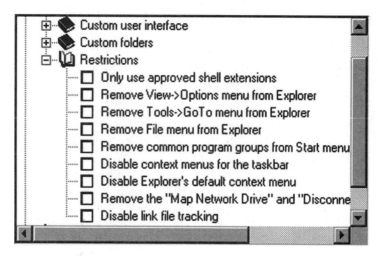

Figure 4-9 *NT system settings.*

- *Remove Tools -> Go To menu from Explorer*

- *Remove File menu from Explorer*

- *Remove Command Program Groups from Start Menu.* This removes only the shortcuts on the Start menu for common groups; it does not stop the running of the EXE files if found by the user.

- *Disable context menu for the taskbar.* Users will be restricted from any right-click options on the task bar.

- *Disable Explorer's default context menu*

- *Remove the Map Network Drive and Disconnect Network Drives options*

- *Disable link file tracking*

User \ Windows NT System

- *Parse Autoexec.bat.* If there is an AUTOEXEC.BAT file in the root of the local hard drive, NT will use the path statement as it exists and append it to the system path.

- *Run Logon Scripts Synchronously.* This setting is useful for the roaming user that has a long and involved login script. This will ensure that the login script executes before the Explorer shell is activated.

- *Disable Logoff.* Stops your users from shutting down the workstation.

- *Disable Task Manager.* CTL-ALT-DELETE is disabled.

The following options disable the following Task Manager buttons:

- *Disable Lock Workstation.* Users can't lock their workstation from Task Manager.

- *Disable Change Password.* Users can't change their password from the Task Manager.

- *Show Welcome tips at logon.* I'm not sure why you would want to turn these tips on again, except for the completely petrified new user.

User \ Windows NT User Profiles

The following options have been needed for several years and Microsoft finally provided these settings when you upgrade to Service Pack 4.

- *Limit profile size.* We can now limit the user profile size and enforce it through a system policy. The registry can also be added to the overall allowed size of the user profile support folders. When their user profile has exceeded your defined size limits, a warning will appear; the profile must be reduced before the user can log off. See Figure 4-10.

- *Exclude directories in roaming profile.* Even better, we can restrict the folders/directories that are included in the roaming user profile. Directory names are entered, separated by semicolons just like a DOS path. Remember them?

WINDOWS.ADM Computer Settings for Windows 95/98

As mentioned at the start of this chapter, this template supports Windows 95 or Windows 98 depending on the date of the template. We will be focusing on Windows 98 but will also indicate what settings apply to Windows 98 clients only. Unless specified, the settings will work on both Windows 95 and 98 clients.

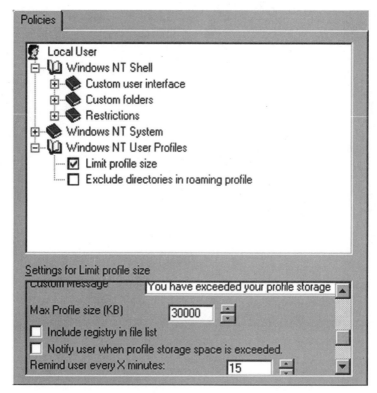

Figure 4-10 *User profile settings can be mandated.*

Computer \ Windows 98 Network \ Access Control

- *User Level access control.* Change the security level from share-level access (the default) to user-level access. This enables "pass through security" to a defined NetWare or NT Server.

Computer \ Windows 98 Network \ Logon

- *Logon Banner.* Define a text logon banner displayed at user logon.

- *Require validation from network for Windows access.* Every time users log onto the network their logon must be authenticated by either an NT or NetWare Server. If your laptop has a docking station, it will not apply to the undocked hardware profile.

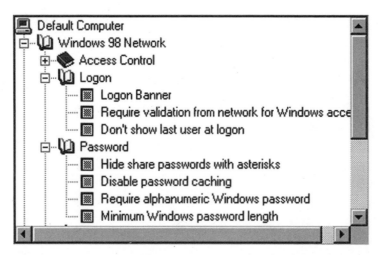

Figure 4-11 *Windows 98 Logon and Password settings for the user or group.*

- *Don't show last user at logon.* Blanks out the user name field each network logon. See Figure 4-11.

Computer \ Windows 98 Network \ Password

- *Hide share passwords with asterisks.* This setting is enabled by default and applies to shared resources on other workstations. Leave it enabled.

- *Disable password caching.* The saving of passwords is not performed. Quick logon for Microsoft networks is also disabled.

- *Require alphanumeric password.* Forces users to use a password that has a combination of numbers and letters.

- *Minimum Windows password length.* Specifies the number of minimum characters in the user's password.

Computer \ Windows 98 Network \ Microsoft
Client for NetWare Networks

- *Preferred server.* Dictates the NetWare server the user is pointed to.

- *Support long filenames.* Provides support for long file names (checked) or removes support for LFNs (unchecked).

- *Disable automatic NetWare login.* Windows 98 uses cached username and password information in the Registry to log on to a NetWare server. Checking this option disables this background action.

Computer \ Windows 98 Network \ NetWare Directory Services

If you have installed Microsoft's Service for NetWare Directory Services (NDS), then you can use these options to control your NDS environment. *This is a Windows 98 option only*. See Figure 4-12.

- *Preferred Tree.* Define the initial NDS tree.

- *Default Name Context.* Define the initial NDS context.

- *Load NetWare DLLs at startup.* Always load specific DLLs for custom NDS applications.

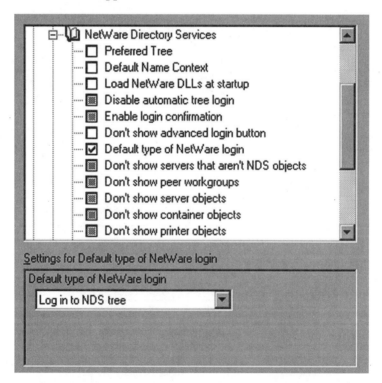

Figure 4-12 *NDS settings if NetWare Directory Services are installed.*

- *Disable automatic tree login.* Always prompt the user to log on to the NDS Tree.

- *Enable login confirmation.* Confirm that the user has logged on successfully.

- *Don't show advanced login button.* Disallow advanced login options.

- *Default type of NetWare login.* Define either a Bindery or NDS login.

- *Don't show servers that aren't NDS objects*

- *Don't show peer workgroups*

- *Don't show server objects*

- *Don't show container objects*

- *Don't show print queue objects*

- *Don't show volume objects*

Computer \ Windows 98 Network \ Microsoft Client for Windows Networks

- *Logon to Windows NT.* Allows the computer to participate in an NT domain for logon and network resources.

- *Workgroup.* When checked the computer will belong to a workgroup and not a domain

- *Alternate Workgroup*

Computer \ Windows 98 Network \ File and Printer Sharing for NetWare Networks

- *Disable SAP advertising.* Stops peer-to-peer workgroups to advertise shared resources.

Computer \ Windows 98 Network \ File and Printer Sharing for Microsoft Networks

- *Disable file sharing*

- *Disable print sharing*

**Computer \ Windows 98 Network \ Dial-Up
Networking**

- *Disable dial-in.* Stops anyone from dialing into this workstation. For Windows 95 users, the server agent must be purchased via the Plus pack.

Computer \ Windows 98 Network \ Update

- *Remote Update.* The path entered under Remote Update tells the Windows 98 Workstation where to search for the system policy file (CONFIG.POL) once system policies have been deployed. The default path is called Automatic, which is one of two locations: either the NETLOGON share on your Primary Domain Controller if your server mix is NT or, if you are using NetWare servers, the default path is SYS:PUBLIC. See Figure 4-13. When you first open this setting no path will

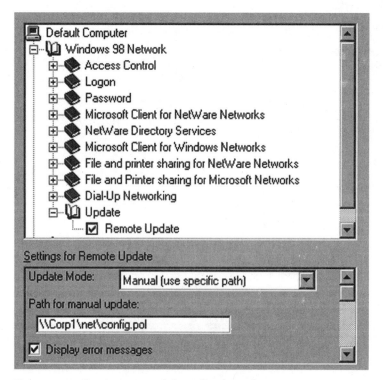

Figure 4-13 *Setting manual download mode.*

appear to be set; you have to first check this value to see the choices. Even though it looks like no choice has been set, the `Automatic` mode is in effect until you select `Manual` mode. You may enter a local path if you wish to enforce a system policy running on the local machine, which may be handy for mobile users. If you wish to change the network location from `NETLO-GON` to another shared network location, you may also do so but make sure that your path is a UNC path as follows: `\\Server\Share\NTCONFIG.POL`. The filename `CONFIG.POL` must be included for the manual path to work. The other choices are `Display error messages` and `Load balancing`.

- *Display error messages.* Checking `Display error messages` will produce an error message if the system policy file is not available.

- *Load balancing.* Checking `Load balancing` allows the workstation to read its policy file from a Backup Domain Controller if they are logging into a BDC. *This setting is for Windows 98 users only; Windows 95 users will look for their policy file setting only on a PDC.*

Computer \ Windows 98 System \ User Profiles

- *Enable User Profiles.* This setting enables user profiles on the Windows NT workstation only. This setting must be set manually on each Windows 95 or 98 workstation before system policies can be activated. We have a catch-22 setting that can't work, as custom user profiles must be active before the system policy `CONFIG.POL` will be looked for.

Computer \ Windows 98 Network \ Network Paths

- *Network path for Windows Setup.* Define a network location for the Windows 98 `CAB` files.

- *Network path for Windows Tour*

Computer \ Windows 98 Network

If you are using SNMP (Simple Network Management Protocol) for remote administration and communication, you can add your settings to a system policy. There are four settings for enforcing your SNMP environment:

1. *Communities.* Adds in one or more groups that query to
   SNMP agent.

2. *Permitted managers.* When checked, this setting lists the only
   IP or NWLink addresses permitted to receive information
   from an SNMP agent. Unchecked means any SNMP agent can
   in turn query the SNMP agent.

3. *Traps for public community.* Lists the trap destinations in your
   SNMP community.

4. *Internet MIB (RFC1156).* Adds the contact name and location
   if you are using Internet MIB.

Computer \ Windows 98 Network \ Programs to Run

At first glance, the following two options seem to be excellent
in deploying software and network services. But there is a catch.
Since these settings are defined in a system policy, they will execute every time the user logs in. They are handy for deployment
but you must make sure that the settings are removed quickly. See
Figure 4-14.

- *Run.* Specifies the applications and utilities to run every time
  this computer is booted.

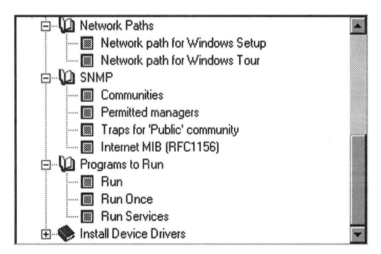

Figure 4-14 *Settings for software installation.*

- *Run Once*. Even handier, this setting allows you to install software or settings across the network.

- *Run Services.* Specifies network services to run at startup, such as dial-up networking services.

Computer \ Windows 98 Network \ Install Device Drivers

- *Digital Signature Check*. Requires all device drivers installed on this computer to be digitally signed by Microsoft. This is supposed to ensure that the driver being installed is good. Cross your fingers.

User \ Windows 98 Network \ Sharing

- *Disable file sharing controls*
- *Disable print sharing controls*

User \ Windows 98 System \ Shell \ Custom Folders

- *Custom Program folders*. UNC path to custom `Programs` folder.
- *Custom Desktop icons*. UNC Path to shared icons and folders.
- *Hide the Start menu subfolders*. If you have a custom programs folder, you'll want to hide the standard `Programs` folder; otherwise, you'll have two folders displayed: the one you want and the one you meant to hide.
- *Custom Startup folder*. UNC path to custom `Start` menu.
- *Custom Network Neighborhood*. UNC path to custom `Network Neighborhood`.
- *Custom Start menu*. Customizes what is listed on the `Start` menu.

User \ Windows 98 System \ Shell \ Restrictions

- *Disable the Run command from the Start menu*
- *Remove Folders from Settings from the Start menu*
- *Remove Task bar from Settings from the Start menu*
- *Remove Find command from Start menu*

- *Hide drives in My Computer* This means no drives from A to Z.

- *Hide Network Neighborhood* The user can't see any servers.

- *No Entire Network in Network Neighborhood* This setting can be handy in restricting the servers that users see in their work area.

- *No workgroup contents in Network Neighborhood*

- *Hide all items on Desktop.* This means all desktop items, files, folders and icons are gone.

- *Remove Shut Down command from Start menu*

- *Don't save settings at exit*

User \ Windows 98 System \ Control Panel \ Display

- *Restrict Display Control Panel.* Choose from restricting the Background, Screen Saver, Appearance, or Settings page. The Settings tab is a definite restriction highlight—you can opt to restrict the resolution, adapter, and monitor settings.

User \ Windows 98 System \ Control Panel \ Networks

- *Restrict Network Control Panel.* Checking this option disables the entire Network icon in Control Panel.

- *Hide Identification page*

- *Hide Access Control page*

See Figure 4-15.

User \ Windows 98 System \ Control Panel \ Passwords

- *Disable Passwords Control Panel.* Checking this option disables the entire Passwords icon in Control Panel.

- *Hide Change Passwords page*

- *Hide Remote Administration page*

- *Hide User Profiles page*

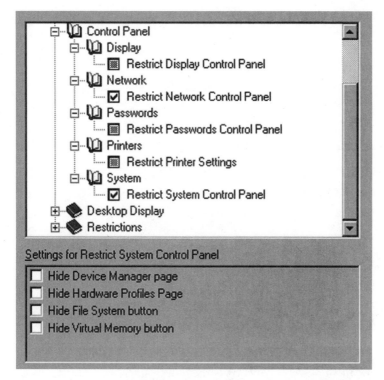

Figure 4-15 *Control Panel settings for the user or group.*

User \ Windows 98 System \ Control Panel \ Printers

- *Hide General and Details pages*
- *Disable Deletion of Printers*
- *Disable Addition of Printers*

User \ Windows 98 System \ Control Panel \ System

- *Hide Device Manager page*
- *Hide Hardware Profiles page*
- *Hide File System button*
- *Hide Virtual Memory button*

User \ Windows 98 System \ Desktop Display

- *Wallpaper*
- *Color scheme*

User \ Windows 98 System \ Restrictions

- *Disable Registry editing tools.* Enabling this option disables Regedit and Tweak UI from executing.

- *Only run allowed Windows applications.* This selection allows you to enter all the Windows 32-bit applications that you wish your users to run. Unfortunately, you must include every EXE file that the user needs, such as Systray.exe, Explorer.exe, and Clock.exe. So it has some drawbacks. If you select this option the user can execute only the applications that were added to the list. See Figure 4-16.

- *Disable MS-DOS prompt.* This option disables the MS-DOS prompt and all MS-DOS applications.

- *Disable single-mode MS-DOS applications.* The most common single mode MS-DOS app is the DOS game.

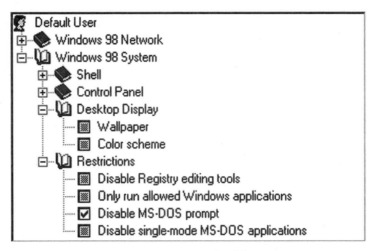

Figure 4-16 *System options we can disable.*

05

Deploying System Policies and User Profiles

In this chapter you will learn:

- How to ask the correct question before deploying system polices and user profiles

- About the possible combinations of policies and profiles and the ramifications

- How to define the user's environment for distinct situations

Deploying System Policies and User Profiles

Having implemented user profiles and system policies in numerous organizations, I can attest to the user's frustration at being locked down without warning. I can understand the complaints of some users; I know full well why others had to be locked down.

When deploying system policies and user profiles you must make sure that you consider all of the possibilities that combining security levels presents. The levels of security are numerous if you decide to implement all of the possible options. For example, you could decide to implement roaming mandatory user profiles with system policies; in effect you would have deployed three additional levels of security.

Questions to Ask Before Deploying System Policies

1. *Would administration be easier by using group settings rather than creating settings for each individual user?* The point of this question is that a well-managed security system already in place will be a bonus when implementing system policies. If you have inherited a network and you didn't set up the existing users and groups, there could be some work to do before a system policy is deployed, as the system policy editor uses existing users and global groups. If a user belongs to more groups than you realize then setting up policies can be a chore. Perhaps creating a new set of global groups for system policies is the answer.

2. *Where are the computers that are to receive policies located on your network?* If you have multiple domains, the location where users log on will be where they should receive their policy and profile settings. If the user is a notebook user or a remote user then the rules will be different. The bandwidth required for roaming user profiles for a remote user connecting with a modem is just not useful.

3. *What type of restrictions do you want to impose on users?*
   Complete lockdown or not too much? Local or on the server?
   Either option will have to be tested to make sure it is workable.
   Do your testing on a local workstation, not on a live network.

4. *Do you simply want to restrict access to specific icons or files?*
   Can a conversion of the user's hard drive partition to NTFS,
   and adding file and directory restrictions through NTFS solve
   the problem, or do you really need a system policy?

5. *Will your policy be controlling computer-specific settings only,*
   and not user settings? If so, you may be able to use the Default
   Computer settings for all your needs.

Questions to Ask Before Deploying User Profiles

1. *How much of the user's environment do you want to control?*
   Would system policies be a better solution? Although a
   mandatory user profile controls the user-specific settings, a
   system policy can control both the user and system portions of
   the Registry. Moreover, a system policy can be deployed
   regardless of where the software is installed.

2. *Do you want your users to be forced to use a specific set of*
   desktop folders and environment settings every time they log
   in? Or do users' tasks change on a weekly or monthly basis. If
   your users' needs are the same day in and day out and you are
   not changing application software for the next year, then
   mandatory user profiles might be a perfect fit.

3. *If roaming user profiles seem attractive, will users be allowed*
   to use the default profile from the client workstation or will a
   standardized server-based default profile be used instead?
   Planning users' profile settings and storing them in a central
   location makes a lot of sense for configuring new users from
   the primary domain controller.

4. *Do you want users be able to make modifications to their pro-*
   files? Is a complete lockdown feasible and workable if some of
   your users need full control of their PCs?

5. *Is the server rock solid and does it ever crash?* Local user profiles and local user accounts may be necessary if your server environment is not stable. User profiles defined and stored only on the file server are obviously not available if the server is down.

6. *Where will the profiles be stored, and is there enough server hard drive space to store them?* Profiles and files can get very big. Do the math first. The average user profile is megabytes in size and growing with every logon.

7. *Where do existing user home directories reside?* Remember home directories are not created by default; you have to create and share home directories for both Windows 98 and Windows NT clients. If existing home directories are in use you may have to migrate the existing settings.

8. *Have you mapped your Windows 98 users to the same home profiles directory on your NT server for your Windows NT users?* There may be some complications if you have user names that are the same among the two client platforms.

9. *Do you have a backup procedure in place for system policies and user profiles?* If roaming user profiles are not in use, your user settings stored in the \PROFILES folder on the local PC are not being backed up.

Implementing Client Security

The levels of security that you can choose to implement along with policies and profiles are:

- Domain or Workgroup authentication
- Directory replication
- User profile type
- Login scripts
- File and folder rights
- Shared network folders
- Shortcuts

Domain or Workgroup Logon

Domains

All of the domain user accounts can be managed from a single point instead of computer by computer. Each *domain* has one database containing user and group accounts, and security settings. All primary and backup domain controllers running NT Server in the named domain have a copy of this database.

Each domain user has one account and one password across the domain. Any changes made to the accounts database must be made at the Primary Domain Controller (PDC). Each domain can have only one PDC, and it must be running NT Server.

The Backup Domain Controller (BDC)

The PDC copies or replicates the domain accounts database to the other Backup Domain Controllers installed in the domain. The BDC can then authenticate and log on domain users from the following Windows NT Workstation and Windows 95/98 clients.

Global Groups or Workgroups

Global Groups

Your users must be created in *global groups* in order for system policies to be deployed. The rules for global groups are as follows:

1. The global group contains user accounts only from the domain from where it was created.

2. The global group cannot contain other user groups, only user accounts.

3. The global group cannot contain local users.

4. A global group is most powerful when used across multiple domains. Its main advantage is that a defined user group can be granted access to "resources" in other trusting domains.

5. A global group is used in system policies in a NT Domain, not a local group.

Workgroups

The *workgroup* is really a collection of nondedicated file servers that serve not only the users sitting in front of the computer system, but also the users that exchange files through the network connection. The disadvantages of the workgroup are:

1. No centralized control

2. No centralized user accounts to manage from one location

3. No centralized security database

The user profiles will have to be local, as there is no PDC to authenticate the logon process. A system policy can be implemented, but the loading must be manual; however, this setting must be manually added to each and every workstation in the workgroup as follows.

1. Log on to the workstation as an Administrator and open POLEDIT.EXE.

2. If this is a Windows 98 Client, load the Windows 98 COM-MON.ADM template into the Windows 98 system policy editor; if this is a Windows NT Client, load the Windows NT COMMON.ADM template into the NT system policy editor.

3. Select the File menu and select Open Registry.

4. For Windows 98 select Local Computer \ Update and then Remote Update. For Windows NT select Local Computer \ Network and then System policies update. Both Windows versions will now show Remote Update.

5. Uncheck and check the checkbox to show the choices.

6. Select the update mode of Manual (use specific path).

7. Enter the local path where you want to store the policy POL file. The path must also contain the name of the POL file or the system policy file will not be read. See Figure 5-1.

8. Do not set the options for displaying error messages or load balancing. These options are not used in a workgroup.

9. Save your settings and close the system policy editor.

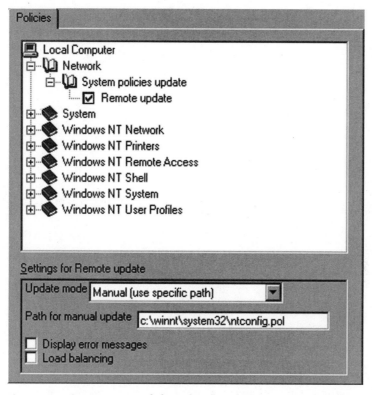

Figure 5-1 *Setting manual download in the Registry mode.*

10. Write down the location where your system policy POL file is to be copied.

11. If NT is the platform, set the NTFS permissions for the POL file to read-only after the system policy file has been created and stored in the correct location.

Directory Replication

When a policy change is made, manual replication of the policy file from the primary domain controller NETLOGON folder to the backup domain controller's NETLOGON share should be done as soon as possible. You can also set up directory replication automatically.

If you implement a System Policy file for Windows NT users and computers, you must be sure that directory replication is occurring properly among all domain controllers that participate in user authentication. With Windows NT, the default behavior is for the computer to check for a policy file in the NETLOGON share of the validating domain controller.

If directory replication to a domain controller fails and a Windows NT-based workstation does not find a policy file on that server, no policy will be applied and the existing settings will remain. This will possibly leave the user with a nonstandard environment or more capabilities than you want that particular user to have.

Perform the following steps to configure the export server:

1. Run the User Manager from Administrative Tools.

2. Create a new account for replication (for example, REP). Specify a password, if desired. The password should be set to not expire.

3. Add the user to the Replicator group. Click OK and then close User Manager. See Figure 5-2.

4. Finally, run the Control Panel and select Services. See Figure 5-3.

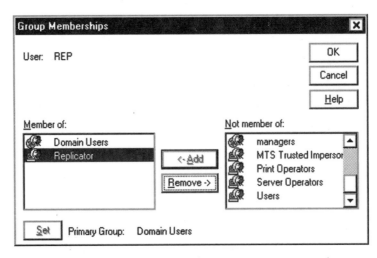

Figure 5-2 *Using User Manager for Domains to create the REP account.*

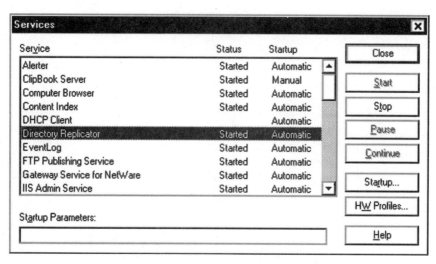

Figure 5-3 *Selecting* Services *and* Directory Replicator.

5. Choose the Directory Replicator service and choose Startup.
   Change the Startup Type from Manual to Automatic. In the
   Log On As control, choose REP. Then choose Add User. Select
   the account created previously and choose Add. See Figure 5-4.

Figure 5-4 *Choosing the replication account.*

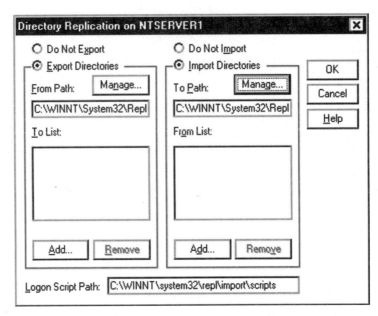

Figure 5-5 *Using Server Manager to start replication.*

6. Type the password for the replication account and choose OK.

7. Run the Server Manager from the Administrative Tools group.

8. Choose the desired Server, then choose Computer and Properties. See Figure 5-5.

9. Choose Add. Specify the name of the domain or computer to act as the import server.

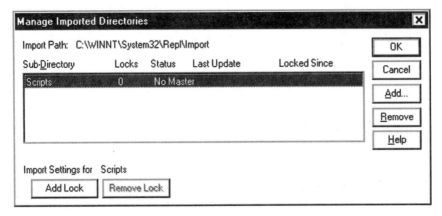

Figure 5-6 *Choosing replication destination.*

10. Choose `Replication`. In the `Replication` dialog box, choose `Export Directories`. The Server Manager displays the default path: `C:\WINNT\SYSTEM32\REPL\EXPORT`. See Figure 5-6.

Specifying the name of a domain replicates the files and directories to any workstation or Windows NT Server in the domain that is configured for import replication.

User Profile Types

The choices for user profile types are:

- A local user profile stored on the local PC
- A roaming user profile that moves with the user
- A mandatory user profile that does not change
- A roaming mandatory user profile that roams with the user but does not change

The release of Service Pack 4 or higher on NT Workstation and Server adds some needed features for controlling user profiles. The updates are found in the template `WINNT.ADM` for both computer and user choices.

Computer \ Windows NT User Profiles

- *Delete cached copies of roaming profiles.* This option is great for users that must occasionally move from computer to computer but also have their own computer system as well. If you think about it, leaving roaming user profiles on other users' computers could be a huge security breech, as Microsoft includes the `MY DOCUMENTS` folder in the user profile.

- *Choose profile default operation.* This setting removes the choice from the end user as to what user profile to use when logging into the domain.

Download Profile
Use local profile

See Figure 5-7.

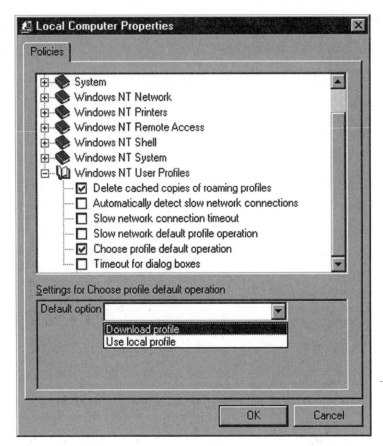

Figure 5-7 *User profile control with WINNT.ADM updates.*

User \ Windows NT User Profiles

- *Limit profile size.* The choices are:

  Max Profile size in KB

  Custom warning message

  Include registry in file list

  Notify user when profile storage space is exceeded

  Remind user every X minutes

  See Figure 5-8.

- *Exclude directories in roaming profile.* The best setting yet for user profiles, with this option you control which all-user profile folders are considered part of the user profile. See Figure 5-9.

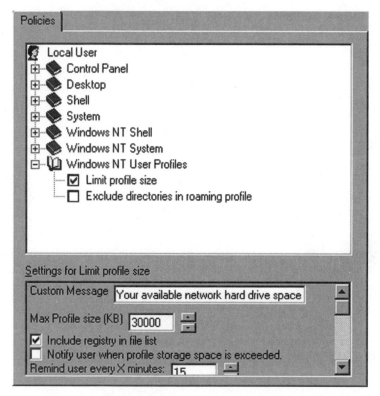

Figure 5-8 *Control your user profile size with these settings.*

If you don't want roving profiles to be enabled on a certain user's Window 98 computer system a Registry edit can control this. Open Regedit and scroll down to the HKEY_LOCAL_MACHINE\ Network key. Highlight the Logon subkey and create a new DWORD value with the value name of UseHomeDirectory with a value of 1.

Note

Login Scripts

The use of logon scripts will allow you to enforce user security on the local PC as well as automate other security options. Both Windows 98 and NT clients support Login scripts. For NT, the file is a text-based file with either .BAT or .CMD as the extension.

The logon script is stored in the WINNT\SYSTEM32\REPL\ IMPORT\SCRIPTS (the NETLOGON share) by default and is enabled

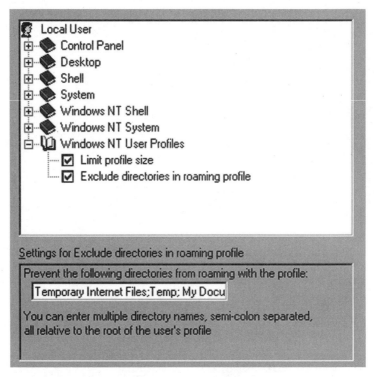

Figure 5-9 *Define the folders considered part of the user profile.*

through User Manager for Domains utility. The location should remain the `NETLOGON` share so that directory replication between PDC and any BDCs will include the logon scripts. The commands that can be included in a login script include:

- Environment variables for NT

- Any `EXE` command you wish to execute

- Any command line-based `NET` command

Note   If you wished to synchronize the workstation's time with that of the domain, delete all system policy template files and remove `Regedit`. Then the following batch file would do the job:

```
@echo off
net time \\Kingston /set /yes
del c:\*.adm > null
del c:\regedit.* > null
```

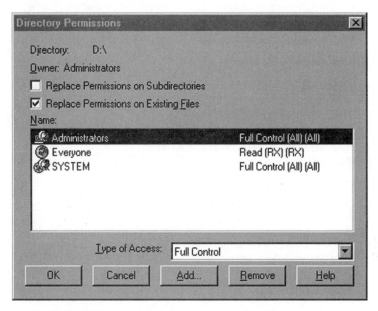

Figure 5-10 *NTFS permissions for file and folders.*

File and Folder Permissions

NTFS file and folder security is certainly the best form of protection; however, you have to ask yourself if your user needs this level of security. The question I always ask myself is, "Where are the data files stored—on the local machine or on the file server?" If the answer is local, then NTFS and NT are the best choice. If the answer is on the file server, perhaps Windows 98 is a better choice.

NT file and folder security is set through the security tab that is available only with NTFS partitions. See Figure 5-10.

The FAT (File allocation table) file system has no real security and should not be used for NT systems if a secure environment is needed. Windows 98 can use FAT16 or FAT32, but there is no security advantage by using either choice.

Network Folders

Any folder that users need access to on the network must be shared to be accessed through the users' network neighborhood.

Shortcuts and Security

For added file security try to ensure that all software files are represented to the end user by a shortcut. In this way, the actual file is sheltered from permanent damage as the shortcut can be deleted but the original file remains.

System Policy and User Profile Combinations

As you now know, we have many choices for implementing policies and profiles for Windows 98 and Windows NT 4.0 clients. In fact, you could be faced with several possible combination options for a typical mixed client environment.

- A default system policy for all users and computers across the domain

- A complete lockdown for specific users and global groups

- A complete lockdown for specific users

- Group lockdown with global groups

- Mandatory profiles for users and or groups and system policies

- Roaming profiles for users and or groups and system policies

- Local system policies and user profiles for peer-to-peer workgroups

- System policies and user profiles for remote users

Note

The template file to use for Windows 98 is ADMIN.ADM along with the system policy editor POLEDIT.EXE, found on the Windows 98 CD-ROM in the POLEDIT folder.

The template file to use for Windows 98 is WINDOWS.ADM along with the system policy editor POLEDIT.EXE, found on the Windows 98 CD-ROM in the POLEDIT folder.

The template files to use for Windows 98 and Windows NT are COMMON.ADM and WINNT.ADM, along with the system policy editor POLEDIT.EXE. They are found on NT Server in the \WINNT folder.

The Default Systemwide Lockdown

This is the recommended minimum system policy to first implement. It is the easiest, as there are only the two default icons, Default User and Default Computer, to attend to. These settings apply to all users on all computer systems, hence the name *default*.

It can also be the trickiest, as all users including Administrator are affected by Default User and Default Computer settings if no other settings are added to the policy.

The default lockdown is concerned with limiting the damage the user can do to the local computer system and operating system components. Think of the settings that you want to be universal. Most of the potential damages a client can get involved with are through Control Panel and Registry settings.

Suggested Windows 98 Client User Settings

These settings would help limit the damage a user could do to the Registry and operating system device drivers.

- Hide Settings tab in Display icon
- Disable the Device Manager page
- Disable the Virtual Memory button
- Disable Registry Editing Tools
- Hide User Profiles page

Suggested Windows NT Client User Settings

- Hide Settings tab in Display icon
- Disable Registry editing tools
- Remove common program groups from Start menu

Suggested Windows NT Client Computer Settings

- Run logon scripts synchronously
- Do not display last logged on user

Lockdown for Named Users and Global Groups

In this scenario proper testing must be done. With multiple groups and users there will be some overlap between the policies and permissions. The settings for all the choices for users and groups are well documented in this book in the respective chapters for each client.

Keep in mind the rules of deployment that can get complicated with users being members of several groups. If the default user settings are getting in the way, remember that you can always remove the default user from the system policy leaving named users and global groups only.

Lockdown for Specific Users

The scenario of using only user settings is workable and your only choice if your server is NetWare. Global groups are not an option for Novell NetWare networks. The default user is quite useful in this example as it becomes your global group, so to speak, affecting all users.

Mandatory Profiles for Users and or Groups

A *mandatory profile* can be implemented along with a system policy if you desire this amount of control. This is a good choice for schools and labs where there are a lot of new users that need the same settings day in and out. Remember that a mandatory user profile is created through the System icon in the Control Panel, and using the User Profile tab to copy the desired local user profile to a network location.

You can also set group rights to the same user profile; however, a mandatory user profile can cause problems in environments where software updates are frequent. Any software installed when a mandatory user profile is active will not be there at the next login—the mandatory user profile is downloaded from the file server every successful login.

Lockdown with Global Groups

The best scenario is to try to manage your system policy with defined global groups. In this scenario, the only possible users in the system policy would be yourself, the Administrator.

Roaming Profiles for Users and/or Groups

Make sure that you want the user to actually roam. This works best with server installed software; however, most software nowadays is becoming too large to properly run from the server. The norm is therefore locally installed software, so make sure that the installed location of all software, user folders, and shortcuts is the same across the board or else problems will occur.

Remember each user has a local registry NTUSER.DAT that holds the path to installed hardware settings for the user. A networked install of software will have different paths in the local Registry. Proper testing must be done to ensure the roaming user profile will really work.

Remember the four golden rules for roaming user profile: **Note**

1. The user profile path must be defined in the user's profile settings found in User Manager for Domains.
2. Windows 98 Clients must have custom user profiles enabled through the Passwords icon in Control Panel.
3. The user profile path must be shared across the network.
4. Software must be installed in the same location on all computer system where the user will potentially roam.

Mandatory Profiles for Users and/or Groups Plus System Policies

This combination makes use of a user profile that never changes plus the advantages of additional system policies. Recommended system policy settings are as follows.

Suggested Windows 98 Client User Settings

- Do not allow computer to restart in MS-DOS mode
- Restrict Display Control Panel
- Restrict Network Control Panel
- Restrict Password Control Panel

- Restrict Printers Control Panel

- Restrict System Control Panel

- Disable Registry Tools

- Disable MS-DOS Prompt

- Disable single-mode MS-DOS application

- Computer Settings

- Disable password caching

The NT client should have NTFS installed as the file system. This allows full file and folder security across the local drive. The settings listed for system policies are a much shorter list than the Windows 98 client due to the higher initial security of NT. The control panel does not have to be locked down, as any changes made require administrative access.

Note

You could however use the "quick and dirty" rename option to rename any Control Panel applet that you don't want to be loaded and displayed when the Control Panel opens.

My favorite to remove is `APPWIZ.CPL`; this applet loads the `Add/Remove Software` **icon.**

Suggested Windows NT Client User Settings

- Hide Settings tab in Display icon

- Remove common groups from Start menu

- Run logon scripts synchronously

- Computer Settings

- Logon banner

- Do not display last logged on user

Local System Policies for Workgroups

If you don't have a dedicated server, then system policies can still be set up in a workgroup environment using the system policies update setting found in the Computer settings for both Windows

98 and NT Clients. When a workgroup model is implemented, the version of Windows being used will determine the level of system security.

System Policies and User Profiles for Remote Users

A remote client that logs into the domain using remote access services is usually using a modem connection that is less than fast. The user profile should be locally stored, not roaming. The client should log in through a defined remote access group that has policy settings for remote access, security, and user profiles.

Suggested Windows NT Client Computer Settings

- Windows NT Remote Access

  Max number of unsuccessful authentication retries
  Auto Disconnect

- Windows NT System

  Logon banner

- Windows NT User Profiles

  Automatically detect slow network connections
  Slow network default profile operation

Special User Environments

I get asked about my suggestions for deploying a secure computing environment for special situations. The most common requests are for these types of clients:

- Students in elementary school or college

- The portable client

  Let's take each situation and work through some suggested solutions. The solution includes the following elements of security we have discussed earlier in this chapter.

Students in Elementary School or College

- *Domain or Workgroup authentication.* Should be logged into a domain for central security.

- *Directory replication*. System policy POL files and login scripts should be replicated to backup domain controllers if available.

- *User profile type*. Local user profiles. Provisions must also be made to back up the local user profiles.

- *Login script*. Used to perform backup of user profiles to a central location.

- *System policy settings*

Suggested Windows 98 Client Computer Settings

- Require validation from network for Windows access

- Don't show last user at logon

- Don't show logon progress

- Disable password caching

- Logon to Windows NT (and specify Domain)

Suggested Windows 98 Client User Settings

- Disable active desktop

- No HTML Wallpaper

- Disable resizing all toolbars

- Remove Run menu

- Remove Find menu

- Don't save settings at exit

- Hide Floppy Drives in My Computer

- Do not allow computer to restart in MS-DOS mode

- Custom Desktop Items

- Custom Program Folders

- Hide Start menu subfolders

- Restrict Display Control Panel

- Restrict Network Control Panel

- Restrict Passwords Control Panel

- Restrict Printers Control Panel
- Restrict System Control Panel
- Disable Registry editing tools
- Disable MS-DOS Prompt
- Disable Windows Update

Suggested Windows NT Client User Settings

- Hide Settings tab
- Remove Run command from Start menu
- Remove folders from Settings on Start menu
- Remove Taskbar from Settings on Start menu
- Remove Find command from Start menu
- Hide Network Neighborhood
- Don't save settings on exit

Suggested Windows NT Client Computer Settings

- Custom shared Program Folders
- Custom shared desktop icons
- Do not display last logged on user name
- File and Folder rights (If NT is the Client then NTFS should be deployed.)
- Shared Network Folders (Create and share a network folder for the user's home directory.)
- Shortcuts (All software on the Start menu should be network shortcuts using `Shell \ Custom Folders` to redirect the user to a read-only network path.)

The Portable Client

- *Domain or Workgroup authentication.* On the road the client needs a local desktop. Windows 98 and Windows NT can obviously handle this. Both Windows 98 and NT can also use dial-up networking to be authenticated to a domain.

- *Directory replication.* This is not an option for the portable client.

- *User profile type.* The user profile must be local.

- *System policy settings.* Any system policy settings are possible, the real question you have to ask is how much user control, is needed on the PC. If you want complete control then any Windows 98, Windows NT, Office 97/2000, or Internet Explorer setting is valid. The system policy POL file will have to be stored locally; see notes earlier in this chapter on how to enable manual downloading of user profiles to a standalone PC.

- *Login script.* This is not an option for the portable client.

- *File and folder rights.* If the client has sensitive data files then NT and NTFS is the best choice.

- *Shared network folders.* This is not an option for the portable client.

- *Shortcuts.* All software on the `Start` menu should be local shortcuts.

Final Steps: Securing the Hives

For a secure Registry, permissions should be reset on the `%SYSTEM-ROOT%\SYSTEM32\CONFIG` directory as follows:

SYSTEM	Full control
Administrators	Full control
CREATOR OWNER	Full control
Everyone	Add and read permissions only

Security Holes to Watch For

Certain software utilities, help files, and executable files can also be security holes to consider plugging.

- *MSINFO32.* If the workstation has any Microsoft Office application installed, the odds are that `MSINFO32.EXE` will be installed. This utility allows users to run the Control Panel and the Registry Editor from the `RUN` box inside MSINFO32. It

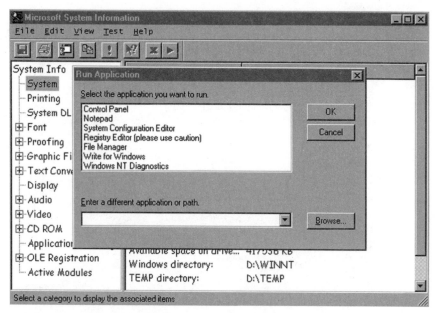

Figure 5-11 *You can run utilities inside MSINFO32 with system polices deployed.*

should be removed. (See Figure 5-11.) These applications bypass the shell name space so they are not monitored or restricted by the System Policy. This allows users to run applications even if they are not listed in the System Policy's "Allowed to run" list or the Control Panel has been locked down.

- *Help Files.* All help files should be checked for security holes. The user can select any of the help files listed and then enter the `Troubleshooting` option in the help file. From here the user can access the Control Panel even if it is locked down. See Figure 5-12.

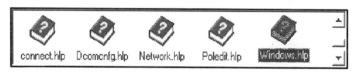

Figure 5-12 *These and other help files can access the Control Panel.*

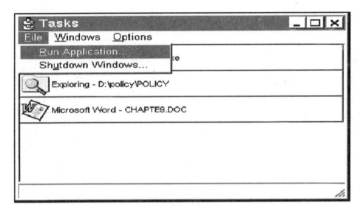

Figure 5-13 *The mostly unknown Task Manager.*

Note

Security hole at the Windows 95 Login: If Windows 95 users are locked down with the setting Require Validation to network for Windows Access and press CTRL-ESC, they can access Task Manager and run any local application(s) they desire. The system policy is in effect; however, the Task Manager runs as a separate process. See Figure 5-13.

The solution is to delete TASKMAN.EXE. Windows 98 does not have this security hole—it has been fixed.

- *Executable Files.* Other executables should also be removed from the local PC to stop potential hacking. See Figure 5-14.

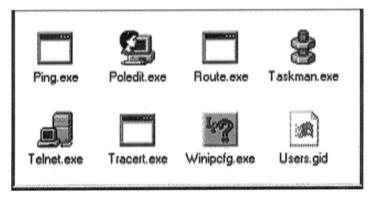

Figure 5-14 *EXE files to consider removing.*

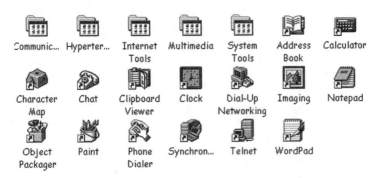

Figure 5-15 *Start menu items should be reviewed.*

- *Start Menu Shortcuts.* The shortcuts found on the Programs menu off the Start menu should be analyzed for possible security breeches. For example, if users have access to the explorer shell, they can do most anything on the local PC. See Figure 5-15.

Fine-Tuning Your Policies' Security Settings for Maximum Safety

Go to the Shell | Restrictions and System | Restrictions and change any gray check boxes to blank. Once you have defined specific user policies, double-click the Users icon and go through the entire list of restrictions, setting every check box to blank, not gray. This protects the users policy from being affected by the default user policy. A gray check box is a do not deploy locally setting; a blank box is a clear command to the local registry for the specified setting.

Check What's Happening with Audit Control

The NT file system has the ability to keep track of most system activities through the use of auditing that can be set on any selected object through the security tab on any NTFS volume. Any object—including files, folders, and Registry hives—can be audited on a user or group level.

Information that is produced when the audit option is implemented is sent to the Event Viewer found in the Administration

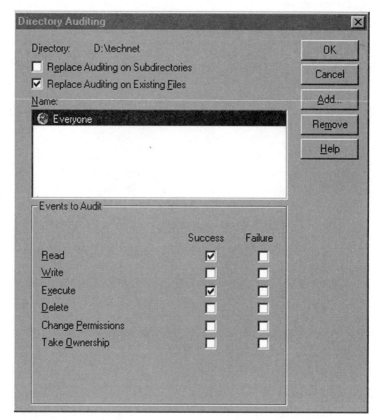

Figure 5-16 *Setting audit levels through the Security tab.*

Tools on the Start menu. This is an extra level of administration that NT supports on both the server and workstation and also for Windows 98 client locations on the file server. See Figure 5-16.

Information that is produced when the audit option is implemented is sent to the Event Viewer. This utility is by default installed in the Administration Tools on the Start menu. See Figure 5-17.

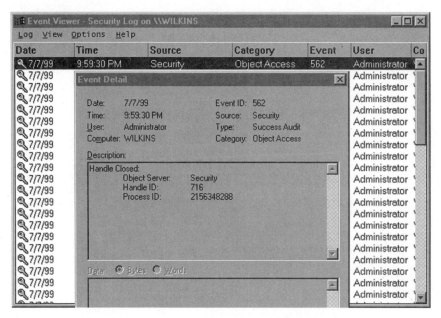

Figure 5-17 *The Event log holds the results of the audit.*

Internet Explorer 5 and Policy Settings

This chapter introduces you to the ever changing world of system polices and how they are deployed through Internet Explorer 5 and the IEAK (Internet Explorer Administrator Kit). You will learn all about the support tools for Internet Explorer 5, as well as:

- What the IEAK is used for
- How to use the Internet Explorer Customization Wizard
- How to set user policy with the Profile Manager
- How and why INS files are created
- Policy settings for Internet Explorer 5

Internet Explorer 5.0 (IE5)

IE5 is the most current Web browser from Microsoft *at this time of writing*. If you are supporting end users migrating to IE5, then a copy of the Internet Explorer Administration Kit is a good resource to get your hands on. It combines a lot of features for the Administrator who needs to deploy IE5 across the corporate network.

System policies are an essential part of deploying Internet Explorer 5 with the IEAK, without using the system policy editor.

IEAK is free on the Web and downloadable from Microsoft at *https://ieak.microsoft.com/*. It combines utilities for the Administrator or ISP who needs to deploy IE5 across the corporate network or to Internet clients.

Administrators can use IEAK to:

- Customize the IE Browser and other optional IE components to suit their users' needs.

- Define installation options and configuration settings before the installation occurs.

- Define custom programs to install during setup.

- Manage the security, connection, and desktop settings that users are allowed to change through INS files.

The main components of IEAK we will explore are the:

- *Internet Explorer Customization Wizard*. This tool steps you through the process of creating a customized IE5 install for multiple clients.

- *Internet Explorer Administration Kit Profile Manager*. A new front end for deploying system policy .ADM template for IE clients, the Profile Manager allows you to make Internet Explorer system policy changes to your users automatically when you are deploying a customized install. This interface is moving us closer to how Windows 2000 handles system policies, as POLEDIT is not used for Windows 2000 at all; it is available only for Windows NT 4.0 and Windows 98 client support of system policies.

There are six major steps involved with creating a custom "Package" with the IEAK. Where system policy settings come into play is at step 5 of the Internet Explorer customization wizard. The general areas that system policy settings can be defined with the Profile Manager are:

- Limiting security levels for Internet Explorer users.

- Specifying intranet server lists for installed components, such as NetMeeting.

- Defining a global page for updating your users' IE settings.

- Outline email client software and settings.

- Predefine your users' connection settings.

We are used to POLEDIT for loading system policy templates and setting user, group, and computer settings in POL files. With the addition of IEAK, you have two choices for setting system policies and restrictions.

1. *With the usual system policy editor and loading the specific IE templates and saving your settings in POL files.* These IE templates are scattered across Microsoft's application software such as Office 97 and Office 2000, and are also included in Windows 98 and 2000 and of course Internet Explorer 5.

2. *Using the IEAK and Profile Manager and saving your custom IE5 configuration as INS files.* These settings are then deployed using the customization wizard or through View | Internet Options | Connections | Automatic Configuration, holding the interval settings for when the INS file is to be checked and deployed. The INS files can also be stored in a central configuration location to be used every time a user runs Internet Explorer or different INS files can be created for different user needs and custom deployment of IE5.

Through INS files we can set policy restrictions in the following user locations:

- *Internet Settings.* These are the same options you'll find when selecting Tools | Internet Options while running Internet Explorer.

- *Initial Wizard Settings*. Choices that are presented during the execution of the Internet Explorer Customization wizard can be predefined as answers for automatic configuration.

- *User Shell Settings*. Define the user's level of interaction with the Explorer shell, file management, and other everyday user tasks.

- *Subscriptions*. Control the user's access and choices with subscription services and channels.

- *NetMeeting, Chat, Outlook Express*. Control file server settings and the presentation of these IE add-in components.

Using the Internet Explorer Customization Wizard

When you deploy the customization wizard you are presented with a splash screen that briefly details the following steps involved with the creation of a custom IE package. The six stages of creation with the customization wizard are:

- *Stage 1*. Gathering information
- *Stage 2*. Specifying setup parameters
- *Stage 3*. Customizing setup
- *Stage 4*. Customizing the browser
- *Stage 5*. Component customization
- *Stage 6*. Deploying the custom IE package

Stage 1

The stage 1 information you provide the customization wizard is basic installation information.

- *Company Name and 10-digit customization code*. By clicking the Get Customization Code button you are directed to the Web location at Microsoft where you can choose your license options and register. They then will email you your 10-digit code so you can complete your IE5 package. See Figure 6-1.

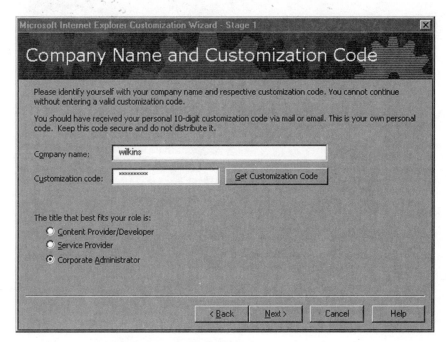

Figure 6-1 *A 10-digit customization code is needed to continue installation.*

- *Your distribution role.* Define whether you are a content provider or developer, service provider, or corporate administrator.

- *The platform for installation of IE5.* Windows 3.11, WFW, 98, NT 3.51 0r 4.0, or UNIX

- *File locations to locate your final Internet Explorer package and customized browser.* See Figure 6-2.

- *The preferred language of IE5*

- *Distribution media.* Download from the Web, intranet, or network location.

- *Features of IE that you want to customize.* Select from a checklist the Internet Explorer components that you want to customize with policy settings for your custom package. You may elect to customize no options at this time, or you may already have defined an existing INS file through the advanced options of file locations. See Figure 6-3.

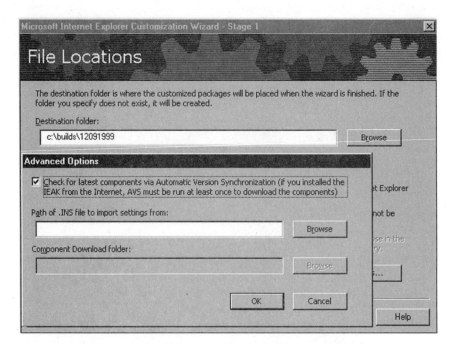

Figure 6-2 *Specify file locations and optional advanced options.*

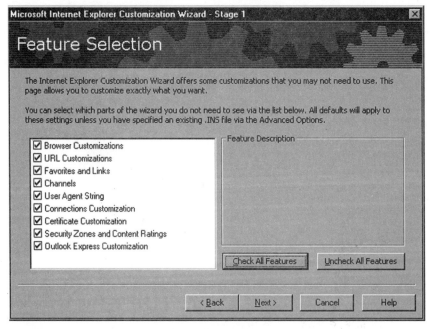

Figure 6-3 *Define the areas of Internet Explorer you wish to customize during the custom package install.*

Stage 2

Stage 2 introduces a feature called *Active Setup*. This allows you to install the latest Internet Explorer 5 components from a Microsoft Web site and include them in your custom package at the time of install. You may have the most up to date IE5 components, but at the rate at which Microsoft updates IE and Outlook express you probably will appreciate this feature.

You can choose to synchronize and update all IE5 components automatically—that is, download all new components—or you can choose the pieces you want to download and update. The major decisions you make in stage 2 are:

- *Component download site.* Provide the Web path to the newer IE5 components.

- *Automatic Version Synchronization (AVS).* Choose the IE5 components to update.

- *Adding custom components.* If your developers have used IExpress for creation of custom components you can enter up to 10 components to include with your package. Other options of interest are:

  GUIDE: This is a globally unique identifier, which tattoos all user action through the Registry. All user email and IE work can be tracked through this unique number. Microsoft hopes the next big thing in management software will be tracking all user activity.

  Uninstall Key: The uninstall string can be entered if you want the user to be able to uninstall custom components through Add / Remove programs in the Control Panel. See Figure 6-4.

Stage 3

You can customize how Setup will appear to your users during installation of IE and selected components. Some of the features of stage 3 you can choose to deploy are:

- Customize the Windows update setup wizard for Internet Explorer and other IE tools.

- Choose to install in silent mode with little or no user interaction.

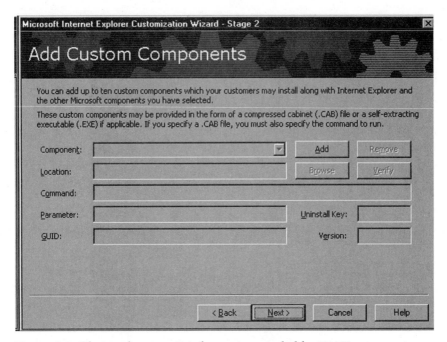

Figure 6-4 *Choices for stage 2 information needed by IEAK.*

- Define up to 10 installation options and decide which components are included with the selected options.

- Preset up to 10 sites from which the custom IE package will be downloaded.

- Define the method in which users will receive updates to their IE components.

- Outline where you want Internet Explorer to be installed and whether the location is fixed or it can be changed.

- Specify that Setup can self-detect existing components and also the components users can customize. Choose also whether IE components that are downloaded will be automatically installed. See Figure 6-5.

- Create or import a new profile with the Connection Manager Administration Kit (CMAK) included with IEAK.

- Specify if you want to automatically install the Active Desktop into your user's desktop and folders.

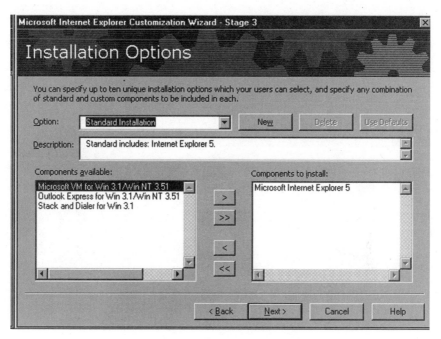

Figure 6-5 *Select advanced components and the installation method.*

Stage 4

This stage is where you customize the look and feel of the IE browser, the location of custom folders, and proxy and security settings. See Figure 6-6. Highlights of stage 4 are defining:

- The browser title bar, toolbar background bitmap, browser toolbar buttons, and IE logo
- Default URL Home, search, and online support locations
- Favorites, Favorites folders, and links for the Links bar
- Startup Welcome page
- Automatic browser configuration
- Connection settings
- Proxy settings
- Desktop toolbar settings
- Active Desktop customization
- Settings for all aspects of security

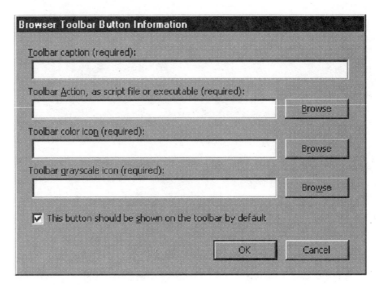

Figure 6-6 *Predefine custom toolbar information.*

Stage 5

This stage allows you to customize the installed components of IE5, including email, news, and domain server settings. System policy settings for IE and installed components can also be defined. Highlights of stage 5 are:

• News and mail servers addresses

• IMAP email server settings

• Custom startup options for Outlook Express

• Outlook Express custom settings

• System policies and settings including options for the Internet Explorer, Outlook Express, security and desktop settings

Stage 6

Stage 6 is where you would actually install the IE package using the executable file IESETUP.EXE and its companion file IE5SITES.DAT. These two files are small enough to fit on a floppy disk together; they are located in the build location specified during the custom IE5 package creation.

IE5SETUP.EXE locates the URL path for the needed IE 5 files from the IE5SITES.DAT file. IE5SITES.DAT is a text file that lists all of the download location information and the path to the .CAB files for each location.

The following steps occur when IE5SETUP.EXE is executed:

1. IE5SETUP.EXE first extracts the setup files into a temporary directory.

2. IE5SETUP then looks at the [String] section of IE5SETUP.INF for the URL location of the IE5SITES.DAT file.

3. Next, Setup goes to the file IE5SITES.DAT to retrieve the URLs for the download sites and then displays the download sites to the client.

4. Setup then downloads the defined .CAB files, which are placed in the directory the client specifies, or if the administrator has mandated a location, that location is used instead.

5. Setup then extracts the .CAB files.

6. Setup finally installs Internet Explorer and each component the administrator specified.

7. After installation Setup prompts the user to restart the computer.

Using the IEAK Profile Manager

The IEAK Profile Manager (PM) is used to create custom user configuration files that can be stored and used for configuring groups of users that will be receiving a custom install of IE5. The Profile Manager first creates a file structure called an *instruction file* (INS) used for autoconfiguration. The creation of the custom INS file, in turn, creates a set of associated CAB files linked to the INS file.

For example, you could use the Profile Manager to create a custom set of configuration settings for installing IE5 for the office group in your company and save the settings as OFFICE.INS. The OFFICE.INS would also be an existing NT global group on your network. The PM would then generate a custom set of CAB files to be used with OFFICE.ADM.

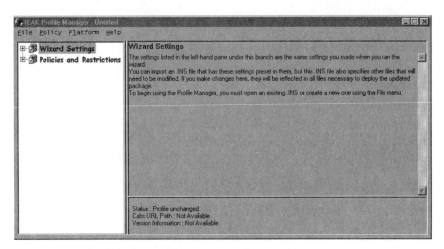

Figure 6-7 *The default Profile Manager choices.*

The CAB files contain installation scripts called INF files that automatically deploy when the CAB files are unpacked. The INF files then deploy the defined system policy restrictions through the user's local Registry.

To start the IEAK Profile Manager, run the executable PROG-MGR.EXE and the screen shown in Figure 6-7 will be displayed.

Selecting any of the visible Wizard Settings you can modify, add, or change the current settings that you want to deploy. There are also 10 system policy templates that you can also modify through the Profile Manager for custom instruction (INS) files. First, let's overview the wizard settings we can control.

- *Browser Title*. Define the title bar text for IE5 plus text in any custom toolbar bitmaps.

- *Animated Bitmaps*. Select a custom logo to replace the IE logo that usually appears in the upper right-hand corner.

- *Logo*. Select a custom logo to replace the IE static logo that usually appears in the upper right hand corner.

- *Digital Signatures*. Software Publishing Certificates and Private Key encryption are two popular digital signatures that IE5 now supports. See Figure 6-8.

- *Favorites and Links*. Predefine the list of favorites and URL

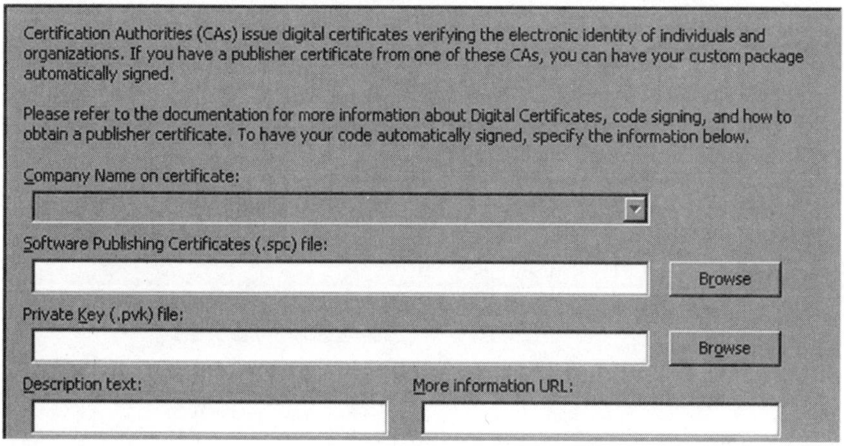

Certification Authorities (CAs) issue digital certificates verifying the electronic identity of individuals and organizations. If you have a publisher certificate from one of these CAs, you can have your custom package automatically signed.

Please refer to the documentation for more information about Digital Certificates, code signing, and how to obtain a publisher certificate. To have your code automatically signed, specify the information below.

Company Name on certificate:

Software Publishing Certificates (.spc) file:

Browse

Private Key (.pvk) file:

Browse

Description text:

More information URL:

Figure 6-8 *Digital signing choices for IE5.*

links that will be added to the top of the list that the user can access while using Internet Explorer.

- *Browser Toolbar Buttons.* Define custom buttons that will be visible on the Internet Explorer Toolbar.

- *User Agent String.* You can specify a default user agent command string that will be used when Internet Explorer first starts. You can track the browser usage and define custom Web content with this command syntax. Full details are available in the Internet Explorer Resource Kit that can be downloaded free from Microsoft.

- *Connection Settings.* You can choose to import your connection setting from the Control Panel to be included in a custom package.

- *Automatic Browser Configuration.* Define the location of INS files to be automatically deployed when Internet Explorer starts. You can also specify an automatic timeframe to deploy these settings as well.

- *Proxy Settings.* Define the proxy settings to use for HTTP:, Gopher, FTP, Secure, and Socks.

- *Important URLs.* Define the start page that is displayed when Home is selected, the search page that is displayed when Search

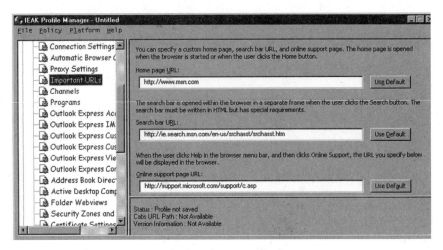

Figure 6-9 *These URLs can be handy to set for new users.*

is selected, and the online support page that is displayed when the user selects Online Support. See Figure 6-9.

- *Channels.* If the user is using channels you can define the channels that will show up on the user's desktop.

- *Programs.* Default program settings can be applied for Email, HTML Editor, Newsgroup, Internet call, Calendar, and Contact list.

- *Outlook Express Accounts.* Define Outlook Express, Internet Mail, and News settings.

- *Outlook IMAP Settings.* Specify file locations and settings for IMAP accounts.

- *Outlook Express Custom Content.* Define a starting Information pane and Welcome message for Outlook Express.

- *Outlook Express Custom Settings.* Define junk mail filtering and Outlook Express as the default mail or news software.

- *Outlook Express View Settings.* Customize folder, toolbar, and other view settings.

- *Outlook Express Compose Settings.* Define HTML as the default for Outlook Express and News message composition. Also add a digital signature to be attached to each email message sent.

- *Address Book Directory Services*. Define the default LDAP server and its search parameters.

- *Active Desktop Components*. Define custom active desktop components to be displayed on users' desktops.

- *Folder Webviews*. Specify custom Web views for `My Computer` and `Control Panel` folders if Active Desktop has been activated.

- *Security Zones and Content Ratings*. Outline security and content ratings to be deployed for Internet Explorer.

- *Certificate and Settings*. Stipulate valid digital certificates and Authenticode trust settings.

Policies and Restrictions and Profile Manager

The IEAK uses 10 system policy templates with the familiar ADM extension. Custom ADM files can also be added to the Profile Manager by selecting Policy and Import. See Figure 6-10.

All policies and restrictions that you deploy using the IEAK are first saved to information (INF) files.

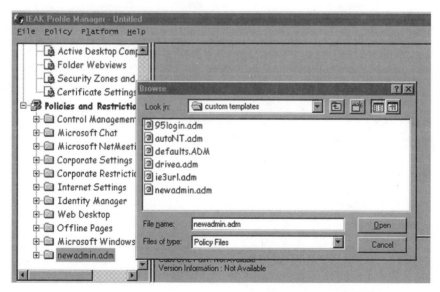

Figure 6-10 *Adding a custom ADM template to Profile Manager.*

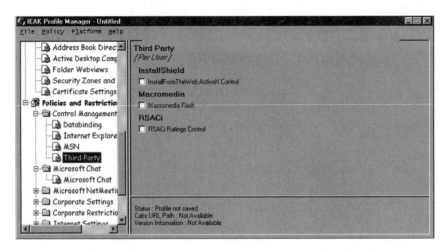

Figure 6-11 *Third Party policy restrictions set through Profile Manager.*

Control Management

- *Databinding*. If you are using Dynamic HTML, you can choose a variety of data source objects: RDS, TDC, or XML.

- *Internet Explorer*. Choose what controls the user can access for the Active Desktop and other IE components such as: Media Player, Chat, and Microsoft Wallet.

- *MSN*. If you use MSN you can specify Installation options and controls available.

- *Third Party*. InstallShield, Macromedia Flash, and RSAC Rating Control can be disabled. See Figure 6-11.

Microsoft Chat

Define chat servers and accessible chat rooms.

Microsoft NetMeeting Settings

- *NetMeeting Settings*. Define all NetMeeting user settings.

- *NetMeeting Protocols*. You can disable the use of TCP/IP with NetMeeting. See Figure 6-12.

Corporate Settings

- *Dial-Up Settings*. Use automatic discovery from Control Panel for dial-up settings.

- *Language Settings*

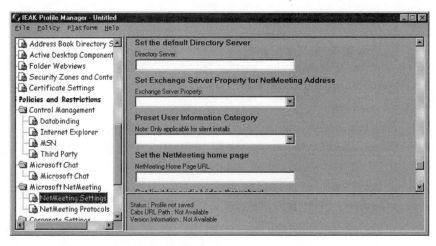

Figure 6-12 *Define NetMeeting user and protocol settings.*

- *Temporary Internet Files (User).* Specify the location of temporary Internet files.

- *Temporary Internet Files (Machine).* Define the local disk space allowed for temporary Internet files.

- *Code Download.* If you are using Active X controls you can specify the only update location that will be allowed for updates.

- *Related Sites and Errors.* Disable Show Related Links and a variety of error messages.

- *Office File Types.* Allow or disallow Office 97 file types from browsing in the same IE Window. See Figure 6-13.

Corporate Restrictions

- *Internet Property Pages.* Disable all or sections of the property pages under Internet Options.

- *General Page.* Disable all or sections of the general tab.

- *Connections Page.* Disable all or sections of the connection tab.

- *Content Page.* Disable all or part of the content tab.

- *Programs Page*

- *Browser Menus.* Disable all or parts of the File, View, Tools, and Help menu as well as right-click options.

- *Toolbars*

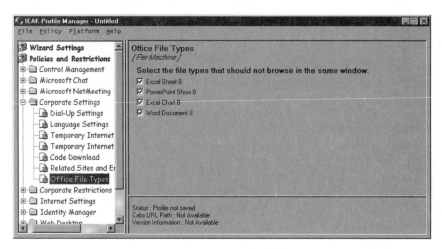

Figure 6-13 *Corporate setting choices with Profile Manager and IE5.*

- *Favorites and Searches*
- *Persistence.* Set file size limits for the local machine and the Intranet Zones.
- *Security Page*
- *Software Updates.* Disable automatic install of IE 5 components and updates.
- *Startup Restrictions*
- *Maintenance Mode.* Disable the `Add / Remove Software` icon

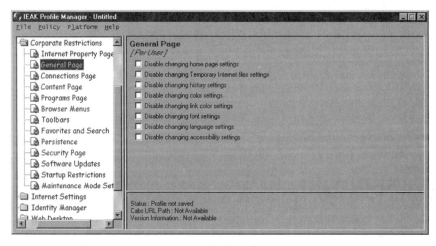

Figure 6-14 *Corporate restrictions for IE5.*

for adding, uninstalling, or repairing IE 5 and its components. See Figure 6-14.

Internet Settings

- *Auto Complete*. Choose how auto-complete is used. It can be handy to track what the user searches for on the Web and what addresses he or she goes to.

- *Toolbars*

- *Display Settings*. Set the default text options while using IE 5.

- *Advanced Settings*. Define the advanced View options.

- *URL Encoding*

- *Component Updates*. Define the URLs for component updates to IE 5.

Identity Manager

Restrict the user from using Identities.

Web Desktop

- *Desktop*. These settings are the same settings found in Windows 98. They allow restrictions of all or some Active Desktop settings.

- *Start Menu*. Restrict all or part of the Start menu items with the exception of Help. See Figure 6-15.

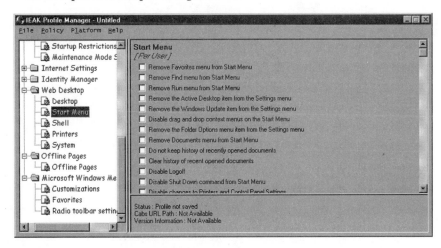

Figure 6-15 *Start menu restrictions for IE 5 clients.*

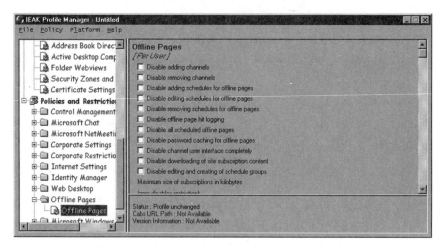

Figure 6-16 *Offline controls and options.*

- *Shell.* Restrict options found in `My Computer`.
- *Printers.* Restrict the deletion or addition of printers.
- *System.* Define the only applications the user can run.

Offline Pages

Define how IE 5 operates while the user is offline. Set controls on channels, subscriptions, and schedules. See Figure 6-16.

Microsoft Windows Media Player

- Customizations
- Favorites
- Radio Toolbar set

See Figure 6-17.

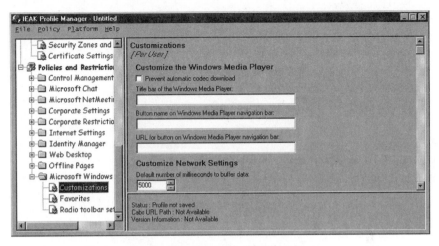

Figure 6-17 *Choices for the Windows Media Player.*

System Policies and the Registry

This chapter introduces you to the Registry, the main operating system database for Windows NT 4.0, Windows 98, and Windows 2000. To be honest, this book is all about the Registry; however, we have been focusing on system policies and user profiles, that is, the Registry settings we can deploy at the Explorer shell level. In this chapter you will learn:

- How and when to remotely edit user's system policy settings

- How to create REG files for automating Registry entries—even remotely

- Where system policy settings live in the Registry

- How to use Regedt32 and Regedit effectively

- About the Registry structure

Sometimes it's hard to remember the power of the system policy editor until we think of it as the Registry editor that it actually is. Either by using Registry editor #1 (the system policy editor, `Poledit.exe`), Registry editor #2 (`Regedt32.exe`), or Registry editor #3 (`Regedit.exe`), we are making changes to the all important system database, called the *Registry*. So what's your choice, Door #1, Door #2, or Door #3?

The reality is that you will use all of the above-mentioned software tools and more in your administrative toolbox. It's not enough just to know how system policies work at the Explorer shell level. When things don't work the way they are supposed to, you'll want to know where to go in the Registry with one of the Registry editors to see what the current settings are, and make a real-time change if necessary. It's essential that you recognize that a system policy is merely a predefined list of Registry settings— this makes it much easier to troubleshoot system policy problems.

Sometimes the task of opening the system policy editor and checking little white boxes and clicking OK, seems much too simple for its own good. Back in the old days of computing (5 long years ago!), real administrators had to go to the DOS prompt to create scripts, batch files, and run utilities to maintain their network.

The reason that the DOS prompt was black was that we were literally in the dark, so to speak. There's just no way you can easily have a global view of your network at a command prompt. Now please don't send me email that you still do a lot of work at the prompt. I know, I know—the point I'm working up to is that you identify with how much work your changes produce because it takes so long and is usually quite involved for carrying out a simple task.

Today we can check off a checkbox in the system policy editor, and lock out everyone on the network. The action of checking or clearing the checkbox produces a direct Registry action once our template changes are saved.

Inside the Registry from a Software Point of View

The basic steps in accessing the Registry from a software point of view are:

1. Open the required Registry key.

2. Carry out the required operation to the key which could be reading, writing, or updating information.

3. Close the Registry key.

When you open a key you receive back a handle to the Registry key, you are *accessing* (hence the name HKEY). This is like obtaining a one time "pass" to perform the desired operation. For example, if you wanted to open HKEY_USERS, you would receive the handle 0x80000003.

Once you have finished the operation, you need to again supply the already obtained pass (that is, you have to give it back), in order to close the key and complete the Registry task. This attention to detail is to make sure that all operations performed on the Registry are single tasked; your operation must always stay unique and not be confused with another Registry requests. The Win32 API (Application Programming Interface), which is the programming rules for Windows NT and Windows 98 software running under the Explorer shell, includes functions for communicating with the Registry and its keys and values. Examples are:

RegOpenKey	This function opens an existing key in the Registry.
RegCreateKey	This function opens an existing Registry key, or creates a new key if the specified key can not be found.
RegConnectRegistry	This function opens a root key on a remote computer system.
RegCloseKey	This function releases the handle of an open key.
RegDeleteKey	This function deletes a key.
RegFlushKey	This function writes all your changes to the Registry right away.

When these functions are used, each function returns an error code that verifies the success or failure of the function. Examples of error codes used are:

- ERROR_SUCCESS
- ERROR_KEY_NOT_FOUND
- ERROR_BADKEY

So the power of the system policy editor can be deceptive—in fact, I think it's much more dangerous a utility in the NT world than in the Windows 98 environment. Now you may be thinking, "Why do you say this?" It comes down to one word—*security*. NT has a security system and Windows 98 doesn't and never will. By default, on an NT workstation you must be an administrator to access and change Registry information directly; on a Windows 98 system, anyone can make changes to the Registry. If you make a change to the Registry in NT you are a member of the Administrators group—you're boss and you're supposed to know what you're doing. So let's open Door #1, the system policy editor in Registry mode.

Using the System Policy Editor as a Registry Editor

Opening the system policy editor, from the File menu we can select the mode of operation. Selecting the option Open Registry, the policy editor responds with the icons Local Computer and Local User. Regardless of what Windows-based platform you are using (Windows 98, NT 4.0), the icons shown in Registry mode will always be the same: Local Computer and Local User. See Figure 7-1.

There are no options available for adding groups or users in Registry mode, which displays a real-time window on the current status of the local Registry on the computer we are sitting in front of or a remote computer we are connected to using the remote features of the policy editor. Any active settings are shown as checked; otherwise, they are not implemented and are shown as cleared.

Remote Registry Editing

Registry modes of the system policy editor fall into two options:

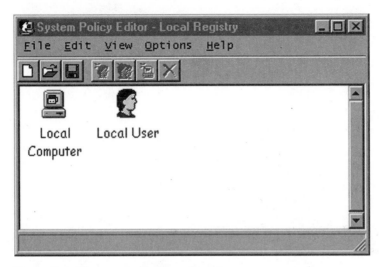

Figure 7-1 *The system policy editor in* Registry *mode.*

- *Option 1*. Editing the Registry of the local computer system that you are using.

- *Option 2*. Editing the Registry of a remote computer system from the computer system you are using.

Local and remote computer systems must be the same OS platform—NT or Windows 98, but not a mix of the two. Registry mode is useful for several tasks, for example:

- Checking on the current status of a computer's system policy settings

- Checking on a remote PC for the current state of its system policy settings

- Adding, changing, or removing a specific Registry change right away

Suppose that you had a user that you wanted to control with a system policy but for some reason the setting that you wanted to apply wasn't working properly. And the system policy setting that you wanted to deploy was not to show the settings tab when the user either opened the Display icon in the Control Panel or by right-clicking on the Desktop and selecting Properties. But for some unexplained reason the setting was not downloading and activating properly and you were almost out of time.

What to do? Well with the Registry mode of the system policy editor we can quickly see at a glance what settings are active and what settings are not and make a change immediately. If the setting I wanted to implement was to hide the settings tab, I could follow the listed steps to remove the settings tab in `Registry` mode.

1. Open the system policy editor.

2. Check to make sure that that correct template is loaded (`ADMIN.ADM` for Windows 95, `WINDOWS.ADM` for Windows 98, and `COMMON.ADM` for NT 4.0).

3. Double-click on the `Local User` icon.

4. Click to open the `Display` option.

5. Check off the `Hide settings tab` checkbox.

6. Select `File` and then `Save`.

7. Select `File` and then `Close`.

8. Close down the system policy editor.

9. Test your setting.

See Figure 7-2.

Pretty cool stuff, isn't it. Now let's suppose that you wanted to check on another computer that was on the 10th floor but still a member of the same network. For this situation we would use remote access.

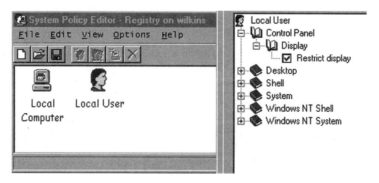

Figure 7-2 *Hiding display options in* `Registry` *mode.*

For NT remote Registry works right out of the box, assuming that you are attached to a network and you have the proper Administrator rights and permissions. You can also use a Windows 98 network service called *remote Registry service* to edit and control the Registry on another computer; however, there are several conditions that must be met on each workstation in order for remote services to be used for Windows 98 workstations. (The notes for the installation and setup are back in Chapter 3, "Installing and Using the System Policy Editor.")

Connecting to a remote workstation is simple. Running the system policy in Registry mode from the File menu, select Connect and then type the name of the computer to which you want to connect. The computer name is the Identification tab found in the Control Panel in the Network applet. See Figure 7-3.

This remote feature might have you reaching for the office furniture catalog but before you place that order for the top-of-the-line Lazy-Boy computer chair remember, *this is a feature that should be used for viewing only.* We still can't control the remote users' uncanny ability to power off their computer system just as we are performing a remote Registry edit. I'm sure you will agree that this scenario could be dangerous.

Now let's look at the Registry editors available for Windows NT: first Regedit and then Regedt32.

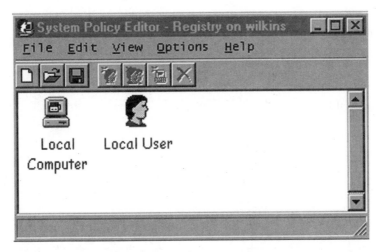

Figure 7-3 *The system policy editor in remote* Registry *mode.*

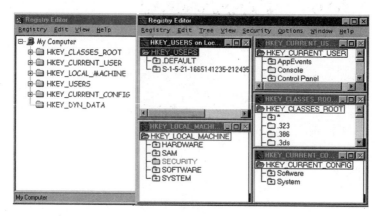

Figure 7-4 *The two Registry editors for NT: Regedit and Regedt32.*

The Windows NT Registry Editors

Windows NT 4.0 has both Regedit and Regedt32; however, a Windows 98 workstation only has one Registry editor called *Regedit*. Regedit and Regedt32 both have their uses in the NT world. Some NT purists will dismiss Regedit as a Windows 98 utility not useful for the NT world. And a lot of NT books quickly dispense with Regedit and focus on Regedt32; however, since we are mainly interested in the Registry as it applies to system policies, don't follow this line of thinking. See Figure 7-4.

The editor that you use really depends on the task at hand: Searching for data values, setting security levels, and defining audit trails are all Registry tasks you can accomplish only by using both editors. With the exception of "Network paths for Custom shared folders," which use a REG_EXPAND_ SZ data value, two types of data values, REG_SZ and DWORD values make up all system policy settings.

Both Registry editors can see both REG_SZ and DWORD data types, but most important, each editor has its own set of specialized tasks you need to know about.

Note   *Registry Hives:* One of the biggest differences between the Windows 99 and Windows NT Registry is how and where the Registry is stored. The NT Registry uses a collection of files called *hives* to replace `SYSTEM.DAT`. NT also replaces `USER.DAT` with `NTUSER.DAT`. The hives are stored in separate files that have no file extensions located in `\WINNT\SYSTEM32\CONFIG` folder. In NT, for every physical hive except for the system hive (which is part of `HKEY_ LOCAL_ MACHINE`) there is a `.LOG` file that records all transactions to each separate hive.

Regedit

Regedit leads a dual life, first as a system utility that is used to install Registry structure during a software installation of either a Windows NT 4.0 or Windows 98 software application, and second as a bare-bones Registry editor. If you've never used Regedit before directly as an editor, you have certainly used it indirectly in background mode while installing 98 or NT applications that have called it from their setup routines adding the necessary Registry structure and settings that WIN 32-based software applications require to run.

A quick list of Regedit features:

- It can edit the two Registry data types that make up most system policy settings.

- The search engine can search on data types; Regedt32 can search only on key values.

- We can create files called `REG` files to automate system policy settings.

- It's easier to use than Regedt32.

Before you get the idea that Regedt32 is not so useful, let me emphasize that it is very useful and can do some tasks that Regedit can only dream about. So we need to know about both editors, but first Regedit.

Viewing the Registry with Regedit

When executed, Regedit initially shows the root keys below `My Computer`. The plus keys indicate that the six root keys can be expanded to show the other subkeys. See Figure 7-5.

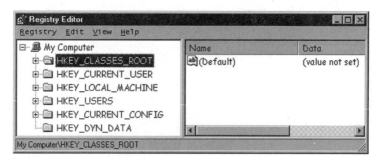

Figure 7-5 *Regedit showing 6 root folders if all is well.*

The Registry is divided into six main sections, each of which is
identified as a HKEY_ "Section Name". Looking at the initial structure (you may not believe this), you should note these six
Explorer-like folders group and display settings for "ease of editing." Although the six root keys look rather complicated, there
are in fact only two physical keys. The other keys are aliases that
point to branches within the two physical keys. The remaining
Registry structure is fairly simple.

Key: A key in the Registry is comparable to the folder we are
familiar with when using Explorer. The familiar folder icon
appears beside each of the six HKEYs in the Registry.

Subkey: A plus sign indicates that there is more to look at; by
clicking on the subkey we can view its contents. Each key and
or subkey contains at least one value with a special name of
Default if no value has been assigned to the key. This value is a
placeholder for the empty folder and is a minimum setting that
can't be removed.

Note   HKEY_LOCAL_MACHINE is a collection of hive files located in
\WINNT\SYSTEM32\CONFIG and HKEY_USERS. NTUSER.DAT is located
in WINNT\PROFILES\"USERNAME".

Moving from top to bottom, the overall Registry structure is as
follows:

HKEY_CLASSES_ROOT. Registered extensions and the software
apps that are registered to the extensions plus OLE, ActiveX,

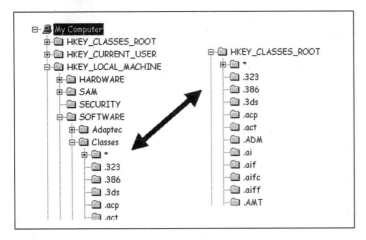

Figure 7-6 HKEY_CLASSES_ROOT *linked to* HKEY_LOCAL_MACHINE\ SOFTWARE\Classes.

and DCOM settings are stored here. Whenever you use the Windows Explorer and perform the task View | Folder Options | File Types you are directly accessing HKEY_CLASSES_ROOT. It is a pointer to HKEY_LOCAL_MACHINE\ SOFTWARE\Classes. You may not be aware of the amazing fact that Windows 3.1 also had a Registry and a Registry editor called regedit that edited its Registry DAT file called REG.DAT. Its official system name was HKEY_CLASSES_ROOT (HKCR). HKCR is present for backward compatibility with Windows 3.1 software running on Windows NT or Windows 98 systems. When a Windows 3.1 application requests information from REG.DAT, HKCR steps in and answers the request. See Figure 7-6.

HKEY_CURRENT_USER. This hive holds custom settings of the current logged on user. We also know this section as the User Profile stored in \\WINNT\PROFILES\USERNAME. This root key is also a pointer to HKEY_USERS\"Logged on User". System policy settings for all users and groups are also found here. See Figure 7-7.

HKEY_LOCAL_MACHINE. Also known as HKLM, this is the main hive for global hardware and software settings, Control Panel and Network settings, as well as startup and shutdown settings. System policy settings for computers are also found here. This folder is used for remote Registry editing of the system

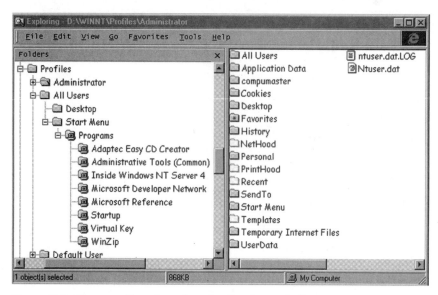

Figure 7-7 *User profiles viewed at the Explorer shell.*

hives. Other hives present in HKLM are SAM, SECURITY, and SOFTWARE.

- *The* SAM *hive* contains existing security information for current user and group accounts installed on this computer such as passwords and domain association.
- *The* SECURITY *hive* contains the user and group security settings. An example of the type of security information would be user rights and file permissions. This information is also hidden by default, although as an Administrator you could use Regedt32—the other Registry editor—to change the default security rights and peer into the security system. SAM is linked to the SECURITY subkey under HKLM\SECURITY\SAM. We normally access this information when we set permissions through the Explorer shell and when we use either User Manager or User Manager for Domains.

HKEY_USERS. I like to call this folder the "Master" of all User settings. It holds the Default User hive profile that is running before you actually log onto your PC, plus the logged on User

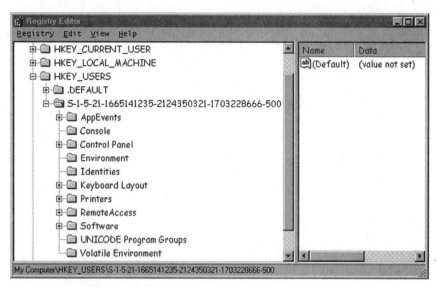

Figure 7-8 *SID identifiers shown under* HKEY_USERS.

profile. When a user is successfully logged on to an NT system, the Default user profile is disabled. Note that the current user's subkey is not the user's name but his or her security identifier (SID). The active user's settings will also be shown in HKEY_CURRENT_USER. HKEY_USERS is also used for remote Registry editing of the current user hive. See Figure 7-8.

HKEY_CURRENT_CONFIG. This is your computer's hardware profile found in the System Icon | Hardware profile in Control Panel. It is also a pointer to HKEY_LOCAL_MACHINE\SYSTEM\ CurrentControlSet\Hardware Profiles. See Figure 7-9.

HKEY_DYN_DATA. This key is not used in NT. Windows 98 uses this key for a memory only listing of active plug-and-play hardware settings that originate in HKEY_LOCAL_MACHINE\Enum. For now it shows up in Regedit because this editor came from Windows 98. So the root folder shows up because of what Regedit expects to find; since it's not present in NT you will receive an "unable to open" error if you try to access this key.

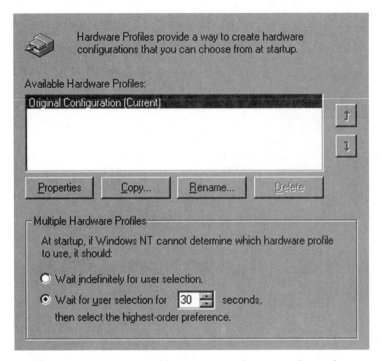

Figure 7-9 *Hardware profile settings in the Control Panel.*

Registry Data Values Used by System Policies

- *String Data Values.* A *string* is a set of characters such as a set of words and decimal numbers, path names, or other text-based information. Think of the entries in INI files, which also have to be in text format. Strings are listed under the data pane heading of Regedit with the tab graphic, and are always enclosed in quotes, as shown in Figure 7-10.

- *DWORD Data Values.* DWORD (which stands for *double value*) is a 32-bit value shown by eight HEX digits. It also is shown under the data pane of the Regidit, displayed with a 0x starting format as shown below. Most of the system policy settings that use the DWORDs usually set the value either as on (1) or off (0). See Figure 7-11.

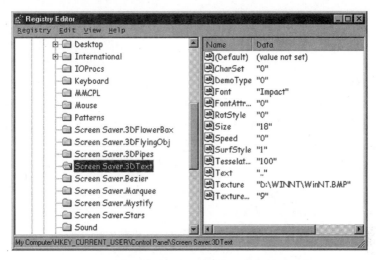

Figure 7-10 *String data values as displayed by Regedit.*

The following additional three string data types are also found in the Registry. The first two, REG_EXPAND_SZ and REG_MULTI_SZ, are supported only by the Windows NT operating system. The third value is REG_BINARY. Both the Windows 98 and Windows NT 4.0 Registry support REG_BINARY values. These three data

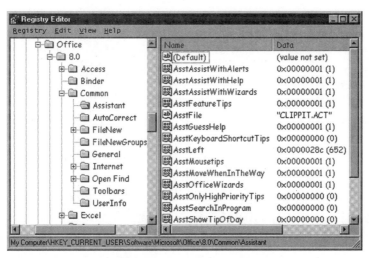

Figure 7-11 *DWORD data values as displayed by Regedit.*

types are not used for system policies but will be briefly described for continuity.

- REG_EXPAND_SZ   (This is an expandable data string, which is text based.)

- REG_MULTI_SZ   (This is a multiple string, or values that contain lists or multiple values in text-based strings.)

- REG_BINARY   (This is a system data value that can be either a binary or hexadecimal value.)

The ability of the Registry to accept a complete choice of string, binary, or hexadecimal data values allows developers complete flexibility in storing hardware and software settings in the Registry.

Searching for Information in the Registry with Regedit

Searching for information in the Registry can be accomplished through the Explorer-style interface, using the hunt-and-peck method; however, this could take a very long time. Using the Find option (CTRL-F) allows you to select what data type you wish to search for. The values searched for can be string, hex, or binary data. Searches are also not case sensitive.

If you are not sure where the item you are looking for is located, make sure the search engine doesn't fool you. The search starts from where you are located in the tree, so if the item you are searching for is above where you searched from, it won't be found. Once the desired data are found, the item will be displayed; to show the next occurrence of the selected item use the Find Next option on the Edit menu or more simply, press the F3 key. The information we view with Regedit is static, as no automatic refreshing is performed. Pressing F5 performs the manual refreshing of the Registry data or by using the View menu and selecting Refresh. See Figure 7-12.

Exporting and Importing Registry Settings

When you want to explore or seriously modify the Registry, the first step is to export the Registry, or a portion of the Registry, to

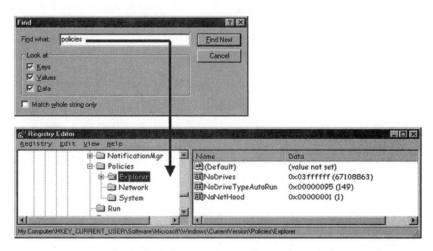

Figure 7-12 *Searching for system policy information with* Find.

a new .REG file. The import and export file is a special formatted text file with a .REG extension. The .REG extension is sometimes used by software applications for adding their own custom Registry settings during installation of the application. If you were a software application developer and you wanted to incorporate your new application's needed keys into the Registry, you would start by using REGEDIT to add your keys. Then you would back up (that is, export) the newly entered keys and values into a new .REG file. This file would then be part of the install process for the new software application and during the install process—the .REG file would be merged or imported into the existing Registry.

The exporting and importing of Registry settings is performed from the file menu. The actual menu labels are quite confusing, so I will perform the needed translation. The export option states Export Registry file, which actually means "Copy all or part of the current Registry to a text file with a REG extension." The import option states Import Registry file; my translation: "Merge into, or overwrite all or part of the Registry from a text file with a REG extension."

How many .REG files are installed on your PC? Click the Start button and use the Find option to see how many .REG files are resident on your PC. You may be surprised.

Note

What's a REG File?

A REG file is one of the best kept secrets of the Windows 98 and NT world; however, if your users are Windows 98, then it can be a nightmare as there is no security system available unless you count the ATRTRIB command (Joke!). If your users are NT Workstation, and NTFS (NT file system) is deployed, you're laughing.

Some of the important reasons to know about REG files are detailed in the next few pages. Make sure that you experiment with REG files, you'll be glad you did. But first some background as to how REG files actually work.

REG files are a feature of Regedit that empower software and hardware developers because these files are designed to be executed during a software or hardware installation merging needed Registry settings into the existing Registry by running Regedit in the background. Keys, Values, and Data Values can be added with REG files. Data value types that can be added are REG_SZ, REG_DWORD (System Policy types), and REG_BINARY. With regards to REG files the key term to understand is *merge*.

Sometimes merge means *overwrite*. What you say, overwrite? Yep. If you did a search for REG files on your computer you would have found a bunch that you would swear that you didn't create. And I'd believe you, because you're right, you didn't—they were left over after you installed your application software and even Windows 98 and/or Windows NT. The cleanup after the install usually doesn't remove these files. And these REG files are sometimes dangerous because they can hold settings that don't match your current computer setup. That's because the choices for the hardware or software components that are installed in the Windows 98 and NT world sometimes are contained in REG files. If these files are left on your PC—or more important, your user's PC—you or they could double-click on a REG file and reset settings that are currently active in your Registry to other settings, messing up your computer! Yikes! The scenario I just described is no longer a merge, it's an overwrite.

Let's look at a REG file now (Figure 7-13). By right-clicking any REG file you can Merge or Edit. Selecting edit opens the file in

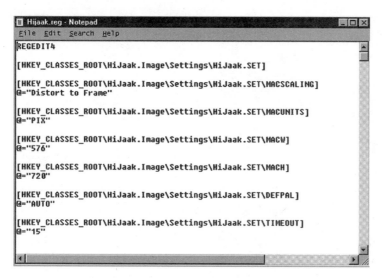

Figure 7-13 *Contents of a* REG *file in Notepad.*

Notepad. Make note of the header at the top of all REG files,
REGEDIT4.

The header tells the operating system to import the settings
found in this listing into the current Registry using Regedit. If the
path specified does not exist, then create the needed keys and
then import the listed data types and values into the specified
location. This is what's loosely defined as a *merge*; settings that
were not there before have been added in. What happens if the
existing path and data types are found in the Registry. Well,
then—the action performed is to replace the existing data values,
that is *overwrite*.

And how do you perform a merge if you find a REG file on your
system? Easy, just double-click the file and presto, it's done. See
Figure 7-14.

NT users can somewhat relax because you have to be an
Administrator or a member of the Administrator's group to be
able to read and write to the Registry; Windows 98 users, however, can do whatever they want anytime, anywhere.

But wait, now the good news for Windows 98 users. By disabling the use of Regedit through a system policy, the user is pro-
tected from making a serious mistake. You could also remove

Figure 7-14 *Message after a* REG *file is merged at the Explorer shell.*

Regedit from all of your users' PCs to be doubly safe. The next four sections detail the power of the REG file when control is squarely in the Administrator's camp, as it should be.

1. *Back up and restore scenarios.* By highlighting a folder in the Registry and selecting Registry | Export Registry file, you can quickly back up the selected contents to a REG file.

2. *Compare Registry information among multiple computers.* Using Microsoft Word or Norton Utilities File Compare, we can compare two different registries to help in troubleshooting.

3. *Remote updates to many computers at one time can be performed using REG files.* Suppose that you had a Registry setting on your computer system that you added because of a Knowledge Base article from Microsoft, and you were faced with adding this setting to every computer in your company, a rather daunting task. Using a REG file, you could export the setting or settings to a REG file stored on your file server. You could then use a login script or a system policy to execute the REG file when your users logged in, saving you hours of Registry editing.

Note   Using Regedit with the syntax /S tells Regedit to run in "silent mode" and not notify the user that changes have been made.

4. *Know when your users have installed software they weren't supposed to.* Since most Windows 98 and Windows NT 4.0 software uses REG files, a simple search of your users' computer system can alert you when they have been installing software and utilities off the Internet.

Using a REG File to Automate System Policy Settings

Let's look at an example that allows you to deploy system policy settings from your login script without using POL files and the system policy editor.

1. Start Regedit.

2. Move to HKEY_CURRENT_USER\Software\Microsoft \Windows\\ CurrentVersion\Policies. (There will already be at least an Explorer key under Policies. You can then add DWORD values set to 1 in the appropriate keys.)

3. In the Explorer key you can add one or all of the following values (see Figure 7-15):

NoFind	Removes the Find command from the Start menu
NoDrives	Hides Drives in My Computers
NoNetHood	Hides the Network Neighborhood
NoDesktop	Hides all system icons on the Desktop
NoRun	Disables the Run command box on the Start menu
NoSaveSettings	Don't save settings on exit
DisableRegistryTools	Disable Regedit and Tweak UI

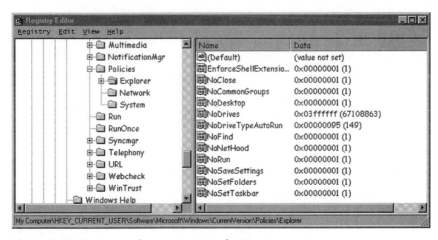

Figure 7-15 *System policy settings in the Registry.*

4. Add a System key under `Policies`. In the System key you could then add one or all of the following value choices as `DWORD` values set to 1 to enable the following options:

`NoDispCPL`	Disables the `Display` icon in Control Panel
`NoDispBackgroundPage`	Hides the `Background` tab in the `Display` icon
`NoDispScrSavPage`	Hides the `Screen Saver` tab in the `Display` icon
`NoDispAppearancePage`	Hides the `Appearance` tab in the `Display` icon
`NoDispSettingsPage`	Hides `Settings` tab off the `Start` menu

5. Once all of the selected edits are done export `HKEY_CURRENT_ USER\Software\Microsoft \Windows\ \CurrentVersion\ Policies` to a `REG` file called `POLICY.REG`.

6. Then copy this `REG` file to your file server, for example, to a folder called `\\SERVER1\control`. Add this command to your system login script:

```
REGEDIT \\server1\control\policy.reg /s
```

The next time your users log in, the settings will be automatically merged into their local Registry and will be in force. You could optionally add the `POLICY.REG` to a startup group for a particular user for an automatic merge with existing values, or perform the import manually.

Importing REG Files

We have three basic options for importing `REG` files while using the Explorer shell. By far the easiest method, and the one you will usually use, is by double-clicking on the `.REG` file that you wish to deploy; it will be automatically imported into the existing Registry. Also the `Registry` menu option `Import Registry File` allows you to import backup `.REG` files into the Registry. Also, when you perform a drag and drop with a `.REG` file onto the `REGEDIT` window, the `.REG` file will instantly be imported.

Using Regedt32

Regedt32 is present in all versions of NT from 3.1 up to Windows 2000. It does not install software settings in the background like Regedit, but is primarily the Registry editor for editing of the five data types used by NT. It also is used to perform remote Registry editing for NT user profiles. If you are used to Regedt32, then by all means use it; however, for system policy settings Regedit is much easier to use. See Figure 7-16.

A quick list of Regedt32 features:

- It can edit the two Registry data types that make up all system policy settings plus the other three NT Registry data types

- Audit trails can be set to track Registry key access by both users and groups

- Security permissions can be accessed and changed

- Remote user profile editing from any NT workstation

Defining an Audit Trail

Using Regedt32, you can track user and group access to any portion of the Registry. But be warned; too much auditing will severely reduce system performance. Auditing is also performed

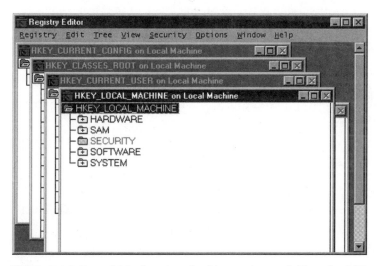

Figure 7-16 *Regedt32 showing the hive and root folders for NT.*

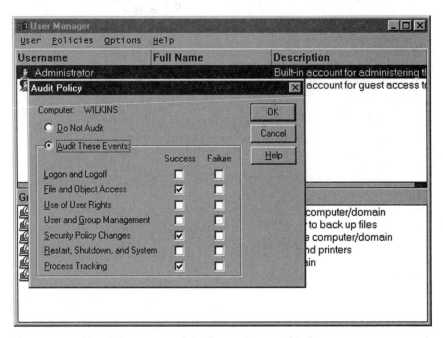

Figure 7-17 *User Manager and Audit settings enabled.*

only on the computer system where auditing has been enabled. If
you want to audit a user's access to your server's Registry, then
auditing must first be enabled before you define the actual audit.
User Manager for Domains is used to turn on systemwide auditing for the specific NT server through the drop-down menu
option Policies and then selecting Audit. For Windows NT
workstation users, we use the Administration Tool User Manager
to enable auditing. (Auditing is not supported on Windows 98
computers; however, if the User has a domain account on a primary domain controller, then you can audit his or her activity on
the server itself.) See Figure 7-17.

The choices we can enable by checking off the desired checkboxes are as follows:

Choices	What's Tracked
Logon and Logoff	Logging on to the computer system or domain
File and Object Access	Auditing printer, file, and directory access

Use of User Rights	How users use their rights that are assigned
User and Group Management	Changes made to the Registry for user and group accounts
Security Policy Change	User and audit rights that are changed
Restart, Shutdown, and System	Turns on the security log for tracking of successful events in the Registry
Process Tracking	Tracks failures

If you wanted to track file and directory access you would check File and Object Access. To enable Registry auditing you would check Security Policy Changes, and Restart, Shutdown, and System to track both successes and failures.

Deploying a Registry Audit

To define an audit trail in the Registry, run Regedt32 and from the Security drop-down menu select Auditing. See Figure 7-18.

From the Registry key auditing screen that is presented, you can choose the key or keys to track access based on the following conditions. Remember that the current security levels of the user are in force—users may try to perform one or more of the following tasks but their security permissions that are currently defined may stop them from carrying out the task. This means that the user that tries to use a REG file but has a user account that doesn't permit this action will be denied the right to use the REG file. However, if the audit trail has been defined and is in force, even the attempt will be recorded. Both success and failures can be monitored.

When users or groups are tracked with one or more of the following audit events, an audit trail will be generated:

Registry Access	The User or Group Tried to
Query Value	Read a value in the Registry
Set Value	Modify a Registry value
Create Subkey	Create a subkey
Enumerate Subkeys	Read subkeys under the audited key

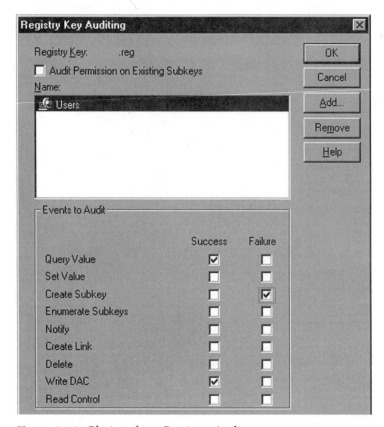

Figure 7-18 *Choices for a Registry Audit.*

Notify	Track changes or updates
Create Link	Create a symbolic link
Delete	Delete a key
Write DAC	Change security permissions
Read Control	Read security permissions

To view all audit trails we use another administrative tool, the Event Log. It is found off the Start Menu | Programs | Administrative Tools. Auditing for NT is split among three logs: system, application, and security logs.

1. *System.* Tracks events produced by the operating system and hardware devices.

2. *Application.* Tracks events by application programs.

3. *Security.* Tracks security permissions, Registry audits, and logon and logoff events.

The event logs are binary files with the names `AppEvent.evt`, `SysEvent.evt`, and `SecEvent.evt`, and are stored with the Registry hives found in the `WINNT\SYSTEM32\CONFIG` folder.

Setting Security Settings

You can also change the permissions on the hives and keys in the Registry from the default values if you wish, although this is not a great idea in the real world. I use this option as a "permissions checker" and not as an option to apply any additional permissions. Selecting the `Security` tab and then `Permissions` shows the current permissions that are assigned. The typical defaults are:

Everyone	Read
Administrator	Full Control
System	Full Control

It is standard in the NT world to be part of the `Administrator`'s group in order to be able to install software. The group `Everyone` is a global group created by the operating system to which all users belong. Finally, the `System` group is the operating system. I guess we should let Windows NT have complete control of the Registry, right?

Using Regedt32 for Remote Editing

If you want to check on another NT system to compare or edit its Registry, Regedt32 is the editor for this task in the NT world. Selecting the `Registry` drop-down menu and then `Select Computer` we can browse, select, and then view the remote Registry on the NT system we connected to. Being a member of the `Domain Administrator` group is usually the norm for complete domain roaming with Regedt32.

The Registry hives that are delivered to your desktop from the remote PC are `HKEY_LOCAL_MACHINE` and `HKEY_USERS`. See Figure 7-19.

This Registry editor can edit the Windows NT Registry as well

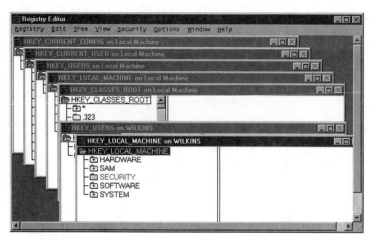

Figure 7-19 *Remote connection to another NT system.*

as the Windows 98 but only if remote Registry services for Windows 98 is installed.

Manually Editing a User's Profile with Regedt32

As system administrator, you may need to change a profile setting to avoid unnecessary user interaction, or to make modifications before setting the profile to mandatory. You can open a specific user's profile or the Default User Profile with Regedt32 and customize it manually. To manually customize a user profile, first locate the profile to be modified.

- If the profile is a server-based profile, locate the \\server\share\username.

- If the profile is a local profile, locate the %systemroot%\ Profiles\username directory.

- If you need to edit the Default User Profile, locate the %systemroot%\Profiles\Default User directory.

1. Start Regedt32.exe, and select the HKEY_USERS on the Local Machine window. Highlight the root key of HKEY_USERS.

2. From the Registry menu, select Load Hive. See Figure 7-20.

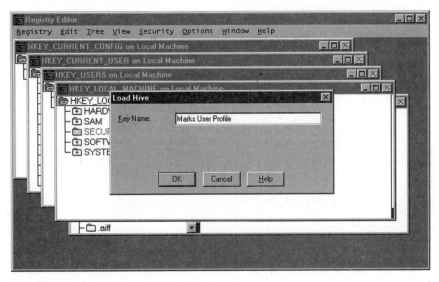

Figure 7-20 *Loading a remote user hive.*

3. Browse for the desired PROFILE directory and select the NTuser.xxx file. A dialog will prompt you to enter a Key Name. I recommend that you use the user's name. This key name is a temporary name only. Click OK. This adds the profile Registry hive as a subkey to HKEY_USERS. Edit the new user profile values as necessary. See Figure 7-21.

4. After completing the changes, highlight the root of the user's profile Registry key and from the Registry menu, select Unload Hive. This saves any changes to the user's profile.

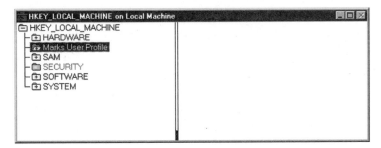

Figure 7-21 *Editing a remote* Registry *hive.*

Modifying the Defaults User Profile
with Regedt32

To modify a Windows NT profile load the `NTuser.xxx` hive into the Registry as detailed earlier, make the necessary changes, and unload the hive (this automatically saves the changes). The workstation `Default User Profile` is located in the `\%systemroot%\Profiles\Default User` directory. To provide users with a `Default User Profile` that contains custom short-cuts, folders, and files that are not centrally managed, place the icons in the appropriate folder within the `Default User Profile`. New users will receive the shortcuts, folders, and files as part of their new profiles.

System Policy Settings in the NT Registry

There are several settings to be aware of when supporting system policies. We want to know what goes on in the Registry when we check and uncheck options while using the system policy editor and enabling user profiles. Settings listed are first for NT and then for Windows 98.

HKEY_USERS \ S-1-5-21-1665141235-
2124350321-1703228666-500

In `HKEY_USERS` the security ID (SID) is found in the logged-on user's user profile `NTUSER.DAT` that it is stamped with. The complete `NTUSER.DAT` is also found under this key. This information is also mirrored in `HKEY_CURRENT_USER`, but the SID is not present at this location—only the contents of the `NTUSER.DAT`.

It's really important to remember that the current logged-on user has loaded his or her own user profile. If that user has problems, you have to be logged on as that user to see the problems and not yourself; otherwise, you are looking at your user profile, not your user's.

HKEY_USERS \ .DEFAULT

This is the only location in the Registry for the default user profile. It is active only when a computer system running NT is on but no one has logged in yet, or a user has just logged out and hasn't logged in again. Although the default user profile is also mirrored with HKEY_CURRENT_USER, we can't access this information on the local machine while it is running. However, we could remote into a computer system which no one had logged into just yet.

HKEY_LOCAL_MACHINE \ SOFTWARE \ Microsoft \ Windows \ CurrentVersion \ Policies

If a system policy is in effect for the current computer, some of the computer settings that were set with WINNT.ADM and COMMON.ADM will be stored under this policy folder. You could back up all of the settings at this location into a REG file if you wanted to apply them onto another user with Regedit rather than through a system policy.

HKEY_LOCAL_MACHINE \ SOFTWARE \ Microsoft \ Windows NT \ CurrentVersion \ ProfileList

This key holds a list of the locally cached user profiles that are stored in the \WINNT\PROFILES folder. They are listed by SID number and not by username. You can view the same listing but by username though the System icon in Control Panel selecting the User Profiles tab.

HKEY_LOCAL_MACHINE \ SOFTWARE \ Microsoft \ Windows \ CurrentVersion \ Explorer \ Shell Folders

This key holds the local paths where the All Users Common Desktop, Common Programs, Common Start Menu, and Common Startup folders are located. The default is on the local PC.

HKEY_LOCAL_MACHINE \ SOFTWARE \ Microsoft \ Windows \ CurrentVersion \ Explorer \ User Shell Folders

This key holds the paths as to where the *custom locations* for the All Users Common Desktop, Common Programs, Common Start Menu, and Common Startup folders could be located.

HKEY_LOCAL_MACHINE\SOFTWARE\Microsoft\ Windows NT\CurrentVersion\Winlogon

This folder holds most of the NT-specific security settings that are set with WINNT.ADM. This is a "global" login folder for all users that use this PC. See Figure 7-22.

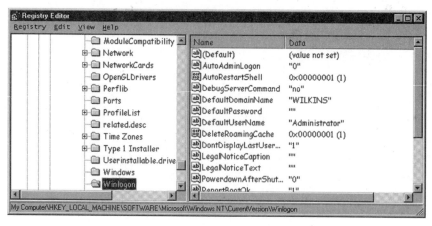

Figure 7-22 *System policy computer settings in Winlogon.*

HKEY_LOCAL_MACHINE \ System \ CurrentControlSet \ Control \ Update

This location specifies the type of download enabled for system policies: automatic or manual. A DWORD of 1 is Automatic, and a DWORD of 2 specifies Manual. The path to the NTCONFIG.POL is also listed here if manual download is enabled. See Figure 7-23.

HKEY_CURRENT_USER \ Software \ Microsoft \ Windows \ CurrentVersion \ Policies

If a system policy is in effect for the current user, most of the user settings that were set with WINNT.ADM and COMMON.ADM will be stored under this policy folder.

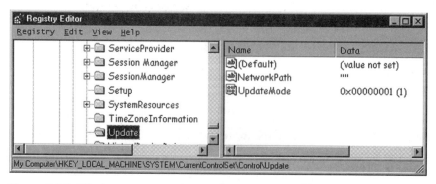

Figure 7-23 *The important settings; where your POL file is located.*

System Policy Settings in the Registry for Windows 98

HKEY_LOCAL_MACHINE \ Network

For Windows 95 users, this location will indicate whether multiple user profiles have been enabled with a DWORD value of 1 for yes and 0 for no. Custom user profiles are enabled through the Passwords icon in Control Panel.

HKEY_LOCAL_MACHINE \ Network \ Logon

A very important setting is found here. The following data string enables support for group system policies: "PolicyHandler" = "GROUPPOL.DLL,ProcessPolicies". If you didn't install group policy support for the workstation this string value will not be present.

HKEY_LOCAL_MACHINE \ SOFTWARE \ Microsoft \ Windows \CurrentVersion \ Profile List

This holds the list of the local user profiles that the system knows about.

HKEY_LOCAL_MACHINE \ System \ CurrentControlSet \ Services \NWNP32 \ NetworkProvider

Another very important setting providing support of groups in system policies. The string value that should be present is "Group Fcn" = "GROUPPOL.DLL". This DLL is used for group policy support.

HKEY_LOCAL_MACHINE \ System \ CurrentControlSet \ Control \ Update

This location specifies whether the user has profiles enabled and the type of download enabled for system policies; choices are automatically downloaded from the NETLOGON share, or manually downloaded from a UNC network path or local path. A DWORD of 1 is Automatic, and a DWORD of 2 specifies Manual. The path to where the CONFIG.POL is also listed here if manual download is enabled.

HKEY_CURRENT_USER \ Software \ Microsoft \ Windows \ CurrentVersion \ ProfileReconcliation

These settings specify where the user's profile folders are located.

Backing up the Registry: NT Registry Software Backup Tools

Backing up the Registry is quite important to your mental health and to your network and users as well. Both operating systems could do a better job of backing up the Registry pieces.

NT has several utilities for backing up and restoring the system hives (HKEY_LOCAL_MACHINE) but has no software tool available for backing up your user profiles (HKEY_CURRENT_USER). First, we will deal with the tools available for the system hives.

If your Registry hive files become corrupted, you will have to provide specific Registry configuration information that should have been saved to the Emergency Repair Disk using RDISK.EXE, which is the command line that can be executed from the command prompt or the Run dialog box to backup the system Registry Hives. If you carefully read the splash screen for RDISK, you will find that Microsoft recommends that you don't use this utility as a backup tool!! What? Well, the reason they slyly make this claim is that if you use the proper syntax—which is RDISK /S—all of the system hives will possibly not fit on one 1.44-MB floppy disk, and so by default SAM, SECURITY, and the DEFAULT User Profile, too. The /S syntax adds the normally left off hives back into the backup mix. See Figure 7-24.

The only time that your system hives won't fit on a floppy disk is if you have a PDC with over approximately 6000 user accounts. But the /S does more than provide a full backup of system hives to the mentioned floppy; it also does a complete backup to WINNT\REPAIR. If these notes are new to you and you've never run

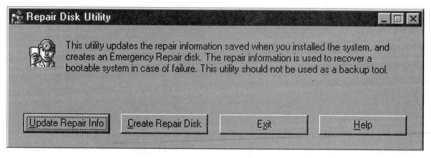

Figure 7-24 *Running Rdisk.*

RDISK then I can tell you with certainty that the hives stored in WINNT\REPAIR were last put there the day your NT systems were installed. So this information is useless. I suggest putting this book down and heading out on a RDISK /S mission to all your servers at the very least. Go on, I'll wait. Back yet? Take a deep breath.

The following hives are on the repair disk and the \WINNT\REPAIR folder:

Autoexec.nt	Used to start the MSDOS environment
Config.nt	Used to start the MSDOS environment
Default._	HKEY\USERS\DEFAULT
Ntuser.DA_	Default user profile
Sam._	HKEY_LOCAL_MACHINE\SAM
Security._	HKEY_LOCAL_MACHINE\SECURITY
Setup.log	CRC file check install information
Software._	HKEY_LOCAL_MACHINE\SOFTWARE
System._	HKEY_LOCAL_MACHINE\SYSTEM

Note also that RDISK does not back up any \PROFILES information!!! **Note**

Using the Emergency Repair Disk (ERD)

The ERD is not a bootable disk. To use the Emergency Repair Disk you must first boot the system with the Windows NT Setup Disk 1. You can create the set of three NT setup disks from your NT CD-ROM. Run the command line WINNT /ox to create the three disks needed. This is another task that should be done before you need the disks. Disk 1 then Disk 2 are inserted and then you will be given the option to repair during the install process by pressing R.

Next you pop in Disk 3 and then the system will then request the Emergency Risk Disk. If you don't have it, the system will try to use the other backup location, the REPAIR folder we just discussed. If you haven't made an ERD or updated the REPAIR folder, you are in trouble. The other option you can select is Inspect

Registry Files. Setup will then display the Registry files that it will try to restore.

- [ ] SYSTEM (System Configuration)
- [ ] SOFTWARE (Software Information)
- [ ] DEFAULT (Default User Profile)
- [ ] NTUSER.DAT (New User Policy)
- [ ] SECURITY (Security Policy)
- [ ] SAM (User Accounts Database)

Windows 98 Registry Structure

The odds are that you will have some Windows 98 users attached to your NT domains. So, a few words on Windows 98. This operating system has no security to speak of and yet it has a Registry quite similar to NT. The entire Registry is contained in two files, USER.DAT and SYSTEM.DAT.

When you open Regedit, USER.DAT and SYSTEM.DAT are opened and presented with six root keys as compared to the five root keys for NT. HKEY_LOCAL_MACHINE is SYSTEM.DAT and HKEY_USERS is USER.DAT. The same pointer structure that we discussed earlier for NT is here as well, plus an additional root folder. Full support for plug-and-play hardware is a feature of Windows 98 and these settings are contained in HKEY_DYN_DATA.

SYSTEM.DAT is always located in the \WINDOWS folder. The default user profile USER.DAT is also always located in \WINDOWS. If user profiles have been enabled, the user's custom USER.DAT will be located in \WINDOWS\PROFILES\Username.

Backing Up the Windows 98 Registry

The Windows 98 Registry is easy to back up because it is not locked by any security system. The good old copy command can be used to back up the Registry, although I prefer using WINZIP. A complete REG file containing the complete Windows 98 Registry can also be created using Regedit.

SCANREG is the software utility that backs up both USER.DAT and SYSTEM.DAT into a CAB file stored in WINDOWS\SYSBACKUP by default. Modifying SCANREG.INI can change this backup location.

Registry Keys Modified by the System Policy Editor

As we now know, the Registry has two root keys or hive locations where policy information is stored. If you run into problems with system policies, this section can be used as a reference section to directly check the system Registry settings in HKEY_LOCAL_MACHINE and HKEY_CURRENT_USER.

Restrict the Display Applet

Found in: Control Panel\Display

Details: Removes or enables tabs from the Display applet

Key: HKEY_CURRENT_USER\Software\Microsoft\
                  Windows\CurrentVersion\Policies\System

Data Values: NoDispCPL REG_DWORD Off = 0 or value
                  removed; On = 1

                  NoDispBackgroundPage REG_DWORD Off = 0 or
                  value removed; On = 1

                  NoDispScrSavPage REG_DWORD Off = 0 or value
                  removed; On = 1

                  NoDispAppearancePage REG_DWORD Off = 0 or
                  value removed; On = 1

                  NoDispSettingsPage REG_DWORD Off = 0 or
                  value removed; On = 1

Color Scheme

Found in: Desktop\Color scheme

Details: Defines the color scheme for the Explorer shell
                  desktop

Key: HKEY_CURRENT_USER\Control Panel\Appearance

Data Values: Current REG_SZ Off = value is removed; On =
                  text of color scheme name

Remove the Run Command from the Start Menu

Found in: Windows NT Shell\Restrictions

Details: Removes the `Run` option from the `Start` menu

Key: `HKEY_CURRENT_USER\Software\Microsoft\Win-`
                  `dow\CurrentVersion \Policies\Explorer`

Data Values: `NoRun REG_DWORD Off = 0 or value is removed;`
                  `On = 1`

Remove Folders from Settings on Start Menu

Found in: Windows NT Shell\Restrictions

Details: `No Control Panel` and `Printer Settings` are
                  available from the `Start` menu

Key: `HKEY_CURRENT_USER\Software\Microsoft\`
                  `Windows\CurrentVersion\Policies\Explorer`

Data Values: `NoSetFolders REG_DWORD Off = 0 or value is`
                  `removed; On = 1`

Remove Taskbar from Settings on Start Menu

Found in: Windows NT Shell\Restrictions

Details: Removes the taskbar choices from `Start Menu |`
                  `Settings`. Removing both the taskbar and the
                  preceding settings (`No Control Panel` and
                  `Printer Settings`) completely removes the
                  `Settings` option.

Key: `HKEY_CURRENT_USER\Software\Microsoft\Windows`
                  `\CurrentVersion\Policies\Explorer`

Data Values: `NoSetTaskbar REG_DWORD Off = 0 or value is`
                  `removed; On = 1`

Remove the Find Command from the Start Menu

Found in: Windows NT Shell\Restrictions

Details: Removes the `Find` utility from the `Start` menu.

Key: `HKEY_CURRENT_USER\Software\Microsoft\Windows`
                  `\CurrentVersion\Policies\Explorer`

Data Values: `NoFind REG_DWORD Off = 0 or value is`
                  `removed; On = 1`

Hide All Drive Icons

Found in: Windows NT Shell\Restrictions

Details: Hides all of your drives found in `My Computer`. In order for all drives to be hidden, a binary number mask must be created for all possible drives from A to Z. This creates a binary number mask as follows:

```
11111111111111111111111111
ZYXWVUTSRQPONMLKJIHGFEDCBA
```

    The binary number 1 represents the corresponding drive letter you want to hide in the correct position from A to Z. Converting this number to decimal will result in the correct number to use. The decimal number 67108863d hides all drives. If you want to customize this number to hide `C:` drive, you would make the third lowest bit a 0. Then convert the binary string to a decimal number and edit the `COMMON.ADM` template file adding the desired decimal number to the `ITEMLIST`.

Key: `HKEY_CURRENT_USER\Software\Microsoft\Windows`
                  `\CurrentVersion\Policies\Explorer`

Data Values: `NoDrives REG_DWORD Off = value is removed;`
                  `On = 3ffffff`

Hide Network Neighborhood Icon

Found in: Windows NT Shell\Restrictions

Details: Hides all access to the `Network Neighborhood`

Key: `HKEY_CURRENT_USER\Software\Microsoft\Windows`
                  `\CurrentVersion\Policies\Explorer`

Data Values: `NoNetHood REG_DWORD Off = 0 or value is`
                  `removed; On = 1`

Hide All Items on Desktop

Found in: Windows NT Shell\Restrictions

Details: This option hides everything on the Desktop except for the `Start` button

Key: HKEY_CURRENT_USER\Software\Microsoft\Windows
                     \CurrentVersion\Policies\Explorer

Data Values: NoDesktop REG_DWORD Off = 0 or value is
                     removed; On = 1

Disable Shut Down Command

Found in: Windows NT Shell\Restrictions

Details: Allows your users to shut down their worksta-
                     tion from the Login dialog box.

Key: HKEY_CURRENT_USER\Software\Microsoft\Windows
                     \CurrentVersion\Policies\Explorer

Data Values: NoClose REG_DWORD Off = 0 or value is
                     removed; On = 1

Don't Save Settings at Exit

Found in: Windows NT Shell\Restrictions

Details: No changes or additions to the users profile will
                     be saved

Key: HKEY_CURRENT_USER\Software\Microsoft\Windows
                     \CurrentVersion\Policies\Explorer

Data Values: NoSaveSettings REG_DWORD Off = 0 or value is
                     removed; On = 1

Disable Registry Editing Tools

Found in: System\Restrictions

Details: Disable Regedit, Regedt32, and Tweak UI

Key: HKEY_CURRENT_USER\Software\Microsoft\Windows
                     \CurrentVersion\Policies\System

Data Values: DisableRegistryTools REG_DWORD Off = 0 or
                     value is removed; On = 1

Run Only Allowed Windows Applications

Found in: System\Restrictions

Details:	Provides a list of 32 bit Windows applications that the user can run. You must include `Systray.exe`; which loads the System tray. Look at the bottom right corner of your computer screen: the graphics that are present there (e.g., the speaker and the time) are activated by the loading of the system tray.
Key:	`HKEY_CURRENT_USER\Software\Microsoft\Windows` `\CurrentVersion\Policies\Explorer`
Data Values:	`RestrictRun REG_DWORD Off = 0 or value is` `removed; On = 1 Name of the executable` `starting with 1 REG_SZ Off = value is` `removed; On = text of application name`

Custom Programs Folder

Found in:	Shell\Custom Folders
Details:	Where the UNC path pointing to custom shell folders is stored
Key:	`HKEY_CURRENT_USER\Software\Microsoft\` `Windows\CurrentVersion\Explorer\User Shell` `Folders`
Data Values:	`Programs REG_ REG_SZ Off = value is removed;` `On = text of UNC path to folder. Default =` `%USERPROFILE%\Start Menu\Programs`

Custom Desktop Icons

Found in:	Shell\Custom Folders
Details:	Where the UNC path for custom icons is stored
Key:	`HKEY_CURRENT_USER\Software\Microsoft\` `Windows\CurrentVersion\Explorer\User Shell` `Folders`
Data Values:	`Desktop REG_SZ Off = value is removed; On =` `text of UNC path to folder. Default =` `%USERPROFILE%\Desktop`

Custom Network Neighborhood

Found in: Shell\Custom Folders

Details: Where the UNC path for a custom Network
                 Neighborhood is stored

Key: `HKEY_CURRENT_USER\Software\Microsoft\Windows`
                 `\CurrentVersion\Explorer\User Shell Folders`

Data Values: `NetHood REG_SZ Off = value is removed; On =`
                 `text of UNC path to folder. Default =`
                 `%USERPROFILE%\NetHood`

Remove Common Program Groups from Start Menu

Found in: NT Shell\Restrictions

Details: Where the UNC path for Common program
                 groups is stored

Key: `HKEY_CURRENT_USER\Software\Microsoft\Windows`
                 `\CurrentVersion\Policies\Explorer`

Data Values: `NoCommonGroups REG_DWORD Off = 0 or value is`
                 `removed; On = 1`

Disable Context Menus for the Taskbar

Found in: NT Shell\Restrictions

Details: Removes any right-click response from the
                 Taskbar

Key: `HKEY_CURRENT_USER\Software\Microsoft\Windows`
                 `\CurrentVersion\Policies\Explorer`

Data Values: `NoTrayContextMenu REG_DWORD Off = 0 or value`
                 `is removed; On = 1`

Disable Explorer's Default Context Menu

Found in: NT Shell\Restrictions

Details: Disables right-click options when using the Win-
                 dows explorer

Key:	HKEY_CURRENT_USER\Software\Microsoft\Windows \CurrentVersion\Policies\Explorer
Data Values:	NoViewContextMenu REG_DWORD Off = 0 or value is removed; On = 1

Disable Link File Tracking

Found in:	NT Shell\Restrictions
Details:	When this option is enabled the configured path for the shortcut is used rather than the absolute path
Key:	HKEY_CURRENT_USER\Software\Microsoft\Windows \CurrentVersion\Policies\Explorer
Data Values:	LinkResolvedIgnoreLinkInfo REG_DWORD Off = 0 or value is removed; On = 1

Parse\Don't Parse Autoexec.bat

Found in:	NT System\Parse Autoexec.bat
Details:	When this value is 1, all environment variables defined in the Autoexec.bat file are loaded and used in the user's environment
Key:	HKEY_CURRENT_USER \Software\Microsoft\ Windows NT\CurrentVersion\Winlogon
Data Values:	ParseAutoexec REG_SZ Off = 0 or value is removed; On = 1

Disable Task Manager

Found in:	NT System\Disable Task Manager
Details:	CTRL-ALT-DELETE will not enable the Task Manager
Key:	HKEY_CURRENT_USER\Software\Microsoft\Windows \CurrentVersion\Policies\System
Data Values:	DisableTaskMgr REG_DWORD Off = 0 or value is removed; On = 1

Remote Update Options of Policies

Found in: NT System\Remote Update

Details: Set either automatic reading of `POL` files
                 from either `NETLOGON` (NT) or `SYS:PUBLIC`
                 (NetWare), or `Manual` (UNC path set by
                 Administrator):

                 With UpdateMode set to 1 (Automatic, the
                 default)
                 With UpdateMode set to 2 (Manual)
                 With UpdateMode set to 0 (Off), a policy file is
                 not downloaded from any system, and therefore
                 is not applied

Key: `HKEY_LOCAL_MACHINE\System\CurrentControlSet`
                 `\Control\Update`

Data Values: `UpdateMode REG_DWORD Off = 0, Automatic = 1;`
                 `Manual = 2`

                 `NetworkPath REG_SZ Text of UNC path for`
                 `manual update`

                 `Verbose REG_DWORD Display error messages.`
                 `Off = 0 or value not present; On = 1`

                 `LoadBalance REG_DWORD Off = 0 or value not`
                 `present; On = 1`

Logon Banner

Found in: Windows NT System\Logon

Details: Enables a logon banner that the user must
                 acknowledge before logging in

Key: `HKEY_LOCAL_MACHINE\Software\Microsoft\`
                 `Windows NT\CurrentVersion\Winlogon`

Data Values: `LegalNoticeCaption REG_SZ Off = value is`
                 `removed; On = text of caption`

                 `LegalNoticeText REG_SZ Off = value is`
                 `removed; On = text of notice`

Logon Dialog Shut Down Button

Found in: Windows NT System\Logon

Details: Adds a shut down dialog box to the `Login` dialog
box

Key: `HKEY_LOCAL_MACHINE\Software\Microsoft \`
`Windows NT\CurrentVersion\Winlogon`

Data Values: `ShutdownWithoutLogon REG_SZ Off = 0; On = 1`

Logon Name Display

Found in: NT System\Logon

Details: Stops the last user name from showing up in the
Login dialog box

Key: `HKEY_LOCAL_MACHINE\Software\Microsoft\`
`Windows NT\CurrentVersion\Winlogon`

Data Values: `DontDisplayLastUserName REG_SZ Off = 0;`
`On = 1`

Do Not Create 8.3 Name for Long File Names

Found in: Windows NT System\File system

Details: Disables the creation of 8.3 names for files

Key: `HKEY_LOCAL_MACHINE\System\CurrentCon-`
`trolSet\Control \FileSystem`

Data Values: `NtfsDisable8dot3NameCreation REG_DWORD`
`Off = 0; On = 1`

Creating Custom System Policy Templates

This chapter introduces you to the art of creating system policy templates. You will learn:

- The structure of system policy templates
- The command language of system policy templates
- How to read the template language
- How to create custom ADM templates
- How to create templates for NT and Windows 98 clients with the Policy Template Editor

What Is a System Policy Template?

We know that a system policy holds the actual Registry settings to be implemented on computer systems, users, and groups of users. The ADM system policy templates that are loaded and used show us the possible changes that can be made with the policy editor. Once the choices have been made and saved, the system policy editor reads the template and translates the choices into Registry edits.

For Windows 98 the system template is WINDOWS.ADM; the templates that are included with Windows NT are COMMON.ADM and WINNT.ADM.

The template files are text files in structure and it's fairly easy to create your own custom ADM templates to control system or software options that Microsoft or other vendors haven't provided choices for. I say "fairly" because, depending on your programming background, the information presented in the chapter may look unreadable.

However, reread this chapter several times and try out the programming examples using the wonderful Policy Template Editor from Simac Software Products that is included with the software tools on the enclosed CD-ROM and I'm sure you will have lots of success.

ADM Template File Structure

The template file is designed to update the two real sections of the Registry: HKEY_LOCAL_MACHINE (the system HIVES, SAM, SECURITY, SOFTWARE, and SYSTEM) and HKEY_CURRENT_USER (NTUSER.DAT). See Figure 8-1.

Each template file is scripted by a varied command set that must be entered correctly in order to have a functioning template. When the template is loaded into the system policy editor the basic structure is parsed and checked. Any errors found will be displayed with the line number and a somewhat cryptic suggestion as to what may be wrong. ADM template files are text based and NOTEPAD.EXE or any text editor can be used for editing and creation of template files.

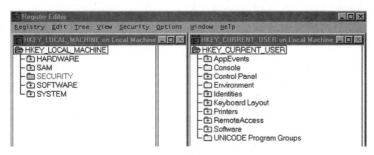

Figure 8-1 *Templates control the two main sections of the Registry.*

There are usually three major sections or groupings in most template files but there could be as little as one section. The sections you will find are either CLASS MACHINE or CLASS USER or both, and a possible third section in square brackets at the end of the template called [strings].

However, you need only one of the CLASS segments to actually have a functioning template, although the norm is the three sections just defined. Let's now deal with the nuts and bolts of the template command language.

CLASS

The CLASS heading is first found at the top of the template file. As mentioned, HKEY_LOCAL_MACHINE and HKY_CURRENT_USER are the two areas that the template file can change through a system policy or direct registry edit.

The CLASS heading informs the policy editor whether the template entry selected affects the computer section of the Registry (HKEY_LOCAL_MACHINE) or the active user's Registry (HKY_CURRENT_USER).

> The CLASS MACHINE section will update only HKEY_LOCAL_MACHINE. **Note**
> The CLASS USER section will update only HKEY_CURRENT_USER. If no class statement is present the policy will still work, but the settings can be only for USER or MACHINE, but not both. The Registry path present in the template will determine the actual class setting in the template file. See Figure 8-2.

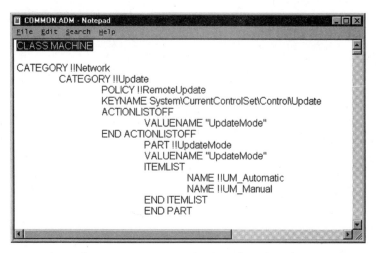

Figure 8-2 *The* CLASS *section is the first found at the top of a template.*

When you view the templates in the system policy editor, the two icons match the two main categories CLASS MACHINE and CLASS USER. Default Computer or Local Computer settings update HKEY_LOCAL_MACHINE. Default User or Local User settings update HKEY_CURRENT_USER. See Figure 8-3.

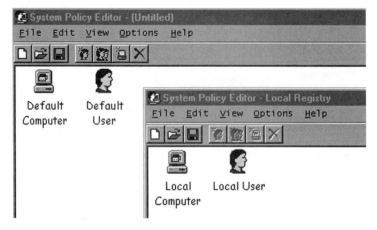

Figure 8-3 *The* Policy *icons directly update* CLASS MACHINE *and* CLASS USER.

CATEGORY

Each of the sections CLASS MACHINE and CLASS USER will contain categories. When you open a template using the system policy editor, the existing categories are shown as blue books when either the Local/Default Computer or the Local/Default User icon is selected. Categories are used to divide the policy into a logical order.

As an example in the WINNT.ADM template the categories for the CLASS MACHINE section (that's the computer side) are Network, Printers, Remote Access, and Shell.

The CATEGORY section must be closed with an END CATEGORY command. Categories can be nested inside a main category. See Figure 8-4.

STRINGS

The category name in the template file can be defined with a text variable used for the category headings that are viewed when using the system policy editor. Notice that double exclamation marks (!!) are used to signify the start of the text variable.

The actual string text value that is used is linked to the [strings] section found at the bottom of the system policy template.

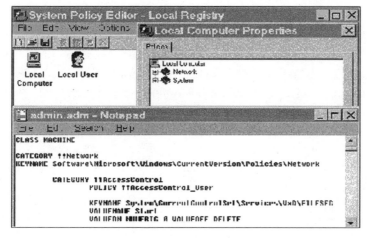

Figure 8-4 *Categories at the policy level and template level.*

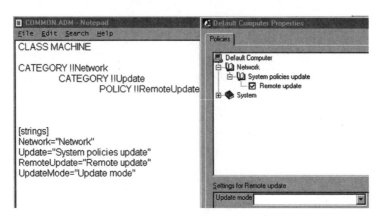

Figure 8-5 *Strings and labels at the policy level and template level.*

The text following the double exclamation marks cannot contain any spaces unless it is placed in quotation marks. Labels for PART, CATEGORY, and POLICY sections of the template can be entered with the text in quotation marks or by a text variable that is always started with double exclamation marks (!!). See Figure 8-5.

Using this method suggested and used by Microsoft, the strings referenced in the [strings] section could be used several times by simply using the same !! text label in the applicable section. However, this seems to me to be the hard way to add text information to a template.

The way I would recommend entering any text information into a template file is by the use of quotations to indicate a text string. The strings can always be listed in quotations at the exact location in the template where the double exclamation marks appear rather than in a cryptic and usually vague text variable linked to the bottom of the template file.

Even if you have text labels that you decide to use several times, it isn't that much extra typing and when troubleshooting your template code it is much easier to read and trace the template code from a top-to-bottom flow. Let's look at an example and you'll see what I mean. The fragment of code in Figure 8-6 is from a template to control the Control Panel applets. The first

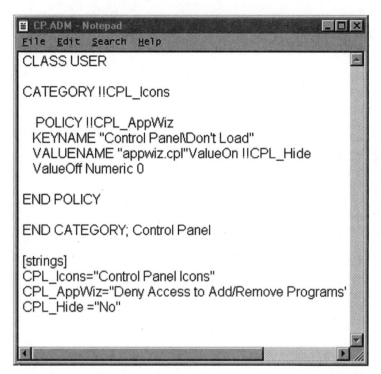

Figure 8-6 *The strings section and text variable labels are hard to read.*

code is for turning off the Add / Remove Software icon using the [strings] section as Microsoft suggests.

Now let's look at the next example (Figure 8-7) using text in quotations at the exact place in the template file where the text is needed.

POLICY

The POLICY variable defines the section or sections in the template file where you define the specific policy choice. It creates the check boxes and the choices available once a main- or subcategory is selected. A policy is set inside a defined category, that is, every category will contain a policy from which a choice can be set. The POLICY section must be closed with an END POLICY command. See Figure 8-8.

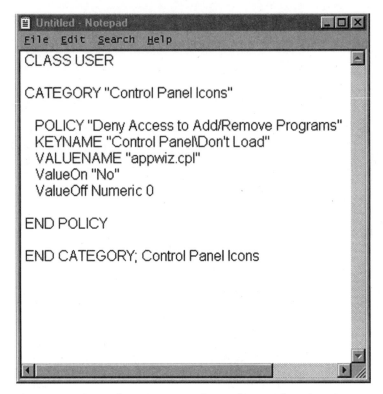

Figure 8-7 *A much easier to read template with strings in quotations.*

KEYNAME

Each policy section must have a KEYNAME with at least one value. The KEYNAME entry is the exact Registry path that the data value will be written to when the template is read. The KEYNAME must also start directly below the POLICY setting.

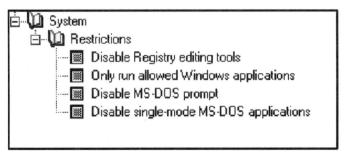

Figure 8-8 *Policies inside a defined category.*

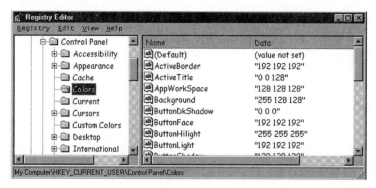

Figure 8-9 *The variable* KEYNAME *defines the exact Registry path.*

Do not start the KEYNAME with a backslash (\) or with HKEY_LOCAL_MACHINE or HKEY_CURRENT_USER. The CLASS section has already defined the section of the Registry that will be used.

The KEYNAME can be listed in either the PART, POLICY, or CATE-GORY section of the template file. It depends on whether the entries are multiple entries inside one CATEGORY or just a single PART or POLICY entry.

Multiple entries will use the defined Registry path if it has been defined in the CATEGORY. See Figure 8-9.

VALUENAME

The VALUENAME is the name in the text description of the Registry data type to be added or changed in the Registry. The VALUENAME is enclosed in quotations, as it is a text value. See Figure 8-10.

(Default)	(value not set)
BuildNumber	0x00000565 (1381)
ParseAutoexec	"0"
RunLogonScriptSync	0x00000001 (1)

Figure 8-10 VALUENAME *labels and data types for policy templates.*

VALUEON

This signifies the type of Registry data that will be entered; the default is REG_SZ. Data values for policy settings can be REG_SZ, REG_DWORD, or REG_EXPAND_SZ, most data entries are REG_SZ or REG_DWORD. We have four choices for value entry types

1. ValueOn "1" or "On"   Data type is REG_SZ

2. ValueOn Numeric 1   Data type is REG_DWORD

3. ValueOff "Off"   Data type is REG_SZ

4. ValueOff Numeric 0   Data type is REG_DWORD

If the data type is to be entered as binary, the NUMERIC designation must be used with VALUE.

Note

> If the text value is to be entered as a REG_EXPAND_SZ, then the variable EXPANDABLETEXT must be added to the PART description. This will then write the value to the registry with data type REG_EXPAND_SZ, for example:
>
> ```
> PART !!MyPolicy EDITTEXT EXPANDABLETEXT
>   VALUENAME ValueToBeChanged
>   END PART
> ```
>
> REG_EXPAND_SZ types in templates are extremely rare.

Template PART Control Indicators

A PART control indicator is like a macro—it defines one or more controls that can be used to set powerful values of a system policy. There can be multiple PART entries.

Each PART entry will usually contain a KEYNAME, a VALUENAME, and value entries. If the KEYNAME entry is defined at a higher level in the template file, in this case, the PART entry will use that KEYNAME. The PART section must be closed with an END PART command. See Figure 8-11. The basic structure of a template is:

- *PART name.* Defines one or more part control indicators that can be used to set values in a system policy. PART names can be defined by text variables and the associated [strings] section, or they can be enclosed in quotation marks.

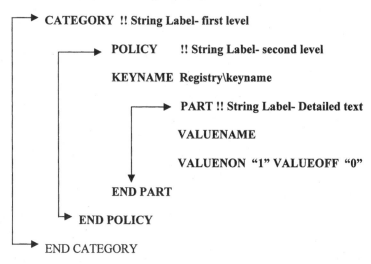

Figure 8-11 *System policy template structure.*

- *END PART.* Each part must be closed with an END PART command.

PART Control Indicators

The definitions for the actions that are defined in the PART and POLICY sections are numerous. The syntax associated with the part controls gives the system policy its power and flexibility.

CHECKBOX

This is the most common PART type. This PART option displays a checkbox that allows the starting, stopping, or ignoring of current system policy. This is used to either deploy or deactivate poli-

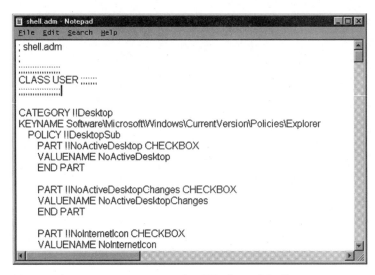

Figure 8-12 CHECKBOX *options for Windows 98 clients.*

cies. An example is shown for the shell options for Windows 98 with SHELL.ADM. (Figure 8-12).

If the box is checked, the VALUEON value is entered; if the box is unchecked, the VALUEOFF value is entered. If the box is grayed out, the checkbox is ignored and the current setting in the Registry remains. CHECKBOX choices are:

- DEFCHECKED. The box is initially checked with a default value.

- VALUEON. If checked, the behavior listed in quotations is written to the Registry.

- VALUEOFF. If checked, the behavior listed in quotations is written to the Registry.

- ACTIONLISTON. Specifies additional optional action to be taken if checkbox is "on."

- ACTIONLISTOFF. Specifies additional optional action to be taken if checkbox is "off."

NUMERIC

This part shows a NUMERIC edit field with spin control. The user can enter a numeric value only. See Figure 8-13.

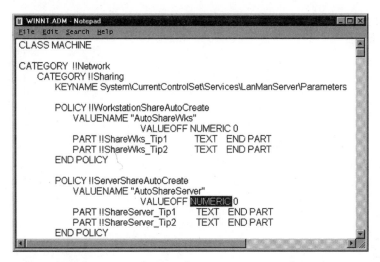

Figure 8-13 NUMERIC *values in the* WINNT.ADM *template.*

Additional syntax choices for NUMERIC are:

- DEFAULT. The edit field shows the default entry but the user can type over the shown entry.

- MAX. Used to set the maximum length of the suggestion up to 9999 characters. Proper syntax is MAX value.

- MIN. Used to set the minimum length of the suggestion up to 9999 characters. Proper syntax is MIN value.

- REQUIRED. This specifies that an entry is mandatory for the part to be enabled. REQUIRED overrides a MIN value of zero.

- SPIN. Shows a spin box that increments the Registry entry a value of 1 every spin of the control.

- TXTCONVERT. Used to convert a binary value into text before being entered in the Registry.

COMBOBOX

A COMBOBOX is an edit field that accepts ASCII text plus a drop-down list. This choice is a joining of a DRODOWNLIST and an EDIT-TEXT box. See Figure 8-14.

The items that can be selected show in a list; however, the user can also add one of his or her own.

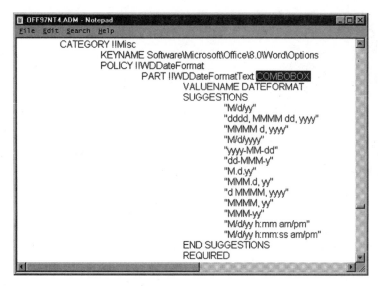

Figure 8-14 COMBOBOX *options in the* OFF97NT4.ADM *template.*

Other syntax options you can use with combobox are:

- ITEMLIST / END ITEMLIST. ITEMLIST holds all the entries that appear in the DROPDOWNLIST. Use END ITEMLIST to close the list of items. Each item contains a NAME, VALUE, or ACTIONLIST.

- NAME. The name is the text that shows in the COMBOBOX.

- VALUE. This is used for the entry chosen from the list. Use VALUE NUMERIC if the data type is either binary or numeric in value.

- ACTIONLIST / END ACTIONLIST. This choice activates an action if the selection is made. ACTIONLIST is activated if NAME is used.

DEFAULT

If used, this text value will show the default entry but the user can type over the shown entry. Other syntax that can be used is:

- MAXLEN. This sets the length of allowable string. Syntax is MAXLEN value (0-255).

- SUGGESTIONS and END SUGGESTIONS. A list of suggestions can be specified in the COMBOBOX. All items are separated by a space.

- REQUIRED. This specifies that an entry is mandatory for the part to be enabled.

DROPDOWNLIST

A DROPDOWNLIST part shows a drop down list to choose from. No manual entry is allowed. See ITEMLIST for the syntax choices for DROPDOWNLIST.

ITEMLIST and ENDITEMLIST

ITEMLIST supports all the entries that appear in the DROPDOWN-LIST. Each item contains a NAME, VALUE, and/or ACTIONLIST. Use END ITEMLIST to close the list of items. Syntax choices for ITEMLIST are:

- NAME. The name is the text that appears in the DROPDOWNLIST.

- VALUE. This is used for the entry chosen from the list. Use VALUE NUMERIC if the data type is either binary or numeric in value.

- ACTIONLIST / END ACTIONLIST. This choice activates an action if the selection is made. ACTIONLIST is used with the NAME entry. ACTIONLIST is activated if NAME is used.

- REQUIRED. This specifies that an entry is mandatory for the part to be enabled.

LISTBOX

Use of the choice shows a list box with Add Item, allowing you to add multiple text entries into the Registry. Other commands used with LISTBOX are:

- VALUENAME. When used with LISTBOX, VALUENAME simply provides the name to the LISTBOX.

- ADDITIVE. Using LISTBOX overrides the current settings in the Registry unless the value ADDITIVE is used. This value tells the policy to add or append the entries onto the current value.

- EXPLICITVALUE. This value creates two columns of data: the first column holds the item name; the second column holds the item data.

REMARK

The use of a semicolon allows you to place comments throughout the template file. See Figure 8-15.

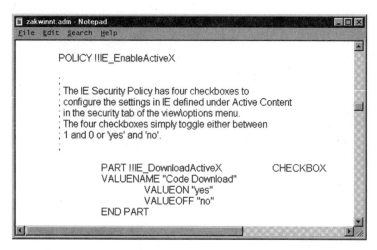

Figure 8-15 *Remarks make code easier to read and understand.*

EDITTEXT

Using this choice shows an edit field that accepts ASCII text. Other commands used with `EDITTEXT` are:

- `DEFAULT`. The edit field shows the default entry but the user can type over the shown entry.

- `MAXLEN`. This sets the length of allowable string. Syntax is `MAXLEN value` (0-255).

- `REQUIRED`. When used, an entry is mandatory to use this part.

Checking Out Template Code Examples

The last few pages of this chapter probably have you thinking that creating system policy templates is too hard. Well, actually it is fairly easy if we start with a very simple example. First, a few template code examples to demonstrate all the command language of the templates. Let's see how using `COMMON.ADM` can restrict the `Display` icon in the Control Panel for NT Clients.

Opening up the template and searching for the `CLASS USER` section we find the `Display` restriction. See Figure 8-16.

Looking at the template, you can see the following code for locking down the `Display` icon in the Control Panel. Let's decipher it line by line.

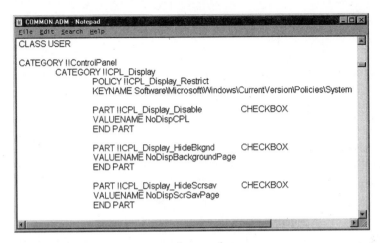

Figure 8-16 COMMON.ADM *template code.*

1. The CLASS USER heading tells us that the settings will be deployed in HKEY_CURRENT_USER.

   ```
   CLASS USER
   ```

2. For this example, we have a category nested inside another category. So we have to open two categories (that is, two blue books) until we are presented with the policy to restrict the display. The policy choice is to Deny Access to Display Icon.

   ```
   CATEGORY "ControlPanel"
   CATEGORY "Display"
   POLICY "Restrict Display"
   ```

3. From viewing the code we can see that the part CHECKBOX is being used so if the value is checked, a DWORD of 1 will be entered into the Registry at the defined KEYNAME path. Then the PART is closed.

   ```
   KEYNAME Software\Microsoft\Windows\CurrentVersion\
   Policies\System
   PART "Deny Access to Display Icon"  CHECKBOX
   ```

4. The VALUENAME is listed that will be activated at the KEYNAME Registry location.

   ```
   VALUENAME NoDispCPL
   END PART
   ```

   By using the system policy template, the system policy editor, and the Registry editor we are able to discover where the policies are being deployed and learn from the structure.

Auto Logon to NT

Let's look at another template for NT that automatically logs us onto the desktop. Again it is a fairly simple template but with a few more details.

Opening the `Default Computer` icon we can see the `Auto Logon to NT` option—that is the `AUTONT.ADM` policy. The rest of the category choices are from the `WINNT.ADM` policy file. Opening the auto login category presents us with the three options that would have to be filled in for this option to work. Obviously this is not the most security conscious template option but as a learning tool, it's perfect. See Figure 8-17.

Let's now look at the template code and see how this template works.

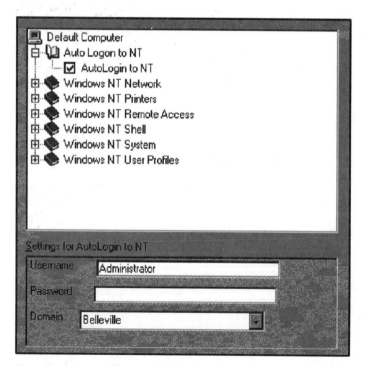

Figure 8-17 *Auto logon choices for NT clients.*

1. Since the `CLASS` is defined as `MACHINE` this policy template will apply to computer settings and `HKEY_LOCAL_MACHINE`.

   ```
   CLASS MACHINE
   ```

2. The blue book `CATEGORY` is `Auto Logon to NT` and the `POLICY` uses the same name.

   ```
   CATEGORY "Auto Logon to NT"
   Policy  "AutoLogin to NT"
   ```

3. The path to the Registry location is listed by `KEYNAME`; the `VALUENAME` specifies the label for the Registry value.

   ```
   KEYNAME SOFTWARE\Microsoft\WindowsNT\CurrentVersion\
      Winlogon
   ValueName AutoAdminLogin
   ```

4. If selected, a string value of 1 will be entered into the local Registry.

   ```
   ValueOn "1"; This is a string value REG_SZ
   ```

5. If the policy had already been in force and it was deselected, then the `ValueOff` and `Delete` would remove the setting. As well, the `ActionListOff` will also remove the settings that were present in the Registry.

   ```
   ValueOff Delete
   ActionListOff
   ValueName DefaultDomainName Value Delete
   ValueName DefaultUserName   Value Delete
   ValueName DefaultPassword Value Delete
   End ActionListOff
   ```

6. If the checkbox is checked, the username must be entered with a maximum length of 15 characters.

   ```
   Part "Username" Edittext Required Maxlen 15
   ValueName DefaultUserName
   Default "Administrator"
   End Part
   ```

7. The password must also be entered with a maximum length of 14 characters.

   ```
   Part "Password" EditText Required Maxlen 14
   ValueName DefaultPassword
   End Part
   ```

8. The Domain or Workgroup must now be entered with a maximum length of 15 characters.

```
Part "Domain" ComboBox Required  Maxlen 15
ValueName DefaultDomainName
Suggestions "NEW YORK" "KINGSTON"
End Suggestions
End Part
End Policy
End Category
```

Creating a Custom Template for Windows NT

The area where Windows NT and 98 is most vulnerable is the
Control Panel. There are some restrictions that policies provide
for, but you probably want more choices. So here's a template
that gives you complete control over the Control Panel. But
before we look at the entire Control Panel template, let's look
at the code again that restricts access to the Add/Remove
Software icon.

```
CLASS USER
CATEGORY "Control Panel Restrictions"
POLICY "Add Remove Software"
KEYNAME "Control Panel\Don't Load"
VALUENAME "appwiz.cpl"
ValueOn "No"
ValueOff Numeric 0
END POLICY
```

Now let's look at the complete code for Control Panel restrictions in the template file CONTROLPANEL.ADM.

```
CLASS USER

CATEGORY "Control Panel Restrictions"

POLICY "Add Remove Software"
KEYNAME "Control Panel\Don't Load"
VALUENAME "appwiz.cpl"
ValueOn "No"
ValueOff Numeric 0
END POLICY

POLICY "Devices"
KEYNAME "Control Panel\Don't Load"
VALUENAME "devapps.cpl"
```

```
ValueOn "No"
ValueOff Numeric 0
END POLICY

POLICY "Inernet"
KEYNAME "Control Panel\Don't Load"
VALUENAME "inetcpl.cpl"
ValueOn "No"
ValueOff Numeric 0
END POLICY

POLICY "Accessibility"
KEYNAME "Control Panel\Don't Load"
VALUENAME "Joy.cpl"
ValueOn "No"
ValueOff Numeric 0
END POLICY

POLICY "License"
KEYNAME "Control Panel\Don't Load"
VALUENAME "liccpa.cpl"
ValueOn "No"
ValueOff Numeric 0
END POLICY

POLICY "Main"
KEYNAME "Control Panel\Don't Load"
VALUENAME "main.cpl"
ValueOn "No"
ValueOff Numeric 0
END POLICY

POLICY "Multimedia"
KEYNAME "Control Panel\Don't Load"
VALUENAME "mmsys.cpl"
ValueOn "No"
ValueOff Numeric 0
END POLICY

POLICY "Modem"
KEYNAME "Control Panel\Don't Load"
VALUENAME "modem.cpl"
ValueOn "No"
ValueOff Numeric 0
END POLICY

POLICY "Network"
```

```
KEYNAME "Control Panel\Don't Load"
VALUENAME "ncpa.cpl"
ValueOn "No"
ValueOff Numeric 0
END POLICY

POLICY "ODBC"
KEYNAME "Control Panel\Don't Load"
VALUENAME "odbccp32.cpl"
ValueOn "No"
ValueOff Numeric 0
END POLICY

POLICY "Ports"
KEYNAME "Control Panel\Don't Load"
VALUENAME "Ports.cpl"
ValueOn "No"
ValueOff Numeric 0
END POLICY

POLICY "Server"
KEYNAME "Control Panel\Don't Load"
VALUENAME "srvmgr.cpl"
ValueOn "No"
ValueOff Numeric 0
END POLICY

POLICY "System"
KEYNAME "Control Panel\Don't Load"
VALUENAME "sysdm.cpl"
ValueOn "No"
ValueOff Numeric 0
END POLICY

POLICY "Telephony"
KEYNAME "Control Panel\Don't Load"
VALUENAME "telephon.cpl"
ValueOn "No"
ValueOff Numeric 0
END POLICY

POLICY "Date and Time"
KEYNAME "Control Panel\Don't Load"
VALUENAME "timedate.cpl"
ValueOn "No"
ValueOff Numeric 0
END POLICY
```

```
POLICY "UPS"
KEYNAME "Control Panel\Don't Load"
VALUENAME "UPS.cpl"
ValueOn "No"
ValueOff Numeric 0
END POLICY

POLICY "Console"
KEYNAME "Control Panel\Don't Load"
VALUENAME "console.cpl"
ValueOn "No"
ValueOff Numeric 0
END POLICY

POLICY "PC Card"
KEYNAME "Control Panel\Don't Load"
VALUENAME "devapps.cpl"
ValueOn "No"
ValueOff Numeric 0
END POLICY

POLICY "Regional Settings"
KEYNAME "Control Panel\Don't Load"
VALUENAME "intl.cpl"
ValueOn "No"
ValueOff Numeric 0
END POLICY

POLICY "FindFast"
KEYNAME "Control Panel\Don't Load"
VALUENAME "findfast.cpl"
ValueOn "No"
ValueOff Numeric 0
END POLICY

POLICY "Services"
KEYNAME "Control Panel\Don't Load"
VALUENAME "srvmgr.cpl"
ValueOn "No"
ValueOff Numeric 0
END POLICY

END CATEGORY; Control Panel Restrictions
```

Viewing CONTROLPANEL.ADM with the system policy editor, the system policy is easy to view and use. See Figure 8-18.

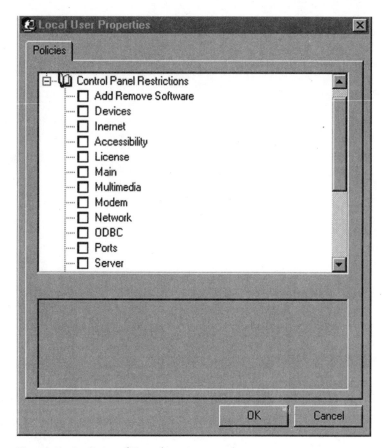

Figure 8-18 *Control Panel options with* `CONTROLPANEL.ADM`.

We now can add complete control by adding this template to the existing NT templates `WINNT.ADM` and `COMMON.ADM` by loading them at the same time into the system policy editor. See Figure 8-19.

Writing Our Own Custom Templates

We can make a policy for any `REG_SZ` or `REG DWORD` value we want, or that exists in the NT or 98 Registry. Let's now look at a great software utility for easily creating your own template files for both Windows 98 and NT 4.0 clients. It is called the *Policy Template Editor* (PTE) and the company is Simac Software Products. You can visit their Web site at *www.tools4NT.com/*. See Figure 8-20.

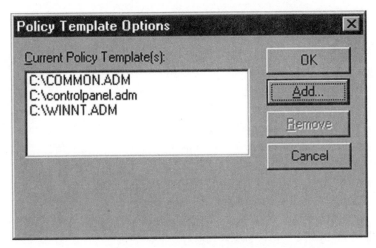

Figure 8-19 *Loading multiple* ADM *templates for NT clients.*

The PTE allows you to view existing system policy templates and also create your own templates using the existing menu structure. I will step through three examples, two for NT clients and one for Windows 98 clients. The template code is written for you as you build your template in object mode.

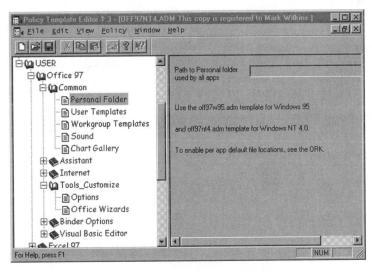

Figure 8-20 *The Policy Template Editor by Simac.*

NT Example: Creating a Template for Setting Your L2 Cache

NT out of the box supports only 256K of your L2 cache. This is also called your *hardware cache* and is located on your motherboard. If you have a Pentium PC, the odds are that you have 512K cache installed. You'll have to check your documentation, or BIOS, or out on the Web to make sure. The reason this is such an important setting is that you must have the right amount of L2 cache RAM in order to maintain a high "hit ratio." If you have 64K RAM, then you should have 512K cache. The problem is, even if you do, NT won't use the L2 cache because of the Registry setting that is tattooed with the default setting of 256K. The Registry tweak to manually update your L2 cache size is as follows:

1. Open `REGEDIT` and navigate to:

   ```
   HKEY_LOCAL_MACHINE\SYSTEM\CurrentControlSet\Control\
       Session Manager\Memory Management
   ```

2. There you will find a value called `SecondLevelDataCache` (see Figure 8-21). It's a `DWORD` with a `HEX` value of 0. The 0 `DWORD` value means that NT will recognize 256K of L2 cache.

The typical values for L2 cache size are: 256(100HEX), 512(200HEX), and 1024(400HEX). So let's build a system policy template that allows you to update your users' cache size to 512K through a computer system policy.

1. Open the Policy Template Editor (PTE). Select the menu item `File` and then select `New` to create a blank template that the PTE will call `New1`. See Figure 8-22.

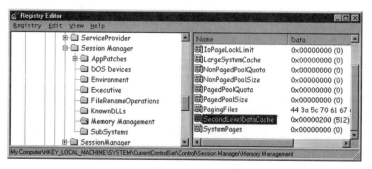

Figure 8-21 *Use Regedit to find the* `SecondLevelDataCache`.

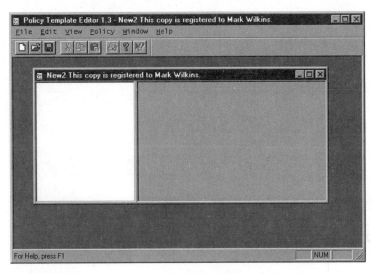

Figure 8-22 *Creating a new template file with the PTE.*

2. Now select the menu item Policy and select New Class. We must select the right one for our registry hack. Since the Registry path is in HKEY_LOCAL_MACHINE, we must select Machine. Then click Apply Now. See Figure 8-23.

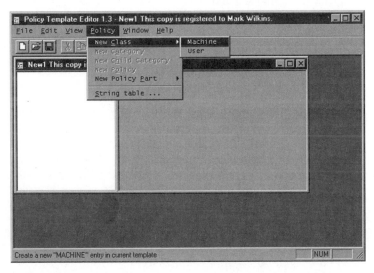

Figure 8-23 *Select* New Class *and* Machine *for this example.*

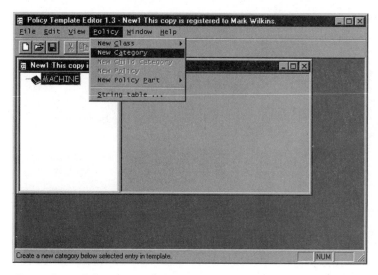

Figure 8-24 *Selecting and naming your* CATEGORY.

3. Next select the menu item Policy and choose New Category. Double-click the blue book Category to name your CATEGORY. Then click Apply Now. See Figure 8-24.

4. Next select the menu item Policy and choose Policy. Double-click the <new> value to name your POLICY and to enter the Registry path, and the value choices for when the value is checked, and when the value is unchecked. Then click Apply Now. See Figure 8-25.

   • The Registry path is
     SYSTEM\CurrentControlSet\Control\Session Manager\
     Memory Management.
   • The Value name is SecondLevelDataCache.
   • The Value when checked is to be a DWORD, so we must check Explicit Value and Numeric and enter the value of 512.
   • The Value when unchecked can be left at the default value of 0.

5. Now save your policy as L2CACHE.ADM.

There, we're done. Let's load L2Cache into the system policy editor and see what our template looks like. See Figure 8-26.

Now you're probably thinking that it would be nice to have a

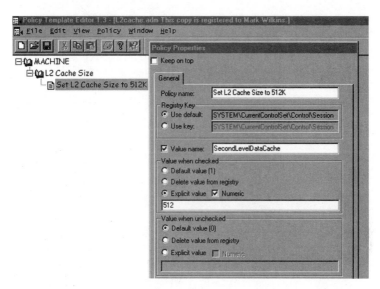

Figure 8-25 *Name your* POLICY *and fill in the required data fields.*

choice of the available cache sizes of 256, 512, and 1024. So let's look at what we would have to do with the Policy Template Editor. We would have to add a part called a DROPDOWNLIST from the Policy menu and then select New Policy Part and DropDownList. Then click Apply Now. See Figure 8-27.

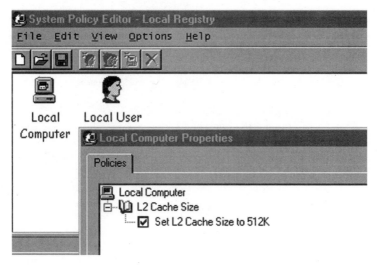

Figure 8-26 L2CACHE.ADM *loaded in the system policy editor.*

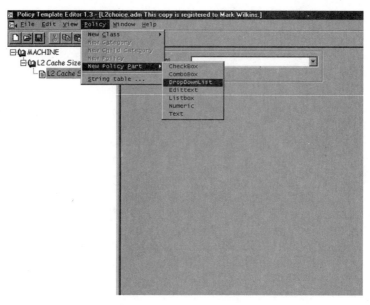

Figure 8-27 *Adding a* DropDownList *part to* L2CACHE.ADM.

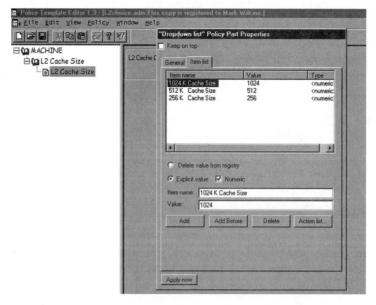

Figure 8-28 *Enter the required data for the* Dropdownlist
choices.

By double-clicking the `Dropdownlist` graphic, we can enter
the data needed for L2 cache choices. Then click `Apply Now`. See
Figure 8-28.

Looking at the updated template in the system policy editor,
we see the choices that we can now choose from a `DROPDOWNLIST`.
See Figure 8-29.

NT Example: Turning on the NumLock Key

This example is much simpler, involving only one registry data
type. The Registry hack for turning the NumLock key on when
you logon to an NT system is to add a `REG_SZ` data value

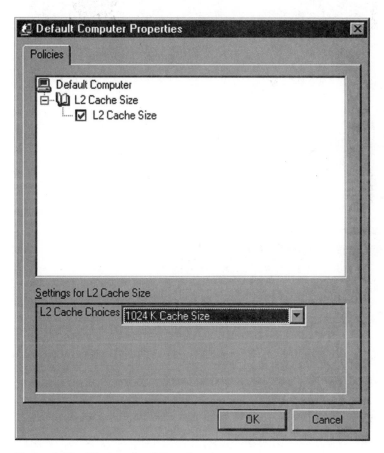

Figure 8-29 *Choices for L2 cache size.*

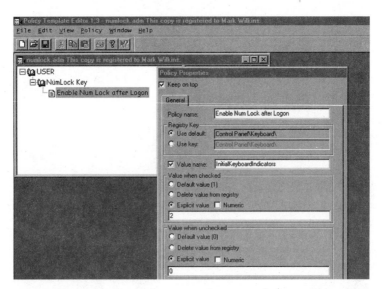

Figure 8-30 *NumLock choices with PTE and the system policy editor.*

KeyboardIndicators of 2 to the Registry path HKEY_CURRENT_USER\ Control Panel\Keyboard.

Using the PTE, we create a CLASS value for USER since the path is for HKEY_CURRENT_USER. The final properties screen for creating this template is what you need to see. See Figure 8-30.

Windows 98 Example: Disabling the Device Manager Update Button

Windows 98 has these annoying update buttons (to me, anyway) that, when clicked, will automatically try to search out on the Web in a vain attempt to fix the hardware or software problem automatically.

The Registry tweak to disable the Update Device Driver wizard in Device Manager is to add a DWORD value NoDevMgrUpdate with a value of 1 to the Registry path of:

```
HKEY_LOCAL_MACHINE\SOFTWARE\Microsoft\Windows\
    CurrentVersion\Policies
\Explorer.
```

1. Using the Policy Template Editor, you would have to first select the menu item File and then New to select a new template.

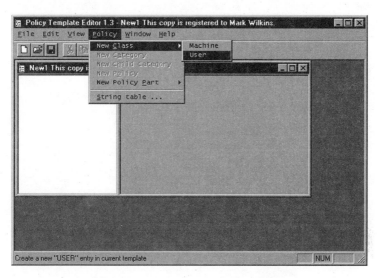

Figure 8-31 *Adding a* CLASS *value with the PTE.*

2. Second, you would have to select your CLASS for your template. In this case it would be User. See Figure 8-31.

3. Then from the Policy menu you would have to select Category and name your Category. Then click Apply Now. See Figure 8-32.

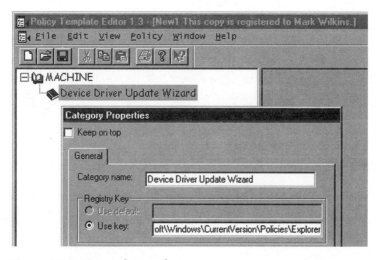

Figure 8-32 *Next select and name your* CATEGORY.

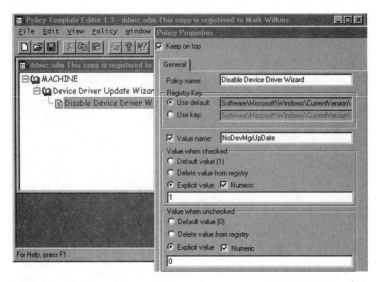

Figure 8-33 *Properties of the* Policy *menu using the Policy Template Editor.*

4. Next you would have to select the Policy menu and select and name your Policy and the required data. See Figure 8-33. The data you would have to enter is:

   • The Registry path of Software\Microsoft\Windows\ CurrentVersion\Policies\Explorer
   • The Value name of NoDevMgrUpDate

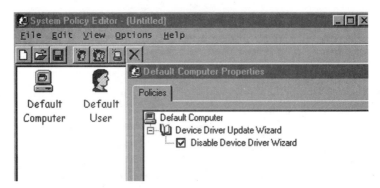

Figure 8-34 *Viewing the new template with the system policy editor.*

- The Value when checked of `Explicit value Numeric 1`
- The Value when unchecked of `Explicit value Numeric 0`

The last task to do is to save the template as an `ADM` file. The system policy editor displays the template in this manner. See Figure 8-34.

For the best Registry tips and tricks, head to *www.jsiinc.com/* for hundreds of Registry hacks for NT.

Troubleshooting System Policies

This chapter is all about troubleshooting with a mixed bag of solutions to common and not-so-common user profile and system policy problems in the NT and Windows 98 world. In this chapter you will learn:

- Troubleshooting basics
- Top 10 list of details and settings to check out when things just won't work
- 21 questions and answers to system policy and user profile problems
- Solving user profile and system policy problems
- Rules about service packs and when to use
- REG file troubleshooting

Troubleshooting 101

The best advice I can give you for troubleshooting when problems occur with system policies and user profiles is always to document your steps and changes on an ongoing basics.

Although documentation may seem old-fashioned in this electronic world, in fact it is essential to solve any type of network problem. Write down these basics and you'll start seeing a much better track record in problem recognition and solving.

1. *DLL versions.* Even the system policy editor uses DLLs.

2. *Software update versions.* The wrong EXE and DLL combination is fatal.

3. *Service pack version.* Service Packs 3, 4, and 5 all have their good points and possibly not-so-good points.

4. *Policy templates used.* There are many templates for both Windows 98 and NT 4.0, some even with the same names. It's a good idea to organize the templates into separate directories along with the corresponding system policy editor.

5. *Error messages.* Writing down and date/time stamping error messages will start an audit trail that will be invaluable in matching problems to fixes when using the knowledge base and other resources.

Be Proactive not Reactive

Who is going to be primarily responsible for the deployment, management, and updating of system policies and user profiles? You should have a master plan written down to help manage system policy and user profile information.

Some suggestions for a successful plan:

1. Back up and label your system policy files `NTCONFIG.POL` and `CONFIG.POL` before you make any changes.

2. Make sure that the collection of templates you think you are using are the actual ones used by the system policy editor. If you forget to reload a template that you used last time, all the settings that the unloaded template controlled will not be updated.

3. Make sure that any template setting you choose not to implement is grayed out.

4. Follow the K.I.S.S. rule and keep it simple. Use the default user settings for a trial or test basis and then copy the default user settings to the desired user and groups.

5. When you create your global groups, make sure that you label them as system policy groups so they stand out in User Manager for Domains and when you add them to a system policy.

The Top 10 Things That Can Mess Up Your Policies and Profiles

1. Make sure your users are being entered into a global group if your file server is NT. If your servers are NetWare, global groups are not supported.

2. Make sure the related policy is set properly inside the policy (.POL) file.

3. Make sure the policy file is located in the right network location, and the network location is accessible from the user running Windows 98 or NT.

4. Check that your users have read access to the NETLOGON share. The security should be Everyone:READ and Administrator: FULL for both the share and normal security settings.

5. Check that you actually made the user a member of the group that you're trying to apply to them.

6. If you are using a home directory the location must be specified as a UNC name.

7. If your users are in the GUEST group, profiles won't get saved!

8. Roaming user profiles get copied back to the server on logout. Make sure you update the profile with the user logged out!

9. Keep access to the system policy editor limited to Administrators.

10. Make sure that your Windows 98 clients have custom user profiles enabled; this also enables system policy support.

Service Packs and System Policies

In order for system policies and user profiles to work, NT Servers and Workstations must be running Service Pack 3 (SP3) at a minimum and preferably Service Pack 4 (SP4) because of the new user profile settings that SP4 features. Service Pack 5 (SP5) has also been released for further Y2K compatibility; you should test, analyze, and plan to install SP5. If you decide to use SP5, it is not necessary to first install SP3 and SP4 because SP5 contains all of the fixes.

Testing and proper backup must be done on test PCs before deploying Service Packs 4 and 5. If you are using custom software or equipment that is not off the shelf, talk to your suppliers as well for their opinion on what Service Pack to deploy. Without a doubt, Service Pack 3 must be installed in order for profiles and policies to work.

Note

> Service Pack 4 comes in two flavors: one for Windows NT 4.0 and one for Windows NT 4.0 Terminal Server. Don't mix them up or else you'll be reinstalling. To check the version of the service pack currently on your NT system use Windows NT Diagnostics found in Administrative Tools (Common).

Service Pack 3 Fixes

The following list details the bugs that Service Pack 3 has fixed as they relate to policy and profiles listed by the associated knowledge base article where you can get more information.

Q172124	Poledit.exe Does Not Get Updated During Service Pack 3 Installation
Q139506	Connections to Share-Level Server May Fail
Q140967	Changing Password in User Manager Does Not Permit Logon
Q143470	Run Logon Scripts Synchronously Not Applied to New Users
Q143472	FPNW Blue Screens Accessing or Creating Folders with Long Paths

Q154710   Cannot View Long File Names on Network in 16-Bit Programs

Q158433   Re-creating Admin Shares Causes Exception Error

Q162774   Policy Editor Crashes When Using Large Custom ADM Files

Q163875   Group Policies Not Applied If DC Name Is More Than 13 Characters

Q164133   Logon Allowed When Access Denied to Mandatory User Profile

Q164507   Any User Can Log on to FTP Server with Disabled Anonymous Logon

Q156520   Logon Validation Fails Using Domain Name Server (DNS)

Q157621   Personal Groups Not Visible If %Systemroot% Is Read-Only

Q157673   Policy Not Updated on Workstation

Q158682   Shortcuts Created Under NT 4.0 Resolve to UNC Paths

Q158994   Windows NT 4.0 Fails to Replicate to Backup Domain Controllers

Service Pack 4 Fixes

The list below details the bugs that Service Pack 4 has fixed as they relate to policy and profiles listed by the associated knowledge base article where you can get more information.

Q142615   Event Log Service Fails to Check Access to Security Log File

Q146965   GetAdmin Utility Grants Users Administrative Rights

Q154694   New Policy Available to Hide Go To on Tools Menu in Windows NT Explorer

Q158581   Icon Position Not Stored When Using Roaming Profiles

Q158682	Shortcuts Created Under Windows NT 4.0 Resolve to UNC Paths
Q169888	User-Defined Path Dropped When User and System Paths Too Large
Q173385	System Policy Editor Will Not Allow More Than 255 Characters
Q175035	Diskless Workstations Cannot Find BOOTP Server with DHCP
Q178109	Roving Profiles for Windows 95 Clients Stop Working
Q178723	Problems with "Run Only Allowed Windows Application"
Q181928	Using POLEDIT to Save Policy Files on NetWare Servers May Fail
Q182918	Account Lockout Event also Stored in Security Event Log on Domain Controller
Q183704	Hide Drives Policy in Common.adm Has No VALUEOFF Statement
Q186434	Slow Network Default Profile Operation
Q188652	Error Replicating Registry Keys

There are no Service Pack 5 fixes that relate to user profiles and system policies. The fixes contained in Service Packs 1 through 4 are fully documented as Knowledge Base articles. You can search the Knowledge Base to find an article about a particular issue by using the *Qxxxxxx* number assigned to the topic. You can also search the Knowledge Base on the Microsoft Web site at *http://support.microsoft.com/support/kb/articles/q150/7/34.asp*.

Warning   To use the emergency repair disk utility RDISK successfully after Service Pack 4 or 5 has been installed, you must manually update your Disk 2 Setup disk of your NT 4.0 three-disk set with the updated version of SETUPDD.SYS, which comes with SP4 or SP5. Copy SETUPDD.SYS from the Service Pack CD-ROM to your Windows NT 4.0 setup Disk 2. If you don't perform this step, your ERD restore won't work! This information is contained in the release notes of Service Packs 4 and 5. Make sure you print out and read the entire document; most people don't.

21 Questions and Answers for Troubleshooting System Policies and User Profiles

Question #1: How can I quickly set up one Mandatory user profile for all my users in a training lab?

Question #2: I created a system policy and it was working, but after performing some updates to my policy, why doesn't it seem to be working?

Question #3: My system policy was working just fine with global groups. I added some specific users to my policy and now some of the user's settings seem to be mixed up. Why?

Question #4: I have a large network with PCSs and BDCs. Why are some of my users getting the proper system policy whereas others are not.

Question #5: My client's computer is configured for manual downloading, yet policies are not being downloaded. Why not?

Question #6: How can I make sure that all my workstations and servers are using the same time?

Question #7: I am using Windows 95 Clients in a large network with PDCs and BDCs. Some of my users don't get the system policy, but others do. Why not?

Question #8: How can I check if my network version of my system policy is actually downloading properly?

Question #9: We recently added an NT Server and changed from a workgroup configuration to a domain. We followed all the steps for setting up roaming user profiles but they don't seem to be working in roaming mode. What could be wrong?

Question #10: Why are my Windows 98 system policy groups not reading their system policy settings?

Question #11: Why is my Windows 98 computer running Microsoft Client for NetWare Networks not downloading policies from a `CONFIG.POL` file on a NetWare server?

Question #12: When I set up group policies for my Windows 98 clients, one or more of the users do not get these group policies when they log on. What can I check?

Question #13: When I attempt to add a group to a system policy I get the following error message: `Unable to save <filename>` or error 1010, or the group I added appears three times in the policy with garbled information. Why is this happening?

Question #14: When I save my system policy `POL` file the error code 1243220 or 1243216 appears. What do these two errors mean?

Question #15: I created a system policy for my client's NT systems. When I attempted to save the `POL` file to the `NETLOGON` share I received the following error message: "An error occurred writing the registry. The file cannot be saved." What does this error mean?

Question #16: I have a problem with users configured for roaming profiles. Their shortcuts don't work on computers other than their own. Why not?

Question #17: The Domain Admins global group is finicky; it doesn't seem to work all the time. Why not?

Question #18: Why is my client's computer not downloading its system policy from a `POL` file on the Windows NT domain? What else can I check?

Question #19: Can I upgrade Windows NT 3.5x user profiles to Windows NT 4.0 roaming profiles?

Question #20: How can I assign a local user profile on an NT workstation to another user sharing the same workstation?

Question #21: I'm moving an NT computer from one department into another. The software setup does not need to be changed but I want to remove all traces of the former user. What user settings can I clean out from the Registry?

Question #1: How can I quickly set up one Mandatory user profile for all my users in a training lab?

Answer:

1. First create the local user profile on the platform of your choice (Windows 98 or NT).

2. Open `Control Panel` | `System` icon and select the `User Profile` tab.

3. Now highlight the user profile you just created, and use the `Copy To` button to copy it to the `\\YOURPDC\NETLOGON\NTUSER.MAN`. At the same time change the extension of `NTUSER.DAT` to `.MAN`.

4. Change the permissions of the user profile to `Everyone`.

5. Add the user profile path of `\\YOURPDC\NETLOGON\NTUSER.MAN` to each user's account.

Question #2: I created a system policy and it was working, but after performing some updates to my policy, why doesn't it seem to be working?

Answer: Check to see whether you used the right version of the SPE. You must use the Win98 SPE to create the `CONFIG.POL` file and only the NT SPE to create the `NTCONFIG.POL` file; otherwise, unpredictable results can occur.

Question #3: My system policy was working just fine with global groups. I added some specific users to my policy and now some of the user's settings seem to be mixed up. Why?

Answer: Check the user policies you just added. The settings in users' policies override the corresponding setting in your group policies as long as they overlap exactly.

You probably have a group policy setting that has not been overridden by the same user setting applied through the user template. Another way of looking at it is that the group setting is checked and the user setting has been grayed out.

Also check for multiple system policies for the same Registry key. When multiple templates configure the same Registry setting, multiple policies can result.

When multiple policies exist, the system policy file listed last in SPE is the one that the domain controller will follow.

Question #4: I have a large network with PCSs and BDCs. Why are some of my users getting the proper system policy whereas others are not.

Answer: First, look at your servers: Check to make sure that the updated POL file is in all NETLOGON folders on all PDC and BDC file servers. In a large network with multiple domain controllers, NT spreads the load over all the controllers for logon.

You can manually update NETLOGON or set up directory replication with Server Manager and Services.

Now check your clients: Make sure that your NT and Windows 98 clients have the checkbox Load Balancing checked either in the WINNT.ADM template in Computer \ Network \ System policies update or the WINDOWS.ADM template in Computer \ Update \ System policies update for Windows 98 clients. This setting allows the reading of the POL files from the backup domain controller by Windows 98 and NT 4.0 clients.

Question #5: My client's computer is configured for manual downloading, yet policies are not being downloaded. Why not?

Answer: Does the path specified for manual downloading include a UNC path along with the name of the policy file itself? Make sure that the user that is logging on to the network has access to the directory in which you placed the system policy POL file.

Question #6: How can I make sure that all my workstations and servers are using the same time?

Answer: Make sure that the clocks are synched between the server and workstation. Use a NET TIME command to do this. See Figure 9-1.

Question #7: I am using Windows 95 Clients in a large network with PDCs and BDCs. Some of my users don't get the system policy, but others do. Why not?

Answer: Windows 95 clients will read the system policy only from the PDC. This is a known bug and the solution is to use

Figure 9-1 *Synchronize workstation/domain times with the* NET TIME *command.*

manual update and specify a manual path on the network where the CONFIG.POL file can be found.

Question #8: How can I check if my network version of my system policy is actually downloading properly?

Answer: POLEDIT has a Select Computer option that permits administrators to establish a remote connection through the Registry mode of the system policy editor. Once the connection is made you can view the existing live settings on the remote client end and make changes if necessary.

To check what remote policy the workstation is actually using to login, go back to the server and connect to the workstation with the system policy editor. Now check the settings in Local Computer and make sure that they match what should be there. See Figure 9-2.

> Windows NT clients need no additional setup in order to use this feature of POLEDIT; however, Windows 98 clients must have Remote Registry Services installed to each client in order to complete the remote connection. This feature is also not cross-platform; from NT you cannot view 98 clients and from 98 you cannot view NT clients.

Note

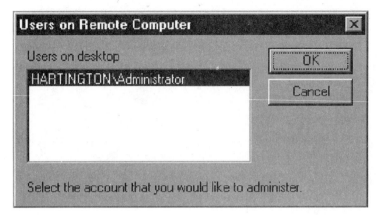

Figure 9-2 *Checking remote users with* POLEDIT.

Question #9: We recently added an NT Server and changed from a workgroup configuration to a domain. We followed all the steps for setting up roaming user profiles but they don't seem to be working in roaming mode. What could be wrong?

Answer: If you have changed from a workgroup to a domain, roaming profiles will not get picked up if the workstation user still has a cached profile from the time it was part of a workgroup. You'll need to remove it, via Control Panel | System | User Profiles.

Question #10: Why are my Windows 98 system policy groups not reading their system policy settings?

Answer: Check to make sure that group support was installed on your client's PC. To set up capabilities for group policies:

1. In the Control Panel, double-click the Add/Remove Programs icon.

2. Click the Windows Setup tab, and then click Have Disk.

3. In the Install From Disk dialog box, click Browse and specify the NETADMIN\POLEDIT directory on the Microsoft Windows 98 Resource Kit CD.

4. Click OK twice in answer to the installation questions.

5. Now in the Have Disk dialog box, select the Group Policies check box, and then click Install.

6. The Windows 98 Setup then copies GROUPPOL.DLL in the Windows System directory on the client computer and makes the required registry changes. Note that just copying the GROUP-POL.DLL to the system directory does not work. The Registry also has several changes added to it.

Question #11: Why is my Windows 98 computer running Microsoft Client for NetWare Networks not downloading policies from a CONFIG.POL file on a NetWare server?

Answer: Make sure that there is a CONFIG.POL in the PUBLIC directory on the SYS: volume of a NetWare 3.x or 4.x server.

Does the client computer have its Preferred Server set to the NetWare server that contains CONFIG.POL?

Make sure that if the client computer is configured for manual policy downloading that a policy file is in the right location.

Remember that NetWare groups are not global groups, so they will not be recognized in a system policy. Only individual user policies are supported.

Question #12: When I set up group policies for my Windows 98 clients, one or more of the users do not get these group policies when they log on. What can I check?

Answer: Is there a policy for that particular user? If there is, then any group policies could be overwritten by the user's own profile. It will be enabled last. Have you checked that user profiles are enabled on the client computer?

Question #13: When I attempt to add a group to a system policy I get the following error message: Unable to save <filename> or error 1010, or the group I added appears three times in the policy with garbled information. Why is this happening?

Answer: This happens if the group name contains more than 39 characters.

Question #14: When I save my system policy POL file the error code 1243220 or 1243216 appears. What do these two errors mean?

Answer: This problem occurs when you use the WINDOWS.ADM template for NT clients instead of the COMMON.ADM. The WINDOWS.ADM template is included on the NT Server CD-ROM but is not supported for either Windows 95/98 or NT. It should be deleted.

Question #15: I created a system policy for my client's NT systems. When I attempted to save the POL file to the NETLOGON share I received the following error message: "An error occurred writing the registry. The file cannot be saved." What does this error mean?

Answer: Check to make sure that you are logged as a Administrator or a member of the Administrator group. You must be a member of the administrators group to save a policy file using the system policy editor on NT computer systems.

Question #16: I have a problem with users configured for roaming profiles. Their shortcuts don't work on computers other than their own. Why not?

Answer: First make sure that the software the user was trying to use is installed in the same location on all computer systems the user logs into. If everything seems OK, then the system policy setting Disable Link File Tracking must be enabled through the WINNT.ADM template.

This setting ensures that shortcut paths remain static and always use the same path. If the original path for the shortcut was C:\PROGRAM FILES\OFFICE\WINWORD.EXE, then that same path will be referenced regardless of where the user logs on.

To activate Disable Link File Tracking, carry out the following steps:

1. Load the system policy editor and load WINNT.ADM.

2. Load the system policy NTCONFIG.POL file.

3. Open the desired user and click Windows NT Shell.

4. Now click Restrictions, and then check Disable Link File Tracking.

5. Save your system policy NTCONFIG.POL file.

Question #17: The Domain Admins global group is finicky; it doesn't seem to work all the time. Why not?

Answer: This is a known system policy bug that is not yet fixed and probably won't be. The workaround is not to use any predefined user groups for system policies.

Question #18: Why is my client's computer not downloading its system policy from a POL file on the Windows NT domain? What else can I check?

Answer: If Auto download has been selected through the system policy template, is there is a CONFIG.POL or NTCONFIG.POL file in the NETLOGON directory on the primary domain controller on the Windows NT network? Other items to check are: Does the user's computer have its domain set properly in the Properties for Client for Microsoft Networks in the Network option in Control Panel?

Question #19: Can I upgrade Windows NT 3.5x user profiles to Windows NT 4.0 roaming profiles?

Answer: When you need to upgrade Windows NT 3.5x roaming profiles (.usr profiles), you do not need to change anything in the profile path configured in the user account. When the user logs on to a Windows NT 4.0-based server and the profile is found to be a Windows NT 3.5x profile, a process automatically looks for the equivalent Windows NT 4.0 profile.

If the profile isn't found, a conversion process creates a new Windows NT 4.0 profile using the settings established in the Windows NT 3.5x profile. During the conversion process, Windows NT 4.0 creates a directory for the new profile in the same location as the existing Windows NT 3.5x profile. The resulting directory has a .pds extension, which stands for *Profile Directory Structure*, rather than the previous Windows NT 3.5x .usr extension.

For example, if the user profile path for the Windows NT 3.5x user mark is \\myserver\myshare\mark.usr, and the user logs on to a Windows NT 4.0-based server, the profile directory mydomainuser.pds would be created within \\myserver\myshare. This allows the user to maintain the old 3.51 profile as well as the new 4.0 profile.

Question #20: How can I assign a local user profile on an NT workstation to another user sharing the same workstation?

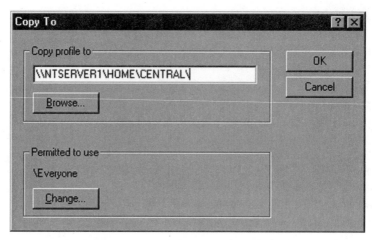

Figure 9-3 *Using the* Copy To *option for moving user profiles.*

Answer: By using the Copy To tool, found in the Control Panel. The five steps are:

1. Log on as an Administrator and open the Control Panel.

2. Double-click the System icon and select the User Profile tab.

3. Select the desired user's profile and click the Copy to button. See Figure 9-3.

4. Under the Windows NT 4.0 directory, click the Profiles subdirectory and choose the user name folder to which you want to assign the administrator profile.

5. Click OK three times to copy and accept and then close all dialog boxes.

Question #21: I'm moving an NT computer from one department into another. The software setup does not need to be changed but I want to remove all traces of the former user. What user settings can I clean out from the Registry?

Answer: (See Figure 9-4)

1. Start Regedt32 and navigate to the following path:

```
HKEY_ CURRENT_USER\SOFTWARE\Microsoft\Windows\
    CurrentVersion\Explorer
```

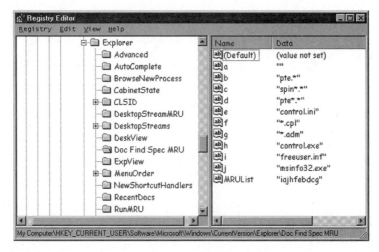

Figure 9-4 *Explorer shell options in the Registry.*

2. There are four locations that you should clean out to remove the activities of the former user. They are:

DocFindSpecMRU   The Find files command usage

RunMRU   The Run commands that have been run

RecentDocs   Documents that have been opened

FindComputerMRU   The Find computers usage

3. As well, navigate to the `WINNT\PROFILES\RECENT DOCS` folder and delete the shortcuts found there.

Programming Errors in Policy Templates

One of the major problems with the acceptance and use of system policies was some sloppy programming of the system policy templates. It was possible to load a template into the system policy editor and check off one setting to deploy, and have two or more settings deployed!

The reason for this bizarre behavior was again template mistakes—but remember templates are merely text files, so mistakes are easy to make. The typical mistakes are the policy checkbox options that are programmed as checked on, even though you didn't actually check the box on. So when you opened up the template to troubleshoot, the checkbox would actually be checked on.

Note

> Remember the system policy script is a program that runs from top to bottom when the selected computer, user, or group's system policy is deployed.

Programming Problem #1

If you disable the `Automatically detect slow connections` policy with the `WINNT.ADM` template the NT computer system will possibly still detect a slow connection. Some early builds of `WINNT.ADM` have coding errors. To fix the template code:

1. Use `NOTEPAD` to load `WINNT.ADM`.

2. Search and find the following segment in the `WINNT.ADM` file:

```
POLICY !!EnableSlowLinkDetect<BR/>
VALUENAME "SlowLinkDetectEnabled"<BR/>
END POLICY
```

3. Make changes to this section of the template as listed adding the proper `VALUEOFF` parameters.

```
POLICY !!EnableSlowLinkDetect<BR/>
VALUENAME "SlowLinkDetectEnabled"<BR/>
VALUEON NUMERIC 1<BR/>
VALUEOFF NUMERIC 0<BR/>
END POLICY
```

4. Save the `WINNT.ADM` template in quotations as `"WINNT.ADM"`. The quotations are necessary to apply the `ADM` extension to a text file.

5. Now load `WINNT.ADM` into the system policy editor and reapply the policy setting.

Programming Problem #2

When you use the `SHELLM.ADM` template file from the Windows 98 CD-ROM to create a policy file, the `Start` menu policies may not take effect. This happens because of a problem with the `SHELLM.ADM` template code. To fix the template code:

1. Use `NOTEPAD` to load `SHELLM.ADM`.

2. Change the order of the following lines found near the end of the `CATEGORY !!StartMenu` from:

```
KEYNAME Software\Microsoft\Windows\CurrentVersion\
  Policies
PART !!MemCheckBoxInRunDlg CHECKBOX
```

to:

```
PART !!MemCheckBoxInRunDlg CHECKBOX
KEYNAME Software\Microsoft\Windows\CurrentVersion\
  Policies
```

3. Now save and close the SHELLM.ADM template file.

Troubleshooting with the USERENV.LOG File

The USERENV.LOG file is a worthwhile tool for troubleshooting the process of loading and unloading user profiles and system policies. Each step in the user profile process is recorded in the log, including informational and error-related messages. USERENV.DLL is included in both the Windows NT Device Driver Kit (DDK) and the Windows NT 4.0 Software Development Kit (SDK).

The checked version of the USERENV.LOG also contains debug flags that you can set and use with the kernel debugger if you are doing development work.

When it is used with a Registry entry it generates a log file that can be used in troubleshooting and debugging problems with user profiles and system policies on Windows NT 4.0 clients.

To enable logging, rename the file USERENV.DLL in the WINNT\SYSTEM32 directory to USERENV.OLD. Then copy the checked version of USERENV.DLL to the WINNT\SYSTEM32 directory of the client machine that you want to troubleshoot.

The checked version of the USERENV.DLL file must match the version of the operating system and Service Pack installed on the client computer. Check the properties of the USERENV.DLL to make sure. Several Registry edits are also required to start the logging process.

1. Start Regedt32 and navigate to the following path:

```
HKEY_LOCAL_MACHINE\SOFTWARE\Microsoft\WindowsNT
  \CurrentVersion\Winlogon
```

2. Next create a new value called UserEnvDebugLevel as a REG_DWORD type. Assign the new DWORD a hex value of 10002. See Figure 9-5.

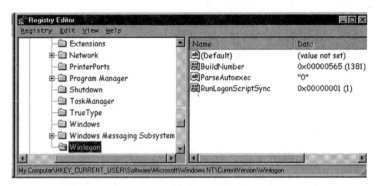

Figure 9-5 *Adding setting to activate USERENV.LOG.*

3. Finally reboot the computer to make the changes active. Logging info will now be recorded in the root of drive C:\> as USERENV.LOG. Notepad or any text editor can be used to view the log file.

USERENV.LOG

```
LoadUserProfile. : Entering, hToken = <0xac>, lpProfileInfo
  = 0x12f4f4
LoadUserProfile: lpProfileInfo->dwFlags = <0x2>
LoadUserProfile: lpProfileInfo->lpUserName =
  <administrator>
LoadUserProfile: NULL central profile path
LoadUserProfile: lpProfileInfo->lpDefaultPath =
  <\\CORP-HQ\netlogon\Default User>
LoadUserProfile: lpProfileInfo->lpServerName = <\\CORP-HQ>
LoadUserProfile: lpProfileInfo->lpPolicyPath =
  <\\CORP-HQnetlogon\ntconfig.pol>
RestoreUserProfile: Entering
RestoreUserProfile: Profile path = <>
RestoreUserProfile: User is a Admin
IsCentralProfileReachable: Entering
IsCentralProfileReachable: Null path. Leaving
GetLocalProfileImage: Found entry in profile list for
  existing local profile
GetLocalProfileImage: Local profile image filename =
  <%SystemRoot%\Profiles\Administrator>
GetLocalProfileImage: Expanded local profile image filename
  = <C:\WINNTDfs\Profiles\Administrator>
GetLocalProfileImage: Found local profile image file ok
  <C:\WINNT\Profiles\Administrator\ntuser.dat>
Local profile is reachable
Local profile name is <C:\WINNT\Profiles\Administrator>
```

```
RestoreUserProfile: No central profile. Attempting to
  load local profile.
RestoreUserProfile: About to Leave. Final Information
  follows:
Profile was successfully loaded.
lpProfile->szCentralProfile = <>
lpProfile->szLocalProfile = <C:\WINNT\Profiles\
  Administrator>
lpProfile->dwInternalFlags = 0x102
RestoreUserProfile: Leaving.
UpgradeProfile: Entering
UpgradeProfile: Build numbers match
UpgradeProfile: Leaving Successfully
ApplyPolicy: Entering
ApplyPolicy: Policy is turned off on this machine.
LoadUserProfile: Leaving with a value of 1
```

Managing User Profiles

In Windows NT 4.0, managing user profiles is done in the `Control Panel System Properties` applet. The `User Profiles` property sheet allows you to view the list of user profiles. See Figure 9-6.

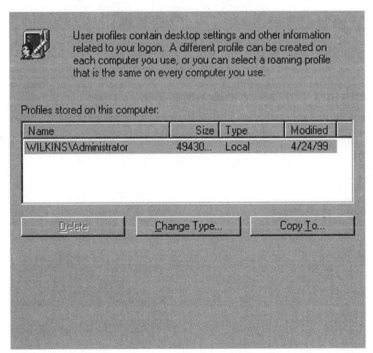

Figure 9-6 *User profile management through the Control Panel.*

From here you can delete, copy, or modify the profile type for each of the profiles listed. Note that the profiles listed here are only for those users who have interactively logged onto the local machine. User profiles that have been created and not used or profiles that are stored for use on remote machines are not included in this list. If a user does not have administrative rights, only that user's profile is listed. Only administrators have permissions to see all available profiles.

Deleting Profiles

The User Profiles property sheet allows users with administrator privileges to delete unused profiles that still exist on a local computer. To delete a user profile, select the profile name and click the Delete button. This deletes the user profile on the local machine, but it does not delete the associated User Account.

Deleting NT Profiles on Remote Computers

If you want to delete profiles on remote computers, the DELPROF utility available in the Windows NT 4.0 Server Resource Kit allows you to perform this task. Windows NT 4.0 user profiles can grow quite large and can take up a lot of disk space, especially if several people are using one computer. With DELPROF, you can reclaim disk space by removing profiles that are no longer needed. This utility deletes user profiles on computers running Windows NT, and it can be used on a local or remote computer running Windows NT 4.0 or earlier.

DELPROF will delete everything contained in a user's profile, including settings, colors, and user documents. Please be aware of any user documents that may be deleted in the user profile sub-folders before using DELPROF.

The syntax of DELPROF.EXE is as follows:

```
DELPROF [/q] [/i] [/p] [/c:\\computername] [/d:days] [/?]
```

/q	Runs in quiet mode, no confirmation for each profile deleted.
/i	Ignore all errors and continue deleting.
/p	Prompt for confirmation before deleting each profile.

`/c:\\computername`	Specifies a remote computer name on which to run DELPROF.
`/d:days`	Specifies the number of days of inactivity. Any profiles with longer inactivity will be deleted.
`:/?`	Displays all command-line syntax.

Changing System Policy Settings in Real Mode for Windows 98 Clients

How can we remove Registry settings if Windows 98 won't even start? One of the powerful files that can be used to modify system policy settings in the Registry is a `.REG` file. The `.REG` file can be used by Regedit to overwrite current Registry entries in the local Windows 98 Registry. A `.REG` file like the one shown below contains two `DWORD`s that will be merged into the Registry removing restrictions on executing certain applications, and also removing the restriction on using `REGEDIT.EXE`. At the command prompt we can use Regedit and the following syntax to merge `REMOVE.REG` with the current Registry.

> With Regedit and Windows 98 there is a new option, the `/D` for delete. The syntax is `/D regpath` (the path to delete). To delete restrictions at the command prompt type `REGEDIT /d Registry path`. The two paths that contain most of the system policy settings are `HKEY_CURRENT_USER\Software\Microsoft\Windows\CurrentVersion\Policies` or `HKEY_LOCAL_MACHINE\Software\Microsoft\Windows\CurrentVersion\Policies`.

Note

Replacing the Windows 98 Registry at the MS-DOS Prompt

If you have a user profile or complete registry that you wish to replace on a Windows 98 PC, you can replace the `USER.DAT` and the `SYSTEM.DAT`, if needed. This is a drastic step to take, but sometimes there may be no choice. At the command prompt, type the following command line to export either the `USER.DAT` or

SYSTEM.DAT portion of the Registry into the root of drive C:

```
REGEDIT /R:<path1> /e <path2> USER.DAT
```

Note that <path1> is the path to the replacement USER.DAT or SYS-TEM.DAT registry file and <path2> is the path to the destination file (\WINDOWS for SYSTEM.DAT and WINDOWS\PROFILES\USERNAME\ USER.DAT for the user Profile).

To replace user Marks user profile if Windows 98 is installed in the WINDOWS folder on drive C: you would type the following line at the MS-DOS prompt.

```
REGEDIT /R C:WINDOWS\PROFILES\MARK\USER.DAT A:\USER.DAT
```

Note   Before performing any registry merges at the MS-DOS prompt you must use the ATTRIB command to change the attributes of USER.DAT or SYSTEM.DAT so they can be overwritten. A failure to do this will result in a message after the merge that the Merge was successful, but it won't be.

```
ATTRIB -S -H -R USER.DAT
```

   or

```
SYSTEM.DAT
```

Creating System Policies for Office 97

One of the ideal uses for system polices is to deploy one or all of the Office 97 system policy template(s) provided by Microsoft to manage your gang of Access, Excel, PowerPoint, or Word users.

What, you say, they don't use Office 97? As we all know Office 97 and 95 are very popular software suites. (I'd bet that Office 97 is being used somewhere on your network; if it isn't, then WordPerfect wins out!)

The Office 97 Resource Kit supplies the template files for Office 97 users running either Windows NT 4.0 or Windows 98. These templates do not support NT 3.51. Although the Office 97 software works exactly the same on NT 3.51, the policies and user profiles of NT 3.51 are not compatible with NT 4.0. The following listing summarizes the templates available for Office 97.

Office 97 Template	What It's Used for
Off97w95.adm	Windows 95/98 clients and Office 97
Off97nt4.adm	Windows NT 4.0 clients
Access97.adm	Settings for Access for Windows 95/98 and NT 4.0
Outlook97.adm	Settings for Outlook97 for Windows 95/98 and NT 4.0

If you do not have access to the Office 97 Resource Kit, you can download the templates and the policy editor from *http://www.microsoft.com/office/ork/*. The other reality is that you may be using Outlook 98 or even considering Office 2000. Those templates and notes are found in Chapters 6 and 13, respectively. See Figure 10-1.

As with most of the Office 97 templates, some settings are for the computer, but most are for the user and groups. You are probably most interested in the user's settings but don't forget to check out the computer settings as well. If you are sharing a PC among multiple users, then these settings can be quite useful. Remember that the computer settings apply to any user that uses the computer system. Since this section is really a resource sec-

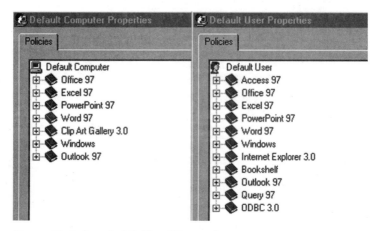

Figure 10-1 *Loaded Office 97 templates.*

tion, it's a great idea to have this book propped up in front of a computer system running the system policy editor with the templates we are discussing. So boot up that workstation and let's continue, shall we?

Office 97 Computer Policy Options

The first template we will check out is the main master template for the entire Office 97 Suite. Regardless of which one of the mighty Microsoft Trio operating systems you are using—Windows 95, 98, or NT 4.0—the system policy settings are the same. Also, a very important point to remember about these Registry settings that we are deploying through system policies is *they're the same, regardless of the Windows platform: Windows 98, Windows NT, or Windows 2000.*

It's a good indication of how similar the Registry settings are for Windows 32-bit software. The Office 97 templates provide system policy settings for both the computer and groups/users. See Figure 10-2.

Keep in mind that every time you deploy computer settings in a system policy these settings are "global" in nature rather than user or group specific. Computer settings are also deployed before user settings are applied, affecting the computer system in the following order:

- Every user that logs onto the named computer

- Every computer system on your network if you apply the setting through Default Computer

Starting with system policy settings for the default or named computer, here are the settings you can deploy and some relevant suggestions for their use.

Office 97 Computer Settings

Computer \ Office 97

- *Default Save.* If your users use the Save as option to save a file to different file formats, you can customize the text message to your user's environment. For example: if you were running

Office 97 Computer Settings (Off97nt4.adm or Off97w95.adm)	Summary of Checkbox Choices
Office97	Saving, password caching, and uninstall locations plus global assistant installation options
Excel97	Microsoft map data and search location plus Windows 2000 file import converter options
Powerpoint97	Windows 2000 file import converter options
Word97	AutoCorrect file location options and custom dictionary locations plus Windows 2000 file import converter options
Clip Art Gallery 3.0	Multiple locations where clip art can be found
Windows	Path information for network software installs for ZAK (Zero Admin Kit deployment)

Figure 10-2 *Quick look at Office 97 computer settings.*

Office 97 and WordPerfect, the text could be `Remember to save the file in WordPerfect 5.0 format.`

- *Disable Password Caching*. Disables or enables password caching on the Office 97 software.

- *Uninstall*. Specifies a new location of the uninstall setup table file used to remove installed Office 97 components or to perform a complete uninstall. The file used is either `Off97pro.stf` (professional) or `Off97std.stf` (standard). The STF file is usu-

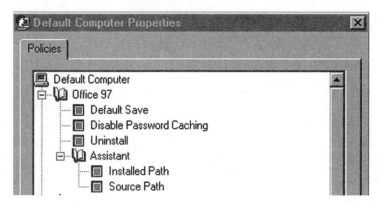

Figure 10-3 *Office 97 computer settings.*

ally found in a local location. Note that this policy setting works only if Office 97 is a complete local install.

See Figure 10-3.

Computer \ Office 97 \ Assistant

- *Installed Path*. This setting provides the location of the assistant files (ACT and ACP files). They could be moved to the server to save space on the local drive. Most of us question why the assistant is even included at all; however, if you want to get creative, check out *www.microsoft.com/ork* for lots of different assistant choices. How about a shape-shifter assistant?

- *Source Path*. OK, you took my advice and downloaded all of the available assistants to keep your users happy. So when Molly in the graphics department is browsing the Assistant Gallery to choose a new assistant, this source path is used to locate the needed ACT files. It's probably wise to define the installed and source path as the same location if you are using this and the preceding option.

Excel Policy Settings for Computers

The following computer settings for Excel 97 are found under the Excel 97 heading when either the default computer or a defined computer setting is selected. See Figure 10-4.

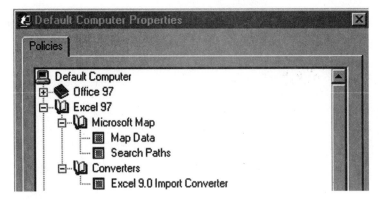

Figure 10-4 *Excel 97 computer settings.*

Computer \ Excel 97

- *Map Data.* In order to use this and the following policy setting, Microsoft Map must be installed. Using the `Insert` drop-down menu in Excel 97, you can select a map to include in your spreadsheet to enhance your data output. This setting defines the directory where map data can be found. Map data on the server would accomplish central storage for common map graphics.

- *Search Paths.* This setting sets the multiple map directories where shared map data are stored. The multiple entries are entered in a DOS pathlike string with semicolons separating the locations.

Note   For example: `\\Server1\Office97\mapdata1;\\Server2\Office97\mapdata2.`

If you have both Primary Domain Controllers and Backup Domain Controllers, you could specify both a PDC and a BDC location for extra redundancy.

Computer \ Excel 97

- *Converters.* This setting will not be used until Office 2000. After installing the new office suite, use this setting to point to the location of the new import converters that will no doubt be needed to properly convert the newer Office 2000 Excel data files to the older Office 97 file formats. This setting would save you from running around to every user's computer adding conversion tools. As Microsoft releases the utilities, just add them to a shared network location and point all users to that location.

PowerPoint Settings for Computers

The following computer settings for PowerPoint 97 are deployed when either the default computer or a defined computer setting is selected.

Computer \ PowerPoint 97

- *Converters*. This setting will not be used until Office 2000. After installing the new office suite, use this setting to point to the location of the new import converters that will be needed to properly convert the newer Office 2000 PowerPoint presentations to the older PowerPoint 97 file formats. This setting would save you from running around to every user's computer adding conversion tools. When Microsoft releases the file converters, just add them to a shared network location and point all users to that location. Again, a nice option to deploy on a large network.

Word Settings for Computers

The following computer settings for Word 97 are found under the Word 97 heading, when either the default computer or a defined computer setting is selected.

Computer \ Word 97 \ Spelling Advanced

- *Default AutoCorrect File*. The word *default* doesn't mean "default"—in this case it means "custom"! If you want your users to use a custom AutoCorrect dictionary, you can start Word and add any entries to the AutoCorrect list through the `Tools Menu -> AutoCorrect`. Your additions are saved to the Windows directory in a file called `Mso97.acl`. This custom `ACL` file also contains all the entries from the default `Mso97.acl`.

Now you can copy this new `AutoCorrect` file to a network location and path by entering a UNC path to the `ACL` file location. It's a great option for users that have different legal or medical or just not standard spelling in their company, like "supercalafragilisticexpealidocious" for instance.

- *Custom Dictionaries*. This sets the path for additional custom dictionaries. The `Value Name` is from 2 to 10 additional dictionary paths, and the value points to the dictionary path. So you can have 9 additional dictionaries to choose from.

See Figure 10-5.

Computer \ Word 97 \ Spelling Advanced

- *New Dictionary Locations*. These are merely examples of some of the dictionaries that Office 97 supports. Actual language choices displayed by this template file can be edited and changed. The four dictionary choices are:

  1. *Spelling*. The file used for the American speller is `MSSP2_EN.LEX`
  2. *Thesaurus*. The file used for the American thesaurus is `MSTH_AM.LEX`
  3. *Hyphenation*. The file used for the American hyphenation is `HY_EN.LEX`

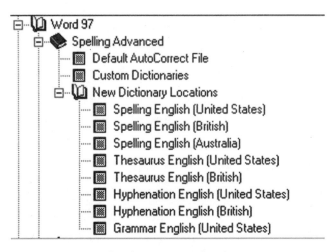

Figure 10-5 *Word policy settings for the computer.*

4. *Grammar.* The file used for the American grammar checker is MSGR_EN.LEX

Computer \ Word 97

- *Converters.* This setting will not be used until Office 2000. After installing the new office suite, use this setting to point to the location of the new import converters that will be needed to properly convert the newer Office 2000 Word presentations to the older Word 97 file formats. Activating this setting would save you from running around to every user's computer adding conversion tools. This was a real problem for users that changed to Office 97 from Office 95 and tried to share files saved from Office 97 with Office 95 users. As Microsoft releases file converters, add them to a shared network location and point all users to that location.

Computer \ Clip Art Gallery 3.0

- *Concurrent Database #1.* UNC Path to database #1
- *Concurrent Database #2.* UNC Path to database #2
- *Concurrent Database #3.* UNC Path to database #3

If your users use a lot of common clip art or if you have custom art for your company, you may find it useful to combine certain clip art in a new Clip Art Gallery database file (CAG files). They could then be stored on a file server for network access. The file formats acceptable to a CAG file is Windows metafiles (WMF), picture files (BMP and GIF), as well as multimedia files (AVI or WAV). You can place three files in three network locations if you wish.

To add images to the Clip Art Gallery follow the steps below: **Note**
1. Click the Insert menu and then select Picture, and then Clip Art.
2. Select the Clip Art tab, and click Import Clips.
3. Search and select the folder that contains the image(s) you're adding.
4. Highlight the image, and next click Open.
5. Finally type in any keywords for the new item(s).

6. Establish the category or make a new category in which to store the image, and click OK.

A great idea would be to point to a CD-ROM server. Using current CD-ROM technology you can create custom locations for your company's clip art.

Computer \ Windows \ Network Install Tab

A Network Install tab can be added to the Add/Remove Programs applet in the Control Panel for providing additional net-

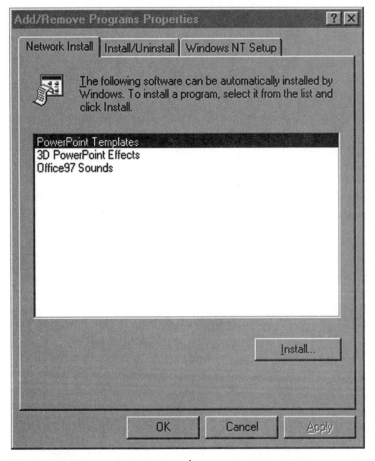

Figure 10-6 Network Install *tab*.

work locations for software installations. The INI settings list the locations of the executable files. Creating an INI file called NETAPPS.INI and placing it in a network location provide the following additional choices. As always, a UNC path is valid only for a network path. See Figures 10-6 and 10-7.

```
[AppInstallList]Developer
PowerPoint Templates=*\\Server1\software1\setup.exe
3D PowerPoint Effects=*\\Server1\software2\setup.exe
Office97 Sounds =*\\Server1\software3\setup.exe
```

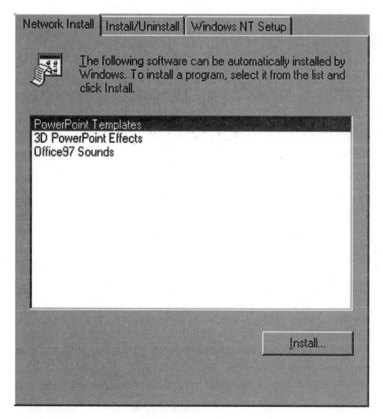

Figure 10-7 New Network *tab in* Add/Remove *software.*

Office 97 User and Group Settings

The User settings can be deployed from one to three ways. Remember the order of deployment as you are gleefully checking off the options.

Default User -> Group #1 -> Group # 2···Named User

- Using the Default User icon affecting all users on the network
- Using a Global Group icon affecting all users of the global group
- Using the named User icon affecting only the logged-on user

See Figure 10-8.

Note

> Just a note as we start this section. The word *common* means "global" to all installed Office 97 applications.

User \ Office 97 \ Common

- *Personal Folders.* This path sets the local or network location of the My Documents folder. When this setting is used under NT, the Registry value is a REG_EXPAND_SZ value allowing the storage of the home directory, username, and user profile. The environment variables that may be in use are %HOMEDIR%, %USERNAME%, and %USERPROFILE%. Once this setting is activated, the new path becomes the path for all Office 97 applications. So this is a global option for the Office 97 user and all data files.

- *User Templates.* This path is used to specify the templates that are shown when New is selected on the File menu.

- *Workgroup Templates.* If you were assigned to a global group, you would probably share the same software and work tasks. Perhaps you would also share common templates. This path sets the path to Workgroup Templates, that is, a network collection of templates. Remember to make the templates in this location read-only so they don't get messed up.

- *Sound.* This check box enables sounds for error messages. Sounds are enabled through the Sound applet in Control Panel.

Office 97 User Settings (Off97nt4.adm or Off97w95.ad)	Choices
Office 97	Settings that affect all installed modules such as common file locations, how your assistant operates, and Internet, Tool Menu, Binder, and Visual Basic choices
Excel 97	Tools Options and Customize choices
Powerpoint 97	Tools Options and Customize choices plus custom help locations and miscellaneous file locations including saving files, templates, and picture folder locations
Word 97	Tools Options and Customize choices plus Web page and Word-Mail choices. Also custom help locations and miscellaneous file locations including saving files, templates, and picture folder locations
Windows	Proxy server settings
Internet Explorer 3.0	Start and search pages when IE starts up
Bookshelf	Location of the Bookshelf content

Figure 10-8 *Quick look at Office 97 user settings.*

- *Chart Gallery.* This setting lists the path to the chart gallery for all Office 97 applications, except Excel, so this means Word and PowerPoint for most users. You could create some common charts that you wished to use in your company and store them in this network location.

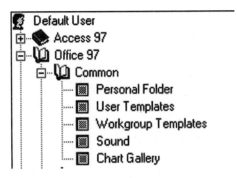

Figure 10-9 *Common settings for users and groups.*

See Figure 10-9.

User \ Office 97 \ Assistant

Just how do you want the talking paper clip to appear when you start Office 97—large and hidden until you make a boo-boo and then exactly 1 inch from the left margin? I thought so.

- *Default State*. Choose from large and visible to small and hidden.

- *Choose File*. What assistant would you like today?

- *Position*. Get out the ruler and be exact (in the top left quadrant of your screen).

User \ Office 97 \ Common \ Assistant \ Options Tab

The Options tab contains a collection of single level on/off options for the Assistant. See Figure 10-10.

- *Respond to* F1 *key*. Manually loads the Assistant

- *Help with wizards*. The assistant knows?

- *Display alerts*. When you get lost in a task

- *Search for both product and programming help*. And now for some new products

- *Move when in the way*. How does it know when it's in the way?

- *Guess help topics*. Based on what you're working on

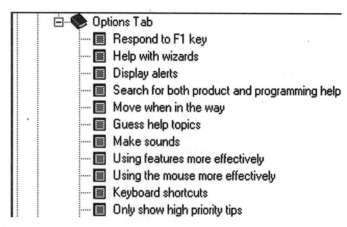

Figure 10-10 *Options tab for the Assistant.*

- *Make sounds.* To keep you company

- *Using features more effectively.* Extra details on Features

- *Using the mouse more effectively.* Right-click tips

- *Keyboard shortcuts.* Real-time tips on keyboard shortcuts

- *Only show high-priority tips.* You mean there's such a thing as a high-priority tip?

- *Show the Tip of the Day.* Ditto

User \ Office 97 \ Internet \ FTP Sites

When running an Office 97 application such as Word, when you select File -> Open or click the yellow File Open folder on the button bar, you next have the drop-down option Look in: to select the location of your data files. See Figure 10-11.

Down at the bottom of the resource listing and you will see two FTP options courtesy of Office 97: first, the ability to search existing FTP locations and second, the option to add or modify the existing FTP sites. Now that you have the background as to why these extra choices appear, perhaps you can put them to good use via your company's intranet.

- *Delete FTP Sites.* This setting deletes the first 10 FTP sites if they actually exist in the File Open | Look in: menu. The Delete FTP sites setting would only be used together with the

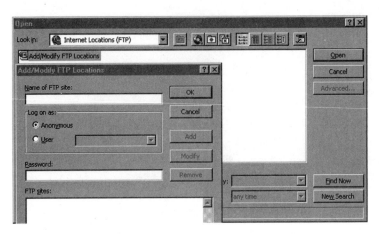

Figure 10-11 *FTP locations.*

setting `Add FTP Sites` listed next. The idea is that if Office 97
users have used a variety of FTP sites, the next time they log on
to the network, the first 10 FTP sites will be removed and the
setting below will add in the 10 FTP sites that you want your
users to see. You get to preload a defined list of FTP resources
for your users' resource list.

• *Add FTP Sites.* See the previous explanation for details.

User \ Office 97 \ Internet \ Web Search \ Internet Lookup Locations

The Internet options shown in Figure 10-12 can be set for the
end user's Internet session. When a lookup is performed, these
values come into service.

User \ Office 97 \ Internet \ Help_Microsoft on the Web

• *Customize submenu.* You can customize the menu displayed
when you select the menu option `Help`, which in turn leads to
the submenu `Microsoft on the Web`. See Figure 10-13. You can
preset up to eight Web locations that are viewable for each
installed Office 97 application.

Values to Define	Description
Server Friendly Name	Defines the name of the index service used
Server Base URL or UNC	Is the URL pointing to web-search.dll? This is installed with WEB find fast
Index Path	Points to the WEB find fast index
Template Path	The template used to display the results
GIF Path	The GIF image used to display results
Properties	The document properties used such as Title, Author, Subject, and Date
Protocol	Sets the listing returned by the search to be FTP or HTTP
Sort By	Specifies the order of the search results

Figure 10-12 *Internet lookup location options.*

Figure 10-13 *Customizing Internet Help.*

Later in this chapter we review the settings for each Office 97 application. This setting appears once again, but when it is shown inside an Office application such as Word, you have a choice of eight additional Web help locations that could be made specific to the Word for the user. Whew. I wish my users used help as much as Microsoft seems to think they really do. Regardless of what customizations you choose to deploy, the last menu option stays—that's the link to Microsoft's home page.

- *Reset submenu to original defaults.* Select this option and you're back to where you started.

- *Disable submenu.* Don't want your users to have access to the Web-based help? This is the only option you'll want to click.

User \ Office 97 \ Tools_Customize

- *Options.* You can also control the Office 97 menu animation.

- *Office Wizards.* Clicking this option provides help with the tools customization wizard.

User \ Office 97 \ Binder Options

If you use the *Binder* feature, you can choose to print the entire binder as a single print job. A Binder as defined with Office 97 is a collection of Office 97 documents, sort of like a project management tool. Check it out under Start | Programs | Office Binder.

Office 97 \ Visual Basic Editor \ Help_Microsoft on the Web

- *Customize submenu.* Customizes the menu displayed when you select the Visual Basic Help menu, which in turn leads to the submenu Visual Basic Help. You can preset up to eight Web locations for VB help locations.

- *Reset submenu to original defaults.* Select this option and you're back to where you started.

- *Disable submenu.* Don't want your users to have access to VB help? This is the only option you'll want to click.

Excel 97 User and Group Options

User \ Excel 97 \ Tools_Options

- *Move Enter Direction.* Sets how the cursor moves when ENTER is pressed.

- *Fixed Decimal.* Automatically sets the decimal place to two places.

User \ Excel 97 \ Tools_Options \ General

- *Recently Used File List.* Shows up to nine recently viewed worksheets displayed on the File menu.

- *Default Sheets.* Sets how many worksheets are to be defined in a new workbook.

- *Font.* Defines the name and the default size of the typeface.

- *Alternate Startup Folder.* Defines an alternate startup file location. When you use this value to define a common network location, you also turn off the MRU (Most Recently Used) files listing held within Excel.

See Figure 10-14.

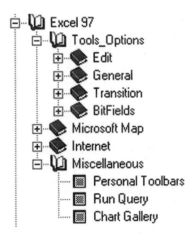

Figure 10-14 *Options for Excel 97.*

User \ Excel 97 \ Tools_Options \ Transition

- *Default Save.* Why this setting is under transition rather than `Tools_Option\Edit` is a mystery to me. This setting can be used to set the `Save` file extension for Excel. The value choices range from all versions of Lotus 123 to all versions of Excel.

- *Menu Key.* Enters the ASCII value for one of the keys on your keyboard (for example, ASCII 47 defines the forward slash) as the launcher for Excel help. Quite handy for former Lotus users.

User \ Excel 97 \ BitFields

- *Options value 3, 5, 6, 95.* These values are not documented anywhere—a Microsoft secret, I guess.

User \ Excel 97 \ Microsoft Map

If you have installed Microsoft map you can define how Excel works with the installed maps:

- Map Matching
- Sizing Units
- Compact Legends
- Auto Correct

User Excel 97 \ Internet \
Help_Microsoft on the Web

- *Customize submenu.* Customizes the menu displayed when you select the menu `Help`, which in turn leads to the submenu `Microsoft on the Web`. You can preset up to eight Web locations for `Excel Help`. Sorry, the last menu option stays—that's the link to Microsoft's home page.

- *Reset submenu to original defaults.* Select this option and you're back to where you started.

- *Disable submenu.* Don't want your users to have access to the Web-based help? This is the only option you'll want to click.

User \ Excel 97 \ Internet \ Converters

- *Future File Format Converters.* This setting will not be used until Office 2000. After installing the new office suite, use this setting to point to the location of the new import converters that will be needed to properly convert the newer Office 2000 Excel worksheets to the older Excel 97 file formats. This setting would save you from running around to every user's computer adding conversion tools. As Microsoft releases file converters, add them to a shared network location and point all users to that location.

User \ Excel 97\ Miscellaneous

- *Personal Toolbars.* This setting sets the path to a custom tool-bar for a roaming user or group. Make sure to leave the trailing backslash when defining the UNC path, or this option won't work. Obviously this option makes sense only when applied to groups. For example: `\\Server\location\toolbar\`.

- *Run Query.* If you run queries with Excel, you can opt to save your defined queries in the defined local or network path entered here.

- *Chart Gallery.* This policy points to the path for an Excel only chart gallery—it's confusing, I know.

PowerPoint User and GroupOptions

The following option can be defined for the default or named user and/or group in your defined system policy.

User\PowerPoint 97\Tools_Options\View

- *Startup dialog.* Defines the startup dialog when PowerPoint first starts.

- *New slide dialog.* Defines each new slide's default dialog when created.

- *Status bar.* Checks if you want a status bar displayed by default.

- *Vertical ruler*. Checks if you want a vertical ruler always displayed.

- *Popup menu on right mouse click*. Turns the right-click menu off or on.

- *Show popup menu button*. Makes the popup menu button available.

- *End with blank slide*. Always end with a blank slide. This option is handy if you create and give presentations.

User\PowerPoint 97\Tools_Options\
General

The settings in this section determine startup options and general user options.

- *Recently Used File List*. This setting determines whether the recently used file list is enabled and, if so, how large it is to be.

- *Macro Virus Protection*. At first glance, this is a handy feature, as long as you remember to update the virus software—too bad we can't. So you need to have an external virus checker for controlling potential macro viruses that are out there.

- *Link Sounds File Size*. How embarrassing, to be known by a goofy sound in your office when your PowerPoint slide show is bigger than a floppy disk. Hey, maybe that's a clever idea.

User \ PowerPoint 97 \ Tools_Options \ Edit

The next few options allow you to customize common edit tasks within PowerPoint. We are really setting the values in the edit tab screen found under `Tools -> Options`.

- Replace straight quotes with smart quotes
- Automatic word selection
- Use smart cut and paste
- Drag-and-Drop text editing
- *Inserting*. Inserted charts assume the current PowerPoint font. This is useful and cuts down on editing time.

- *Undo*. How many undo choices would you like? 99? OK.

User \ PowerPoint 97 \ Tools_Options \ Print

- *Background Printing*. This option enables or disables the background printing services.

User \ PowerPoint 97 \ Tools_Options \ Save

The first three options are simple toggle options depending on your point of view.

- Allow fast saves

- Prompt for file properties

- Full-text search information

The next two options are powerful; make sure that you consider both of them.

- *AutoRecovery*. Sets the saving of AutoRecovery information by Office 97 and sets the elapsed time until the AutoSave feature starts. Set this to 5 minutes—better safe than sorry. See Figure 10-15.

- *Default Save*. You can also set the default file format when saving data files to any version of PowerPoint.

User \ PowerPoint 97 \ Tools_Options \ Spelling

The spelling options presented in this option allow you to control the flow of the auto-spell check and to set the criteria for which words and numbers are checked.

- *Background spelling*. Toggles background spelling off or on.

- *Hide spelling errors*. For the spelling bee champ in your office, turn on; for the rest of us, leave well enough alone.

- *Suggest*. As you type, Office 97 will suggest the word you're about to type. Sometimes this option is helpful for automating repetitive typing tasks.

- Always ignore words in UPPERCASE

- Ignore words with numbers

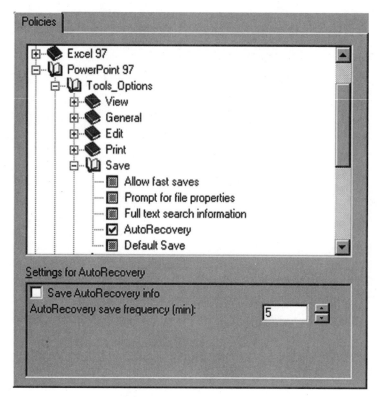

Figure 10-15 *Setting AutoRecovery.*

User \ PowerPoint 97 \ Advanced

- *Picture.* There are two options to consider: the first is a check-box that, when checked, enables the rendering of 24-bit bitmaps at the highest quality available; the second deals with pictures that are exported from PowerPoint to another Office 97 program. Choices are best for either printing or on-screen viewing.

User \ PowerPoint 97 \ Internet\ Help_Microsoft on the Web

- *Customize submenu.* Customizes the menu displayed when you select the menu Help, which in turn leads to the submenu Microsoft on the Web. You can preset up to eight Web locations for `PowerPoint Help`. Sorry, the last menu option stays—that's the link to Microsoft's home page.

- *Reset submenu to original defaults.* Select this option and you're back to where you started.

- *Disable submenu.* Don't want your users to have access to Web-based help? This is the only option you'll want to click.

User \ PowerPoint 97 \ Internet \ Converters

- *Future File Format Converters.* This setting will not be used until Office 2000. After installing the new office suite, use this setting to point to the location of the new import converters that will be needed to properly convert the newer Office 2000 PowerPoint presentations to the older PowerPoint 97 file formats. This setting would save you from running around to every user's computer adding conversion tools. As Microsoft releases file converters, add them to a shared network location and point all users to that location.

User\PowerPoint 97\Miscellaneous

- *Personal Toolbars.* Sets the path to a new local or network location for a custom roving toolbar. The backslash is *not* required in the path, unlike the Excel option. The next three options define the network locations for graphics used by your users. Central locations for AVI, WAV, and clip art can be defined for the user or groups of users. The user cannot set these three options within PowerPoint; so he or she also can't change these locations once they have been defined and implemented through a system policy. See Figure 10-16.

- *Multimedia Directory.* Sets a network path for multimedia files that are inserted with the menu commands `Movie from File` or `Sound from File` with the extensions `AVI` and `WAV`.

- *Template Directory.* Sets a network path for background template files that are added by the menu command `Apply Design` from the `Format` menu.

- *Picture Directory.* Sets a network path for the clip art files inserted into a presentation using the `From To` command found on the `Insert` menu.

Figure 10-16 *Setting graphic options for PowerPoint users.*

- *No Edit Time.* Clicking this option gives you the right to say with a straight face, "Yep, this presentation took me no time at all." Total Editing Time, shown on the Properties and Statistics tab of the file, will back you up by always showing an editing time of zero minutes.

Word 97 User and Group Options

User \ Word 97 \ Tools_Options \ General

- *Help for WordPerfect users.* If your users are migrating from WordPerfect to Word, this can be quite a helpful option to turn on.

- *Macro Virus Protection.* At first glance, a good option; yet there is no upgrade for the virus-checking software and macro viruses have become even more pronounced since 1997. Turn it on, but remember you also need an up-to-date virus checker as well.

User \ Word 97 \ Tools_Options \ Edit

- *Picture Editor.* We can decide on the software that will edit pictures; it's a fixed drop-down box with these two choices: either Word or Microsoft Photo editor.

User \ Word 97 \ Tools_Options \ Print

- *Background Print.* Background printing can be enabled or disabled.

User \ Word 97 \ Tools_Options \ Save

- *Default Save.* You can define the default format in which to save Word documents, including Word, Microsoft Works, WordPerfect, Rich Text Format, and HTML.

- *Background Save.* Turn on or off the option of background saves while you work. I'd vote for this option always to be turned on.

User \ Word 97 \ Tools_Options \ Spelling & Grammar

This section allows you to turn off the checking of spelling and grammar in the background.

- *Background Spelling.* Checks spelling as you type.

- *Background Grammar.* Checks grammar as you type.

User \ Word 97 \ Tools_Options \ File Locations

This section sets the locations for clip art pictures and the path to the AutoRecover folder. Typically, you would be setting network locations with these options.

- *Clip Art Pictures.* Sets the location for clip art files used by Word.

- *AutoRecover Files.* Sets the path to where the AutoRecovery files are stored.

- *Tools.* Sets the path to the folder containing dictionaries, filters, and text converters.

- *Startup.* Sets the path to the startup folder.

User \ Word 97 \Tools_Options \ Tools_AutoCorrect

- *Autoformat.* This section allows you to turn off the default action of Word in autoformatting plain-text word mail documents.

User\Word 97\Internet\Help_Microsoft on the Web

- *Customize submenu.* Customizes the menu displayed when you select the menu Help, which in turn leads to the submenu Microsoft on the Web. You can preset up to eight Web locations for Word Help. Sorry, the last menu option stays—that's the link to Microsoft's home page.

- *Reset submenu to original defaults*. Select this option and you're back to where you started.

- *Disable submenu*. Don't want your users to have access to Web-based help? This is the only option you'll want to click.

User \ Word 97 \ Internet \ Converters

- *Future File Format Converters*. This setting will not be used until Office 2000. After installing the new office suite, use this setting to point to the location of the new import converters that will be needed to properly convert the newer Office 2000 Word presentations to the older Word 97 file formats. This setting will save you from running around to every user's computer adding conversion tools. As Microsoft releases file converters, add them to a shared network location and point all users to that location.

User \ Word 97 \ Tools_Options \ Web Page Authoring

This section is useful if you use Word as your primary tool for Web page design. You would probably use another software editor, but you could define the following network or local path values for Web resources for a group of Word users:

- Bullet Path
- Dialog Bullet Path
- Horizontal Line Path
- Dialog Horizontal Line Path
- Local Content
- Workgroup Content
- Local Page Styles
- Workgroup Page Styles
- Clipart URL
- Template URL
- AutoUpDate
- AutoUpDate Address

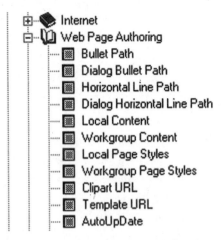

Figure 10-17 *Web options defined with system policies.*

See Figure 10-17.

User \ Word 97 \ Tools_Options \ Miscellaneous

If you work for a company that has specific date and time formats you can mandate your company standards with these first two options—or you can start a new trend! The third option for disabling edit time is another of those policy settings that make you wonder.

- *Date Format.* Year-date-month or date-month-year?

- *Time Format.* From hours-minutes to hours-minutes *and* AM/PM.

- *No Edit Time.* Turns off how long it took you to do your work. Big Brother is watching.

User \ Office 97 \ Windows

- *Internet Settings.* This section allows you to set the Proxy settings for how the user will access the Internet. Settings include `Proxy Server`, `Proxy Override`, and `Proxy Enable`.

User\Internet Explorer 3.0

- *Options_ Navigation.* Sets the start and search pages for your Office 97 users.

- *User\Bookshelf*. Location of Bookshelf Content. If you use the bookshelf CD that was bundled with Office 97, you can specify the network location.

Access 97 System Policy Settings for Users and Groups

If you use Access 97 across your network, these settings allow you to control how Access 97 executes. There are no Computer system policy settings in the Access 97 system policy. These may be useful in a beginning-programming environment where you want to define the startup view and other options. The following options are usually set through the `Tools | Options` menu.

User \ Access97 \ Tools_Options \ View

This section configures the initial Access 97 view shown for the user with check box on/off settings. A checked box enables or shows the selected option; a cleared checkbox does not show the selected option.

- Status Bar
- Startup Dialog
- Hidden Objects
- System Objects
- Macro Names Column
- Macro Conditions Column

User \ Access97 \ Tools_Options \ General

This section sets the default sort order and hyperlink settings. In addition, printing margins can be defined for the user that uses specific forms.

- *Sort Order*. The sort order defaults to general, but you can specify the language you are working with.
- *Sound*. Provides feedback with sound. Handy for data entry with fields that are set for specific data entry types.
- *Hyperlink Colors*. Defines your hyperlinks for viewed and not-viewed data.

- *Hyperlink Underline*. Sets your hyperlinks to be underlined or not.

- *Hyperlink Address*. If you are using hyperlinks, you can choose to have the address of the hyperlink show up in the status bar. The security setting would be to turn off this default feature.

- *Print Margins*. Presets your top/bottom and left/right print margins. Quite useful if you are controlling printer access as well.

User \ Access97 \ Tools_Options \ Edit

- *Find\Replace*. This section sets the default responses to find and replace: either a fast search, a general search, or search using the first character (Start of Field Search).

- *Record Changes*. Sets to always confirm/not confirm record changes before making the change.

- *Document Deletions*. Sets to always confirm/not confirm document deletions.

- *Action Queries*. Sets to confirm/not confirm action queries.

User \ Access97 \ Tools_Options \ Datasheet

This section is used to set the default fonts, colors, and guidelines for the data sheet.

- Default Colors

- Default Font

- *Horizontal Gridlines/Vertical Gridlines*. Shows or does not show the horizontal and vertical guidelines.

- Column Width

- *Cell Effect*. Defines the default background of the cell.

- *Animations*. Shows any animation that may be preset, or in the case of a Web database you may choose to turn this option off.

UserAccess97 \ Tools_Options \ Tables \ Queries

This section sets field sizes and autoindex options and the ability to autojoin tables. Run permissions can be set for the user or the owner of the database. Details are provided for options other than the obvious on/off options.

- Field Size

- Field Type

- *AutoIndex*. When you either import records or create new records in an existing database this option when checked will automatically reindex your records.

- Show Table Names

- Output All Fields

- Enable AutoJoin

- *Run Permissions*. This allows you "Run" security with databases when you wish to control who is allowed to run them.

User \ Access97 \ Tools_Options \ Forms \ Reports

This section sets the selection behavior and procedures for your forms and reports. Default templates can be specified as well.

- *Selection Behavior*. This option defines how controls are selected on a form; either some or all of the existing control options can be specified.

- Form Template

- Report Template

- *Event Procedures*. When enabled, this option automatically starts the procedure that was chosen when you choose the builder button on any property sheet for any event. This will bypass the typical choices that are presented: the expression, macro, and code builder options.

User \ Access97 \ Tools_Options \ Keyboard

This section defines the conditions of the keyboard and entering data. These allow you to mimic the keystrokes for data entry that the user was used to before migrating to Access 97.

- *Move After Enter*. Where the cursor moves next to the next record or field, or no move at all.

- *Arrow Key Behavior*. To the next character or field.

- *Behavior Entering Field*. Moves to the start or end of the field or selects the entire field.

- *Cursor Stop*. Have the cursor stop at the first field when left unchecked, or go to the last field when checked.

User \ Access97 \ Tools_Options \ Module

This section sets the defaults for creating a new database.

- *Font*. Sets the default font to be used.

- *Coding Options*. All of the listed options are either checked to activate, or unchecked not to implement.

- Auto Indent

- Auto Syntax Check

- Require Variable Declaration

- Compile on Demand

- Auto Statement Builder

- Auto Quick Info

- Auto Value Tips

- Tab Width

User \ Access97 \ Tools_Options \ Module \ Windows Options

The following options are also on/off options for how you want Access 97 to respond when you are creating a database.

- Full Module View

- Procedure Separator

- Drag-and-Drop Text Editing

- Debug Window on Top

- Margin Indicator Bar

User \ Access97 \ Tools_Options \ Advanced

The section controls some advanced coding specs with DDE, OLE, and ODBC controls for network databases for which you want to control responses.

- *Default Record Locking.* Defines how Access deals with record locking: selects no locks, all records, or just on edited records.

- Ignore DDE Requests

- Enable DDE Refresh

- *OLE/DDE Timeout.* Sets the OLE/DDE Timeout in seconds.

- *Update Retries.* Sets the number of update retries.

- *ODBC Refresh.* Sets the rate of your ODBC refresh interval in seconds.

- *Refresh Interval.* Sets the refresh interval in seconds.

- *Update Retry.* Sets the update retry interval in seconds.

- *Default Open Mode.* Defines the mode of operation of your Access database when opened—either exclusive to a group of users or shared to all.

User \ Access 97 \ Internet Help_Microsoft on the Web

You can customize the menu displayed when you select the menu `Help`, which in turn leads to the submenu `Microsoft on the Web`. You can preset up to eight Web locations for `Access Help`. Sorry, the last menu option stays—that's the link to Microsoft's home page.

- *Reset submenu to original defaults.* Select this option and you're back to where you started.

- *Disable submenu.* Don't want your users to have access to Web-based help? This is the only option you'll want to click.

Outlook 97 and System Policy Options

Most of us think of Outlook only for sending and receiving email. Actually Outlook 97 is trying hard to be your total information center. If you use it in a networked environment, then these settings allow you to define its complete operation. There are both computer and user settings to consider.

Computer \ Outlook 97

- *Use Scheduler*. Defines whether Schedule+ 7.0 is used. If this setting is checked, the only calendar to be used is Scheduler 7.0.

Outlook 97 User and Group Options

Outlook 97 \ Tools_Options \ General

- Warn Before Deleting
- *Synchronize Folders*. Synchronizes all folders when exiting Outlook while online.

Tools_Options \ Email

This section sets the defaults for sending and receiving email. You can also choose to use WordMail as the default email editor and define the WordMail template.

- Process delivery, read, and recall receipts on arrival
- Process requests and responses on arrival
- Delete receipts and blank meeting responses after processing
- WordMail
- WordMail Template

Outlook 97 \ Calendar

This section allows you to define how the calendar option in Outlook 97 starts and views. In addition, the last setting doesn't belong here since it's defined on the computer side.

- *Work Week*. How many days of our work week the `Calendar` applet tracks.
- First Day of Week
- First Week of Year
- Working Hours
- Appointment defaults
- Show Week Numbers
- Use Schedule+

Outlook 97 \ Tasks/Notes

This section sets up the defaults for the `Notes` and `Tasks` applets within Outlook 97.

- Reminder Time
- Set Reminders
- Track Tasks
- Send Status Reports
- Task color options
- Work Settings
- Note Defaults

Outlook 97 \ Journal

This applet can be set up to be the catch-all for Outlook by defining what's automatically recorded, as well as any Office data file. In addition, you can define the startup conditions of the `Journal` applet.

- Automatically record these items
- Email message
- Fax Meeting cancellation
- Meeting request
- Meeting response
- Task request
- Task response

   Also record these file types:
- Microsoft Access
- Microsoft Office Binder
- Microsoft Excel
- Microsoft PowerPoint
- Microsoft Word
- Journal Entry Options

User \ Outlook 97 \ Reminders

- *Reminder Options.* This section sets the reminder options, either as a visual display or a sound reminder.

User \ Outlook 97 \ Spelling

The most important option when it comes to sending email. There is nothing worse than sending or receiving misspelled email.

- Suggest Replacements

- Check Spelling

- Ignore Uppercase

- Ignore Numbers

- Ignore Original

User \ Outlook 97 \ Internet Help_Microsoft on the Web

- *Customize submenu.* Customizes the menu displayed when you select the menu Help, which in turn leads to the submenu Microsoft on the Web. You can preset up to eight Web locations for Outlook Help. Sorry, the last menu option stays—that's the link to Microsoft's home page.

- *Reset submenu to original defaults.* Select this option and you're back to where you started.

- *Disable submenu.* Don't want your users to have access to Web-based help? This is the only option you'll want to click.

User\Outlook 97\Internet \Converters Future File Format Converters

This setting will not be used until Office 2000. After installing the new office suite, use this setting to point to the location of the new import converters that will be needed to properly convert the newer Office 2000 Outlook presentations to the older Outlook 97 file formats. This setting would save you from running around to every user's computer adding conversion tools.

This was a real problem for users that changed to Office 97 from Office 95 and tried to share files saved from Office 97 with

Office 95 users. As Microsoft releases file converters, add them to a shared network location and point all users to that location.

User \ Outlook 97 \ Miscellaneous

- *Disable Forms Designer*. Removes the user's ability to design forms for use with Outlook 97.

Creating System Policies for Windows 2000

With the release of Windows 2000 Server, Advanced Server, and Windows 2000 Professional, Microsoft has taken the step into the world of large corporate enterprise networks— ready to take on UNIX and the mainframe world—and to try to make everything Microsoft. According to a prerelease briefing from Microsoft, "Windows 2000 presents the most significant release of the Windows platform since the release of Windows 3.0 in 1990." And if *significant* means *lots of changes*, they are certainly right.

This new version will be a huge change for most corporations in the next few years, but I'd be quite surprised if there was a huge outcry for Windows 2000 right away. Microsoft knows this as well—this product has been carefully planned for the long run, because there are too many changes to digest and implement without testing, and more testing.

Looking at the prerelease candidate of Windows 2000 has been an interesting experience of experimentation, testing and reading tech notes over and over and *over*.

The concepts in this chapter are focused mainly on system policies and user profiles, as this book addresses these subjects. So you will learn about Windows 2000 in the following areas:

- The structure of Active Directory

- Group policy

- How system policies are deployed in Windows 2000

- How Windows 98 and NT 4.0 fit into the overall picture

- Windows 2000 and User profiles

Active Directory

Active Directory (AD) is finally introduced in Windows 2000. It is important to understand the Active Directory concepts so *group policy* (the replacement utility for system policies and user profiles) under Windows 2000 can be understood. This is a huge change for NT deployment, as Active Directory is not deployable for Windows NT 4.0—it's an all-or-nothing concept. You can upgrade NT 4.0 computers into Active Directory containers, but there is no real path with backward compatibility—there are just too many changes.

Active Directory is a compatible X.500 directory service with strong ties to NDS/NetWare and StreetTalk/Banyan Vines. It is secure, partitioned, and replicated, terms I explain later in this chapter.

Whereas a typical NT 4.0 directory stores objects, a directory service Active Directory includes not just the directory but also the services that provide the directory replication itself. The

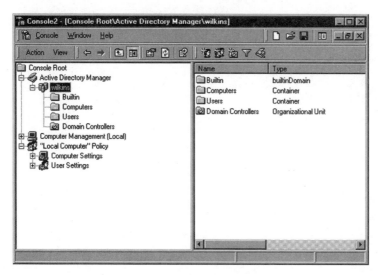

Figure 11-1 *The Active Directory Manager.*

Active Directory Manager is the software tool for managing all objects found in the Active Directory world. See Figure 11-1.

When users log onto and into the Active Directory world, they have access to all of the resources on the global network through the active directory and its services. Active Directory also provides an administrator a single point of administration across the entire corporate network.

Querying

Using the attributes of any AD object, an interrelated *global attribute catalog* is created and maintained that can be used to find any other AD object. The NT security permissions further control access to the objects your users can access throughout the Active Directory world. If desired, access can be granted or removed for each specific Active Directory object. See Figure 11-2.

The security of NT with Active Directory supports both the inheritance and the delegation of permissions. An object's permissions set can also be copied to all of its child objects. Administrators can delegate the desired authority and administrative rights to containers and subtrees to all other individuals and groups.

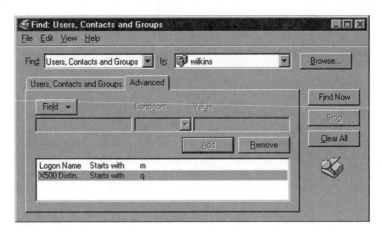

Figure 11-2 *Active Directory searches by attributes.*

Replication

Each server within a domain running Active Directory will store and maintain a complete copy of the domain directory. Any time information is changed at one of the servers running Active Directory, it is replicated to the other servers through a process called *multimaster replication.*

The directory of each domain stores information only about the objects located in its domain. Active Directory is completely *extensible*, which means that you can add new attributes to existing objects by custom programming or by using the Active Directory Schema Manager utility. Active Directory also uses the Domain Naming System (DNS) for name resolution and name-to-address resolution. An Active Directory server will have a name in DNS format, such as *Headoffice.companyname.com*, as domain names are stored and referred to in DNS format. Active Directory fully supports versions 2 and 3 of the Lightweight Directory Access Protocol (LDAP). See Figure 11-3.

Domains

Domains within Active Directory use a new domain model, the *multimaster peer-control model*. This means that all domain controllers (DCs) within a domain can receive changes and replicate those changes; there are no Backup Domain Controllers within AD. Each domain has its own security boundary so that security

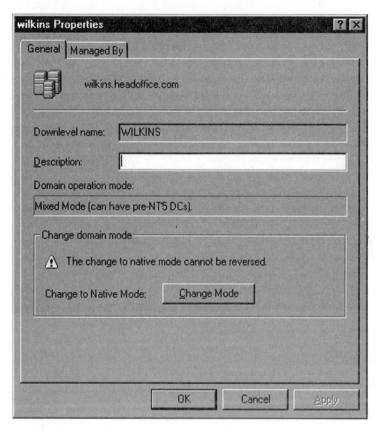

Figure 11-3 *DNS Names are standard for defining Active Directory servers.*

policies and settings will not cross from one domain into another domain.

The administrator of a domain has the absolute right to set group policy only within that domain.

Domain Trees

A *domain tree* is constructed by several domains that share a common schema, forming a seamless namespace. The first domain in a tree is called the *root* of the tree; the additional domains in the same tree are called *child* domains. The domain immediately above a domain in the same tree is called the *parent* of the child domain.

All domains that are in trees are associated with each other by two-way transitive trust relationships. Trust relationships in AD and Windows 2000 are based on the Kerberos security protocol. A trust relationship is now *transitive and hierarchical,* which means if domain A trusts B and domain B trusts C, domain A will also trust C. Trusts can also be viewed through the namespace of the domain tree.

Forests

A *forest* is a set of one or more trees (two or more domains linked together through a common schema) that do not form a common namespace. Trees share a common set of cross-relationship objects and Kerberos trust relationships known to the member trees in the forest.

Sites

A *site* is a place in a network that contains Active Directory servers. Sites are also defined as one or more TCP/IP subnets.

Organizational Units

Organizational units (OUs) are logical containers into which you can place users, groups, computers, and other OUs. An organizational unit is an electronic container, as it were, that you use in the Active Directory world to organize each domain into a logical grouping for your company. See Figure 11-4.

The OU can contain the following familiar objects: users, computers, security groups, printers, applications, security policies, file shares, and more.

Active Directory supports the delegation of administration of containers and subtrees to other users and groups. You could decide to create a tree of OUs inside each domain and then delegate authority for certain parts of the OU tree to a user or group of users. See Figure 11-5.

Global Catalog

The *global network* is a new Windows 2000 network service that holds directory information from all domains in your company. It answers queries about objects anywhere on the network, even across domain trees. The *global catalog* works on an

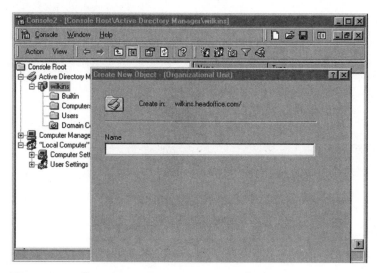

Figure 11-4 *Creating a new organizational unit.*

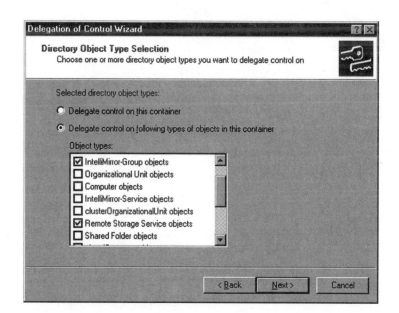

Figure 11-5 *Delegating control of directory objects through Active Directory.*

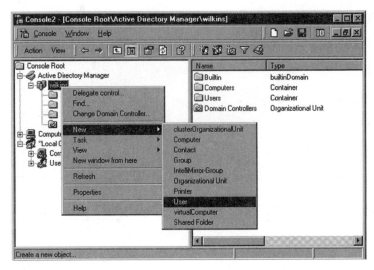

Figure 11-6 *Active Directory object class examples.*

attribute search that is carried out across domains to find the desired object.

A global catalog is created automatically on the initial domain controller in the forest and is stored on specific servers throughout the enterprise on domain controllers that also act as global catalog servers.

Schema

Although this is a hard word to digest at first, *schema* is the formal definition of all object classes and the attributes that make up the defined object classes that can be stored in the Active Directory. The object classes that can be defined are: users, groups, computers, domains, organizational units, and security policies. See Figure 11-6.

Windows 2000 and Groups

Windows 2000 Server has three types of security groups: universal, global, and domain local groups.

1. *Universal Groups.* Universal groups can contain members from any domain in a forest. In addition, they can be used in an access control list (ACL) on any defined object in a forest.

Global groups can contain members only from the same domain; however, they can be used on any ACL. All Windows 2000 groups—universal, global, and local—can be nested.

> You may have a marketing division in your company that includes design, layout, and manufacturing. The marketing division could be considered a universal group. Global groups that nest within the production universal group could represent the design, layout, and manufacturing departments. The permissions you assign to the objects in the marketing group may be inherited through all of its members, with additional group object-specific Access Control Lists that can be assigned to each member.

Note

2. *Global Groups.* The Windows 2000 global groups are similar to NT 4.0 global groups, except you can now place users and other global groups into global groups. The replication for global groups takes place only within a domain boundary. Global groups cannot contain domain local or universal groups; they can contain only other global groups or individual users. See Figure 11-7.

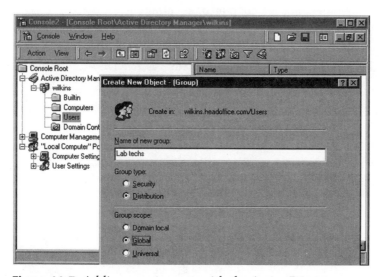

Figure 11-7 *Adding a new group with the Active Directory Manager.*

3. *Domain Local Groups.* A domain local group membership is valid only in the domain where it is first defined, and is not replicated to the global catalog. Domain local groups can contain members from any domain, but can be referenced only in the Access Control Lists in their domain.

You can combine individual users and global groups from your domain and other trusted domains. Universal groups can also be combined and joined together.

User Accounts

Windows 2000 has two types of user accounts: *domain user* accounts and *local user* accounts, similar to the NT 4.0 user account structure.

Group Policy

NT 4.0 included the system policy editor (as we well know). Well, how do you like surprises? *Surprise!* The system policy editor lives no more in the Windows 2000 world—its job has been taken over and enhanced by group policy. Settings that you create with group policy are contained in a *group policy object* (GPO) that are, in turn, associated with the available Active Directory system containers: sites, domains, and organizational units (OUs). The group policy modules are linked to Active Directory in the following structure:

- GPO Name [DomainName.com] Policy
- Default Domain Policy [Wilkins.wilkinshq.com] Policy

Each namespace is further divided into "parent nodes" of `Computer Configuration` and `User Configuration`.

Note

Comparing Windows NT 4.0 and Windows 2000 Policy
1. In Windows NT 4.0, system policies are applied to domains, domain users, and global groups.

2. In Windows 2000, system policies can be applied to Active Directory containers such as sites, domains, and organizational units.
3. In Windows NT, system policies settings are written to the local Registry and are in effect until they are overwritten.
4. In Windows 2000, policy registry settings written to the registry are cleaned up when a previous group policy object no longer applies.

With group policy you can define and mandate system policy (from now on called *group policy*) as well as the following objects:

- Groups of computers and users
- Registry-based policy settings
- Security settings
- Software installation
- Scripts
- Folder redirection

The other term used by Microsoft to describe group policy and Active Directory is *Intellimirroring*.

Group Policy snap-in extensions depend on *dynamic link library* files (DLLs) that control each group policy feature:

Administrative Templates	GPTEXT.DLL
Security Settings	WSECEDIT.DLL
Scripts	GPTEXT.DLL
Software Installation	APPMGR.DLL
Folder Redirection	FDE.DLL

Group policy uses a defined object called a group policy object (GPO), as mentioned earlier, to store group policy settings. These group policy objects are further associated with particular Active Directory containers such as sites, domains, and organizational units. See Figure 11-8.

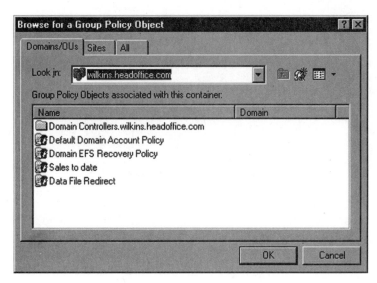

Figure 11-8 *Group policy objects are associated with the existing network structure.*

The data inside each GPO are read and applied to the affected client, group, or computer. GPOs that are defined and used within Active Directory follow a default order of preferences that mirrors the hierarchical nature or pecking order of Active Directory itself. First, sites are defined; next domains; and finally, each organizational unit. Definitions for these new components of the Active Directory were presented earlier in the chapter.

Creating Group Policy

Group policy is created through a new graphical interface (if you haven't been involved with Internet Information Server 4.0 or greater) through the Microsoft Management Console (MMC) adding the group policy editor as a *snap-in*. There are many snap-in options that you can add to the MMC; in fact, this feature allows us to customize the utilities we want to see and use. See Figure 11-9.

The modules that make up group policy are all joined at the hip, so to speak, with the MMC. The administrative template settings for Windows 2000 are found in SYSTEM.ADM and INETRES.ADM, providing Registry stored policy that controls the

Figure 11-9 *Adding the group policy editor to the MMC.*

appearance and behavior of the Active Desktop shell and other operating system components, such as remote OS installation and disk quotas. The other group policy modules are briefly explained below; by selecting any of the group policy modules and right-clicking each option, through properties we can manage, add, or change all displayed group policy options assuming we have the rights to do so.

Group Policy Scripts

Scripts can be created for the control of the startup and shutdown of the computer system and the user logon and logoff. We can now control any system process or backup procedure you want to mandate for your users via a script file. The *Windows Scripting Host* (WSH) was first introduced with Windows 98 and is now a standard with Windows 2000. WSH also integrates with

VB script and PERL-type scripting, among others. There are five
scripts that exist by default in Windows 2000:

1. *Legacy logon scripts.* These are active on the User object; they
   also support WSH scripting for Windows 2000 and Windows
   98 clients by default. Support for WSH can be installed on
   Windows 98 and NT 4.0 Clients.

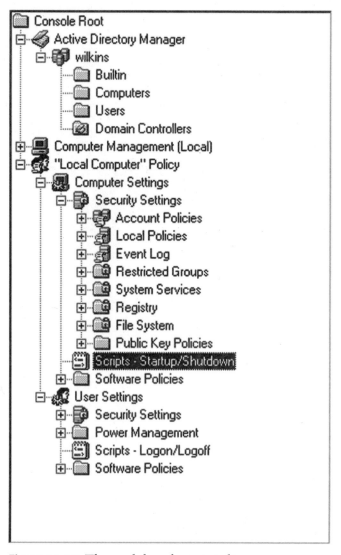

Figure 11-10 *The modules of group policy.*

2. Group policy logon scripts

3. Group policy logoff scripts

4. Group policy startup scripts

5. Group policy shutdown scripts

See Figure 11-10.

Security Groups

Security groups are a new feature; your membership in a security group allows filtering of group policy settings on computers and users across Active Directory. To filter group policy, the Security tab found on every Group Policy Object Properties page can be used to define DACL permissions. The editing of security policy is similar to editing Regedit DWORD values. See Figure 11-11.

The security areas that can be defined for computer group policy include security settings for the local computer, domain, and network. Security settings are contained in information (INF) files that match the type of Windows 2000 environment you are creating or moving toward.

> *Security Templates for Windows 2000 Upgrades*   **Note**
> Windows 2000 includes several security templates, called *incremental security templates*, stored in \SECURITY\TEMPLATES. These apply only to new Windows 2000 Professional workstations that have been installed onto a clean NTFS partition; in other words,

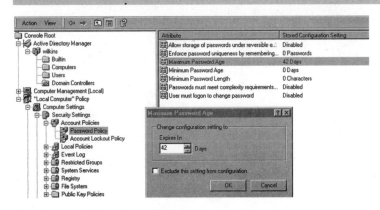

Figure 11-11 *Security policies.*

they contain preset security settings that are applied on the first successful boot and logon. See Figure 11-12.

Any computer systems that have been upgraded from NT 4.0 Workstation should not use these incremental policies; instead, a Basic security template should be applied, bringing the upgraded computer up to the default security settings. The security settings will be fully deployed only on NTFS, although FAT is still supported.

For new installations, Windows 2000 contains three templates called *Basic*. These new default security settings are applied only to Windows 2000 computers that have been installed onto an NTFS partition. The Basic template sets the default security levels for Windows 2000; these can also be added later once your computer systems attain the minimum Windows 2000 level.

1. `BASICWK.INF` for workstations
2. `BASICWS.INF` server
3. `BASICDC.INF` for domain controllers

Security Configuration	Computer	Templates	Description
Compatible	Workstation and server	`COMPATW.INF`	For users that use older legacy applications
Secure	Workstation, server, and domain controller	`SECUREWS.INF` and `SECUREDC.INF`	Increased security settings are applied to account policy, auditing, and relevant registry keys.
High Secure	Workstation, server, and domain controller	`HISECWS.INF` and `HISEDC.INF`	For Windows 2000-only environments (Windows 2000 applications only). This is not likely to be implemented any time soon. This security model would not allow communications with older Windows environments.

Figure 11-12 *Security scripts for new installs.*

Account Policies

Account policies allow you to define computer settings for password lockout, lockout policy, and Kerberos security levels policy in domains.

Local Policies

Local policies define the security settings for computer and user policy, as well as audits of files and folders, user rights and how they are mandated, and other local security options. For example, you could define who had network or local access on a particular computer system. See Figure 11-13.

Event Log

Group policy settings can be defined for security levels for the application, security, and system event logs. The Event Viewer is still used to view the log files.

Restricted Group

Group policy settings can be defined for those who should belong to a *restricted group*.

System Service

The *system services* control the security options for: computer startup and network; file and print services; telephone and fax services; and Internet connections. In NT 4.0 the Control Panel

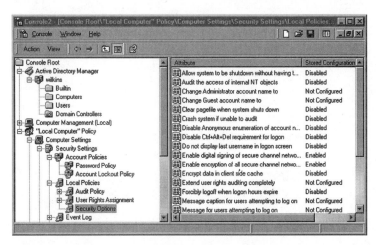

Figure 11-13 *Security options for local policies.*

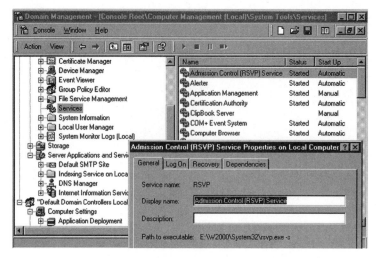

Figure 11-14 *Services can be set by right-clicking each displayed option.*

Services applet was used to set and control these system options. See Figure 11-14.

Registry

We can set the Registry access for keys and folders within the Registry, including access control, registry auditing, and ownership. In NT 4.0 this was performed through the registry editor Regedt32 and the security drop-down menu. See Figure 11-15.

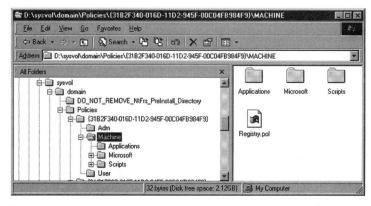

Figure 11-15 *Registry policies.*

File System

Define the permission settings for file access, file and folder auditing, and ownership. Hard drives must be converted to NTFS version 5.0 in order to deploy full Windows 2000 security. In NT 4.0 we used the `Property` tab of the folder or file to set file permissions.

Software Installation

Software can be centrally installed and managed from a central network location. Software can also be assigned and published for users and groups of users and computers.

Software Policies for Computers and Users

This section of group policy will be the most familiar. The software policies use `.ADM` templates to define similar and new policy settings. Group software policy settings are written to either the `Local Machine` or `User` portion of the Registry just as Windows NT 4.0, but the Registry location has changed for the Windows 2000 settings. See Figure 11-16.

- User policy settings are written to `HKCU\SOFTWARE\POLICIES`.

- User configuration is stored in the `\USER\REGISTRY.POL` file.

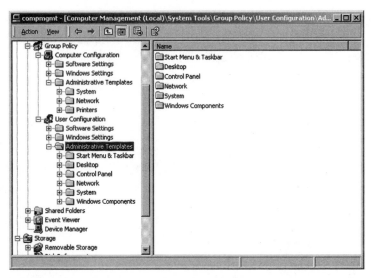

Figure 11-16 *User and computer configurations.*

- Computer policy settings are written to HKLM\SOFTWARE\ MICROSOFT\WINDOWS\CURRENTVERSION\POLICIES.

- Computer configuration is stored in the \MACHINE\REGISTRY.POL file.

- The Registry trees are secure and cannot be modified by a non-administrator.

The NTCONFIG.POL file for Windows NT 4.0 operating system is a binary file, whereas the REGISTRY.POL created by the group policy snap-in is a text file with embedded binary strings. When group policy changes, for any reason, these trees are cleaned, and the new policies are then rewritten.

Computer Group Policy Configuration

The *computer group policy configuration* includes the computer-related policies that specify and mandate the following:

- Operating system behavior

- Desktop behavior

- Software application options

- Security settings

- Startup and shutdown scripts

Computer policy is deployed when Windows 2000 first boots and also during a periodic refresh cycle. Computer policy is processed and completed before the Logon dialog box (CTRL-ALT-DEL) is available and then again in the background, approximately every 90 minutes thereafter.

User Group Policy Configuration

The *user group policy configuration* includes the user-related policies that specify and mandate the following:

- Desktop settings

- Application settings

- Security settings

- Assigned and published application options

- User logon and logoff scripts

- Folder redirection options

User group policy is applied when the user first logs onto the computer and during a periodic refresh cycle. User policy is processed and finished before the Explorer shell has finished loading. This loading mode is called *synchronous*.

User policy is applied at user logon and then approximately every 90 minutes after logon. Both Registry and security settings are always applied.

Folder redirection and software installation periodic background processing are not carried out while the user is currently logged on.

By default, all client group policy settings update their policy settings only when there are any new or changed settings. This is a departure from policy settings in NT 4.0, where they are reapplied at every logon; however, to attain the highest level of policy security, we can activate the setting `Process even if the Group Policy Objects have not changed` to each client extension that you desire.

The Refresh Cycle of Group Policy   **Note**

Group policy can also be set to be processed and applied between domain controllers every 90 minutes rather than the default of 5 minutes. Folder redirection and software installation occur only during initial computer startup and user logon.

Remote Group Policy Deployment

The defaults for remote computers and group policy deployment across slow links are:

Security Settings	ON
Administrative Templates	ON (and cannot be turned off)
Software Installation	OFF
Scripts	OFF
Folder Redirection	OFF

Note   By default, group policy is inherited and cumulative; therefore, it
affects all computers and users in an Active Directory container.
Group policy is processed in the following order: site, domain, and
OU.

The default inheritance is to deploy group policy starting with
the Active Directory container furthest from the computer or user
object. The Active Directory container closest to the computer or
user can override the group policy that was set in a higher level
Active Directory container. However, there are options that you
can set to force the policy set at the domain level to be applied to
all levels of OU under that domain.

The Loading of Group Policy Within Active Directory

The following steps list the processing of group policy:

1. The network and network services start.

2. Computer group policy is applied in synchronous mode.

3. The startup scripts are executed in synchronous mode, one
   after the other.

4. The user is presented the choice of logging in with CTRL-
   ALT-DEL.

5. The user name and password are verified and the user profile
   is loaded.

6. User group policy is applied in the order of local, site, domain,
   and OU.

7. The logon scripts are run.

8. The Explorer shell is started.

When a user logs onto a domain that has both Active Directory
and group policy implemented, first the local group policy is
found and deployed, after which domain policy is deployed. If an
inconsistency occurs between domain and local policy, the domain
policy takes precedence. If the local computer has not logged onto
a domain, then local group policy will have precedence.

Group policy is deployed to the user and computer based on where the active user and computer are defined within Active Directory. If your users move about the network, you may want to have the computer object take precedence over the user object. If you have folder redirection and software installation enabled in your group policy, a user may get applications installed on multiple computer systems when you do not want this to happen.

Group Policy on Standalone Windows 2000 Professional Workstations

Group policy can be deployed on computer systems that do not belong to a domain. The group policy snap-in that applies to local computers is called a *Local Group Policy Object* (LGPO), and can be accessed by loading the Microsoft Management Console (MMC) and adding the local group policy snap-in to the MMC console. The `Local Group Policy Object` is the template portion of group policy and is located in `%SYSTEMROOT%` `SYSTEM32\GROUPPOLICY`.

The following group policy snap-ins can be accessed on a local computer.

- Security settings

- Administrative Templates

- Scripts

Software installation and folder redirection are not deployed on a standalone Windows 2000 Professional workstation, as there is no central domain controller available to perform this task.

Enabling Local Group Policy

To enable the group policy snap-in on Windows 2000 Professional:

1. First click `Start` and select `Run`; enter `MMC` and press ENTER.

2. The `MMC` console will load. In the `MMC` window, on the `Console` menu, click `Add/Remove Snap-in`.

3. On the `Standalone` tab, click `Add`. See Figure 11-17.

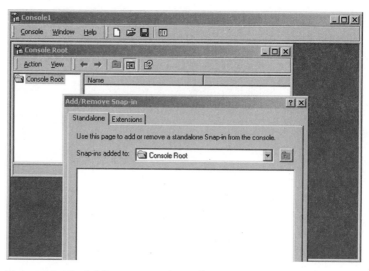

Figure 11-17 *Adding a snap-in to the Management Console.*

4. Select `Group Policy` and then click `Add`. See Figure 11-18.

5. From the `Select Group Policy Object`, click `Local Computer` to edit the `Local Group Policy Object` (**LGPO**), or `Browse` to find the GPO that you want to use. You can also choose the

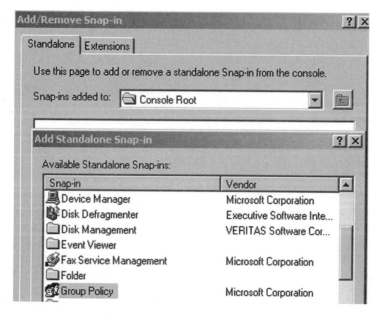

Figure 11-18 *Adding the group policy snap-in.*

group policy extensions that you want to enable or add. See Figure 11-19.

6. Click Finish and then OK.

Requirements for Deploying Group Policy with Active Directory

In order to set group policy for a particular Active Directory container, a Windows 2000 domain controller must first be installed. You must also be an administrator with read/write permissions to access the SYSVOL folder that is found in the system volume of each domain controller and modify rights to the selected directory container.

Note the new term *domain controller*, as there are no backup domain controllers in the new NT world. However, with the

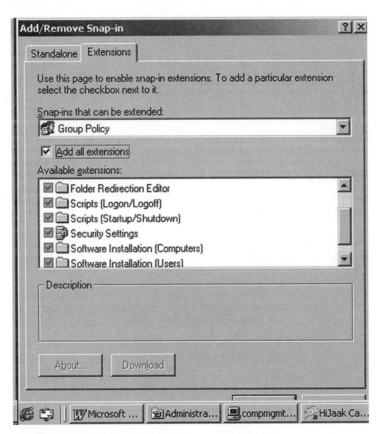

Figure 11-19 *Group policy folder extension.*

Intellimirror and Active Directory features, domain controllers (DC) should have much improved and more flexible methods of data and security replication.

Group Policy Layout

The group policy container is an Active Directory container that stores GPO properties, GPO information, and other system components. The Group Policy Template is a set of subfolders found in the SYSVOL volume folder of all domain controllers in the Policies subfolder. Administrative policy templates, security settings, applications that have been tagged up for automatic software installation, and script files are also stored here as well. See Figure 11-20.

- *ADM.* This location holds all of the ADM files for Group Policy Template.

- *SCRIPTS.* This folder holds all of the script and related files for this Group Policy Template.

- *USER.* This folder contains a REGISTRY.POL file that holds the Registry settings that are to be applied to the users through the active HKCU portion of the Registry. Subfolders include APPS and FILES:

    APPS. This folder holds .AAS files, called *advertisement files*, used by the Windows installer.
    FILES. This folder contains the application files to be deployed.

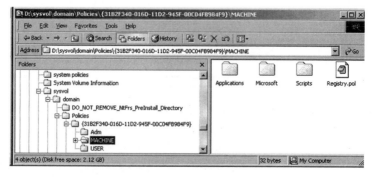

Figure 11-20 *Folder structure of group policy.*

- *MACHINE.* Contains a `REGISTRY.POL` file that holds the Registry settings that are to be applied to computers through the active `HKLM` portion of the Registry. Subfolders include `APPS` and `FILES`:

  APPS. This folder holds `.AAS` files, called *advertisement files*, used by the Windows installer that are applied to computers.
  FILES. Contains the application files to be deployed that are applied to computers.

Choosing a Domain Controller for Enabling Group Policy

Through group policy you can specify which domain controller will be used to edit and store the group policy choices. There are three options:

1. *The one with the Operations Master token for the PDC emulator.* This option forces the group policy snap-in to always use the same DC.

2. *The ones used by the Active Directory Snap-ins.* This option uses the DC that the snap-in tools are currently using.

3. *Use any available domain controller.* This option allows the group policy snap-in to choose any available DC.

All of the preceding options can be overwritten by the primary domain administrator who can mandate which domain controller is to be used for group policy.

Creating Group Policy Objects

Only domain administrators, enterprise administrators, group policy administrators, and the operating system can create new group policy objects by default. Other groups or users must be added to the Group Policy Administrators security group before they can create group policy.

If a non-administrator gains the right to create a group policy object, he or she becomes the creator and owner of the GPO. It does not, however, give the non-administrator rights to other group policy objects created across the domain.

Editing Group Policy Objects

By default, the group policy objects allow Domain Administrators, Enterprise Administrators, the operating system, and the GPO creator full control. The *apply group attribute*, however, is not assigned to them, which means they can edit and create the GPO but the policies contained in that particular GPO will not apply to them. All authenticated users have read access to the group policy object with the apply group attribute assigned. To edit a GPO, the user must be one of the following:

- An administrator

- A creator/owner of the object

- A user that has been granted access to the group policy object

Note

If you wanted to change the control of an organizational unit from an administrator to a non-administrative user so that a group of users (or user) can select from existing group policy objects, but not create new group policy objects, you would:

1. In the Active Directory Users and Computers snap-in, right-click the Organizational Unit that you want to delegate, and select Delegate Control.
2. In the Delegation of Control Wizard, click Next to go past the introduction page. You will be asked to confirm the OU that you wish to delegate.
3. Click Next. You will be prompted for the names of the users and groups to which you want to delegate control.
4. Select a previously defined group (or user), and then click Next.
5. In the list of Predefined Tasks, select Manage Group Policy links, then click Next.
6. Click Finish to accept and complete the changes.

NT 4.0 Compatibility with Windows 2000 Policies

Windows 2000 group policy snap-ins do not support Windows NT 4.0 and Windows 95/98 clients. Support for these older clients is done by installing the Windows 2000 Administrative

Tools (ADMINPAK.MSI) from the I386 folder on the Windows 2000 CD-ROM providing POLEDIT and the templates WINDOWS.ADM, COM-MON.ADM, and ADMIN.ADM.

This installation also installs the Administrative Tools menu on the Start button for support of Windows NT 4.0 networks and clients. The POL files for Windows 95/98 and NT 4.0 clients are stored in the familiar NETLOGON share located on Windows 2000 in SYSVOL\DN.

Windows 2000 Server and Windows 2000 professional will not process NT 4.0 system policies unless the group policy option is turned on to do so. Problems can occur at this point, however, because both Windows 2000 and NT 4.0 policies will be applied. This is a strange attempt by Microsoft to make a mess out of the mixture of NT 4.0 and Windows 2000, to persuade you to migrate to Windows 2000.

ADM Files and Windows 2000

In Windows 2000 ADM template files have been updated with Explain and Version tabs. Remove an ADM template from the group policy snap-in console by right-clicking the Administrative Templates node and selecting Add/Remove Templates.

The first time group policy is started for a particular group policy object, the SYSTEM.ADM template file is copied from the INF directory to the active GPO. The .ADM files shown in Figure 11-21 are included in Windows 2000.

ADM File	Version of Windows	Action
SYSTEM.ADM	Windows 2000	Loaded by Default
INETRES.ADM	Windows 2000	Loaded by Default
WINNT.ADM	NT 4.0	Used with POLEDIT
COMMON.ADM	NT 4.0	Used with POLEDIT
WINDOWS.ADM	Windows 95/98	Used with POLEDIT

Figure 11-21 *ADM templates included with Windows 2000.*

At the root of each `Group Policy Template` folder is a file called `GPT.INI`. This `INI` file stores policy information for local group policy objects informing Windows 2000 version information, whether or not the user or computer portion is disabled, and the organization of user and computer information in the group policy object.

The administrative templates snap-in extension of `Group Policy` saves its information in ASCII files called `REGISTRY.POL`. These files hold the customized settings that are specified by using the group policy snap-in that are applied to the `Machine` or `User` portion of the Registry.

Template Settings for Windows 2000

The `SYSTEM.ADM` template is new for Windows 2000. Available template settings are numerous. They are now grouped under the main headings of `Computer` and `User Configuration` in the subfolder `Administrative Templates`.

Computer \ Administrative Templates \ System \

The new options are for Terminal Server Clients, Microsoft Installer, and logon, logoff, and shutdown status messages.

Logon

Logon options are for configuring startup and shutdown scripts and user profile operation. See Figure 11-22.

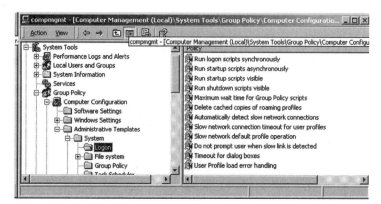

Figure 11-22 *Logon computer options for Windows 2000.*

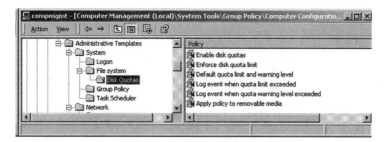

Figure 11-23 *Disk quota computer options for Windows 2000.*

- *File System \ Disk Quotas*. Settings for enforcing any disk quota restrictions. See Figure 11-23.

- *Group Policy*. Defines settings for how the pieces of group policy are applied. See Figure 11-24.

- *Task Scheduler*. Defines how the task scheduler runs for each workstation. See Figure 11-25.

Computer Configuration \ Administrative Templates \ Network

- *Offline Files*. Completes setup options for files that are cached offline. See Figure 11-26.

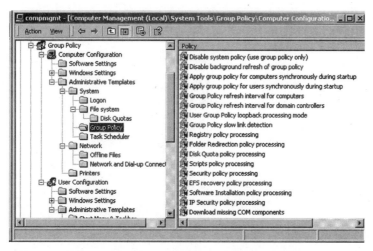

Figure 11-24 *Group policy computer options for Windows 2000.*

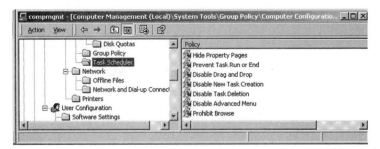

Figure 11-25 *Task scheduler computer options for Windows 2000.*

- *Network and Dial-up Connections.* Mandates that users can't change dial-up connections.

User Configuration \ Administrative Templates \ Start Menu & Taskbar

- Define the Start Menu and Taskbar settings

User Configuration \ Administrative Templates \ Desktop

- Define and mandate Desktop settings

User Configuration \ Administrative Templates \ Control Panel

- *Add \ Remove Programs.* Controls Add / Remove icon settings.

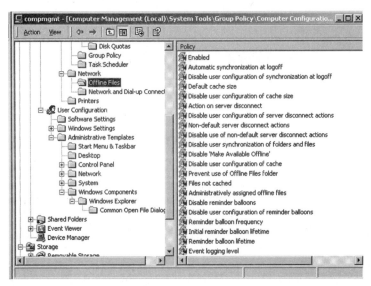

Figure 11-26 *Offline folder computer options for Windows 2000.*

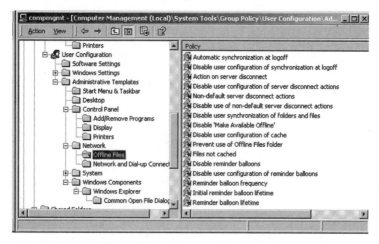

Figure 11-27 *Offline folder user options for Windows 2000.*

- *Display.* Controls the `Display` icon in Control Panel.

- *Printers.* Controls the `Printer` icon in Control Panel.

**User Configuration \ Administrative Templates \
Network**

- *Offline Folders.* User settings for offline folders and cache settings. See Figure 11-27.

- *Network and Dial-Up Connections.* Sets the user RAS and dial-up connections.

**User Configuration \ Administrative Templates \
System**

- Define date / time in what century, Disable registry tools. See Figure 11-28.

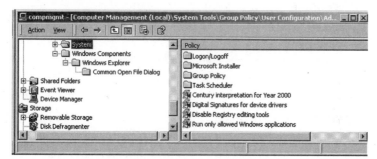

Figure 11-28 *System user options for Windows 2000.*

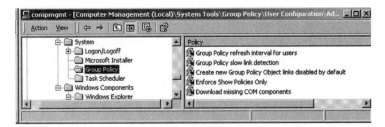

Figure 11-29 *Group policy deployment options for Windows 2000.*

- *Logon \ Logoff.* Sets logon script conditions and user profile settings.

- *Microsoft Installer.* Mandates Microsoft Installer settings.

- *Group Policy.* Defines the group policy refresh interval and other settings. See Figure 11-29.

- *Task Scheduler.* Defines user settings for Task Manager.

User Configuration \ Administrative Templates \ Windows Components

- *Windows Explorer.* Sets the default conditions of the Explorer shell.

- Common Open File Dialog

Windows 2000 and Roaming User Profiles

Windows 2000 has added several new features that expand the flexibility of roaming user profiles. The features are File Deployment, Folder Redirection, and Offline folders, all deployed as part of group policy.

The roaming user profile consists of the user's registry NTUSER.DAT, shortcuts, and folder structure found in the shared user profiles folder on the server.

When the user has a roaming user profile and logs onto a machine and runs software and then logs off, the user profile is copied back to the designated server location. At a later time, the user logs onto a computer system that is not the usual one; all of the user's profile information is copied to the computer system that the user is logging into.

Setting Up Roaming User Profiles with Windows 2000

The first task you will have to perform when setting up roaming user profiles with Windows 2000 is to create a shared network location for the roaming user profiles on a selected Windows 2000 server.

To create a shared folder to store roaming user profiles on a Windows 2000 server:

1. Run the Windows NT Explorer.

2. Right-click and select New, and select Folder.

3. For the New Folder name, type the name of the new shared location for user profiles.

4. Now highlight the new folder just created in step 3 and right-click and select Properties.

5. Select the Sharing tab and select Shared As. See Figure 11-30.

In Windows 2000, the familiar utility User Manager for Domains has been replaced with the Active Directory Manager. To convert an existing user into a roaming user:

1. Click the Start button, point to Programs, then to Administrative Tools, and click Directory Management.

2. Double-click through the folders present until the user's folder is located.

3. Right-click the user you wish to change to a roaming user, and select Properties from the context menu. Note the tabbed selections have replaced the button options found in NT 4.0 and User Manager for Domains. See Figure 11-31.

4. Click the Profile tab. For the profile path, type \\SERVER-NAME\HOMEDIR\%USERNAME%. %USERNAME% is an environment variable. In this case, %USERNAME% will map to Mark Wilkins' user name Mark. When Mark logs on to a computer, Win-

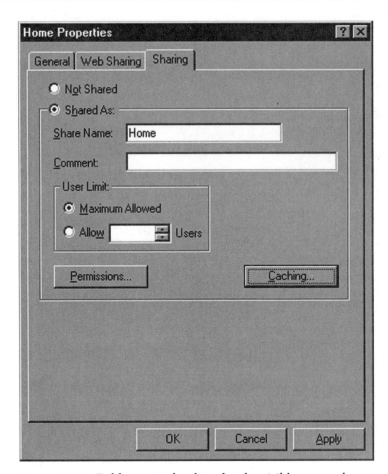

Figure 11-30 *Folders must be shared to be visible across the network.*

dows NT will create the directory Mark in the Profiles share on the selected Windows 2000 server. See Figure 11-32.

File Deployment

In the NT 4.0 world, through system policies we could specify the files, folders, and applications that a user could access and use through system policies and custom folders; however, it was almost impossible to set up properly. With Active Directory and

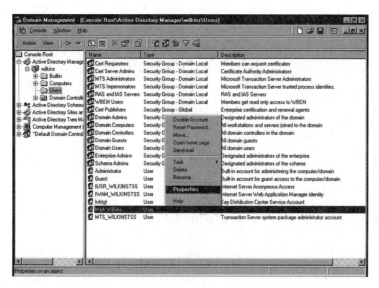

Figure 11-31 *Selecting users with the Active Directory Manager.*

Kerberos security, we can now determine the objects and permissions that we wish to make available to the user or group of users.

Suppose that you wish to deploy a shortcut to a file that will appear on all of your users' desktops. You would first log on as an administrator, then create the file and a shared directory for the file. Then you will use the group policy editor to deploy the shortcut to the desktop of every user within the desired organizational unit.

1. To create a directory for deployed files, run Windows NT Explorer and select the network drive for the shared folder. Right-click and select New and then Folder.

2. For the new folder name, type in the desired name. For this example, I'll call the folder Sales. Next, right-click the Sales folder and select Properties.

3. Click the Sharing tab and select the Shared As option button.

4. Click OK.

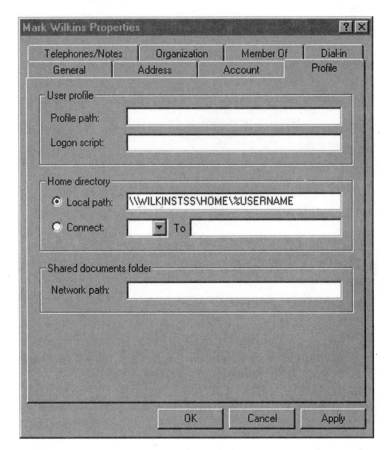

Figure 11-32 *User properties for Windows 2000 Professional client.*

To select the file to be shared, use the NT Explorer to choose the desired file and copy it to the shared location. Now we have to use group policies to deploy the file to each user's desktop.

1. Click the `Start` button, point to `Programs`, point to `Administrative Tools`, and click `Directory Management`.

2. Highlight the domain on which you wish to share the file. For this example, I'll use `WILKINSTSS`.

3. Right-click `WILKINSTSS`, select `Task`, and click `Manage Group Policy`. See Figure 11-33

4. On the `Group Policy Properties` page, click `Add`.

Figure 11-33 *Select the domain to manage group policy from.*

5. Right-click and select New to create a New Group Policy Object icon.

6. For the New Group Policy Object name, type the desired name. For example, let's suppose that you wanted a sales-to-date Word summary to be available on every user's desktop—you could call the new group policy Sales to date.

7. On the Group Policy Properties page, click the Sales to date document and click the Edit button. See Figure 11-34.

8. In the Group Policy Editor edit window, click User Settings.

9. Next click User Documents and Settings, then User, and then Desktop. See Figure 11-35.

10. Right-click on the Desktop folder and select New, and File.

11. For the File name, type \\SERVERNAME\SHARED FOLDER\ FILENAME.

12. Close the Group Policy Editor window and on the Group Policy Properties page, click OK.

13. On the Active Directory Manager window, click Console, and then click Exit.

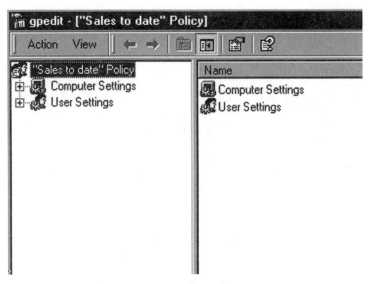

Figure 11-34 *Editing a group policy object.*

When the selected users log onto the domain with the acti-vated file deployment feature within the selected organizational unit, the `Sales to Date` policy will apply. The Word document will be available on every user's desktop in the `WILKINSTSS` domain.

Folder Redirection

Users and administrators can specify through group policy the redirection of a folder's path to either a local or network share location. The user can work with a shared document on the

Figure 11-35 *Adding the file location to Desktop.*

server even though it seems that the share is on the local drive. Folder redirection is an effective way to preserve user documents on a network drive that has proper security.

To redirect users' My Documents folders to the network:

1. Click the Start button, point to Programs, point to Administrative Tools, and click Directory Management.

2. Highlight the domain on which you wish to share the file. For this example, I'll use WILKINSTSS.

3. Right-click WILKINSTSS, select Task, and click Manage Group Policy.

4. On the Group Policy Properties page, click Add.

5. Right-click and select New to create a New Group Policy Object icon.

6. For the New Group Policy Object name, type Data File Redirect and click OK. See Figure 11-36.

7. Highlight the policy object Data File Redirect and click Edit.

8. Now select User Settings, then User Documents and Settings, and finally User.

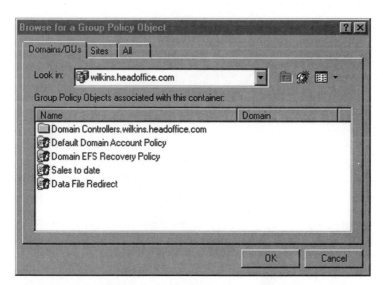

Figure 11-36 *Creating a new group policy object.*

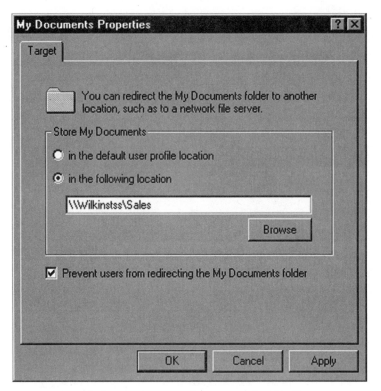

Figure 11-37 *Selecting a network location for My Documents.*

9. Right-click My Documents and from the Action menu, click Properties.

10. On the My Documents Properties page, select the desired network location to redirect My Documents to \\SERVERNAME\MYDOCS\%username%.

11. Select the Prevent users from redirecting the My Documents folder check box. See Figure 11-37.

12. Click OK and select Yes to confirm the move.

Offline Folders

Files and folders can be enabled through group policy to be available as offline folders. These folders are cached locally and updated once the network connection has been restored.

A user could then create a new data file and save it to his or her My Documents folder that is already redirected to a network share by the administrator.

The user could then specify that the file is to be available offline, log off the network, and take his or her notebook computer home.

Later the user can edit the particular file. The next day when the user arrives at work and connects the notebook computer to the network and logs in, the user can synchronize, or update, the server copy of the file.

To make a file in My Documents available for offline use:

1. From the desktop, double-click My Document.

2. In the My Documents folder, right-click the file and choose Make Available Offline.

To synchronize offline documents with the server:

1. On the desktop, double-click My Documents.

2. Click the file you wish to update, then right-click and select Synchronize.

The older version of the data file that was stored on the server is replaced with the newer file from the local machine.

12

System Policies for Windows 98

This chapter concentrates on Windows 98 Second Edition, which is quite similar to Windows 98 first version in the system policy area. Only a few settings are new—these will be noted. Although the book is directed toward NT administrators and covers NT in general, most networks have some Windows 98 clients that are also included in the "NT network," simply because they log into the domain for their user profile and resources just like their NT workstation counterparts. Or, you may have only NT servers and all Windows 98 clients.

The big change for Windows 98 was the Active Desktop and the built-in Internet Explorer Browser that wouldn't go away. This chapter is going to deal primarily with the Active Desktop settings found in SHELLM.ADM. The other Windows 98-specific template is WINDOWS.ADM. Chapter 4 deals with the template settings for Windows 98 (the first version); we will explore the changes added into WINDOWS.ADM template for Windows 98 Second Edition. The other templates bundled with Windows 98 are actually Internet Explorer system policy settings; they get their own chapter, Chapter 6.

Active Desktop Settings and the SHELLM.ADM Template

The SHELLM.ADM template has system policy settings for users and groups of users, but not for computers. The settings are the same

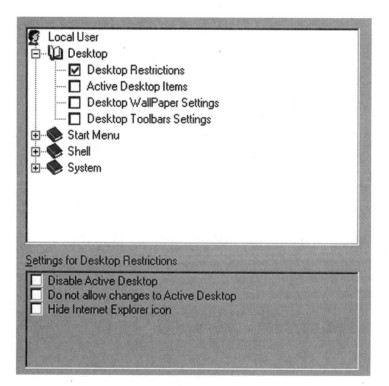

Figure 12-1 *Active Desktop restrictions.*

for all versions of Windows 98, although on certain builds of
Windows 98 the template is called SHELL.ADM; the contents are the
same as SHELLM.ADM.

User \ Desktop

- Desktop Restrictions (see Figure 12-1)

  Disable Active Desktop. From the Display icon Web tab and
  Start Menu | Settings | Active Desktop.
  Do not allow changes to Active Desktop. Mandates Active
  Desktop settings that can't be changed.
  Hide Internet Explorer icon. IE is still present; however, it is
  not available as a shortcut. The DLLs that IE uses are common
  to Windows 98, so uninstalling IE is never a good idea.

- *Active Desktop Items.* These settings are self-explanatory. We
  have five choices for the level of disable (see Figure 12-2):

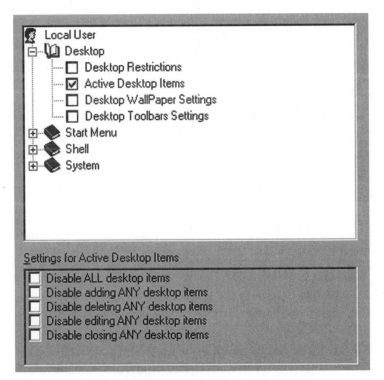

Figure 12-2 *Disable options for the desktop.*

Disable ALL desktop items
Disable adding ANY desktop items
Disable deleting ANY desktop items
Disable editing ANY desktop items
Disable closing ANY desktop items

- Desktop Wallpaper Settings

  No HTML wallpaper. This can be handy for stopping the common procedure of right-clicking on any graphic found on the Internet and "Saving it as Wallpaper."
  Disable changing wallpaper. If you have systems in public areas or use wallpaper to identify the type of Microsoft Windows client, this setting can help.

- *Desktop Toolbars Settings*

  Disable dragging, dropping, and closing ALL toolbars
  Disable resizing ALL toolbars

User \ Start Menu

The first settings are for Windows 98 only, even though you would think that Windows NT desktops with Internet Explorer 4 and 5 installed also have the Active Directory as well. Well, they don't work with NT, only with Windows 98. The Registry settings for Active Desktop are in different locations for each platform. These settings are toggle settings: when checked, the option is hidden or disabled; when grayed out, they're available. The last two settings in this section are for NT only. See Figure 12-3.

- Hide Network Neighborhood icon

- Hide all items on Desktop

- Remove Favorites menu from Start Menu

- Remove Find menu from Start Menu

- Remove Run menu from Start Menu

- Remove the Active Desktop item from the Settings menu

- Disable drag and drop context menus on the Start Menu

- Remove the Folder Options menu item from the Settings menu

- Remove Documents menu from Start Menu

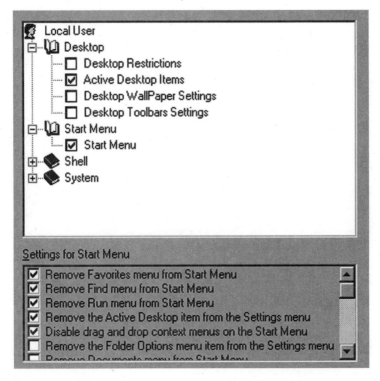

Figure 12-3 *Start menu restrictions for Windows 98.*

- Do not keep history of recently opened documents
- Clear history of recent opened documents
- Disable Logoff
- Disable changes to Taskbar and Start Menu Settings
- Disable context menu for Taskbar
- Hide custom Programs folders

    The next two settings are for Windows NT clients only:

- Hide common program groups in Start Menu
- Run DLG Checkbox for New Memory Space

User \ Shell

More Explorer shell choices for restrictions are found in this section. See Figure 12-4.

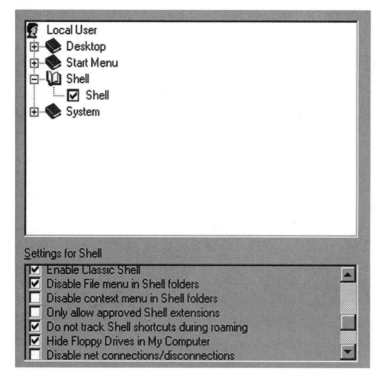

Figure 12-4 *Explorer shell restrictions for Windows 98.*

- *Enable Classic Shell.* Forces the Explorer shell to always be classic—this is not Active Desktop.

- *Disable File menu in Shell folders.* This action stops creation of shortcuts and folders within folders.

- *Disable context menu in Shell folders.* This action stops cut and paste and Send to locations.

- *Only allow approved Shell extensions.* Stops users from using extensions that the Registry doesn't know about. This, in turn, stops the Open with choice that pops up when Windows doesn't recognize the file type.

- *Do not track Shell shortcuts during roaming.* If the user has a roaming user profile, this setting stops the date and time stamping of shortcuts when they are created.

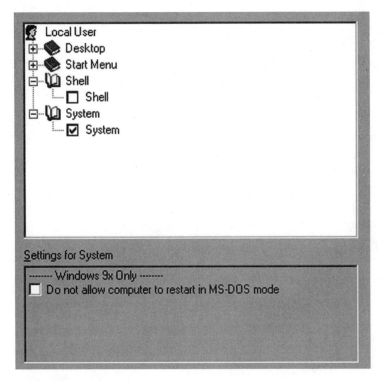

Figure 12-5 *Disabling the MS-DOS Mode prompt.*

- *Hide Floppy Drives in My Computer.* This restriction hides the floppy drives only in Explorer; if users enter a path directly to a floppy drive, they will gain access to that floppy.

- *Disable net connections/ disconnections.* Stops mapping and unmapping of Network drive connections.

User \ System

- *Do not allow computer to restart in MS-DOS mode.* Lots of users assume that MS-DOS Mode is just the MS-DOS prompt— and they're right, sort of. Clicking the MS-DOS shortcut on the Start menu is the 32-bit Command prompt; selecting MS-DOS Mode reboots your computer to the 16-bit prompt for Games. It's worth disabling. See Figure 12-5.

Windows 98 Second Edition: Additions to the WINDOWS.ADM Template

Computer \ Windows 98 Network \ Proxy Server

• Disable Automatic location of proxy server

Computer \ Windows 98 System \ Windows Update

At the top of the Start menu on Windows 98 clients there is a shortcut called Windows Update that points you to a Microsoft Web site that will attempt to fix your PC with updates automatically (see Figure 12-6). Uh-huh. Disable this option for your sanity.

• Disable Windows Update

• *Override Local Web Page.* Points your users to a local Web page when they start Internet Explorer.

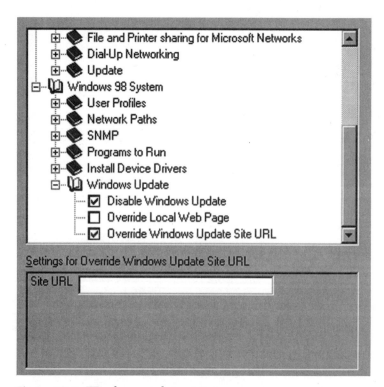

Figure 12-6 *Windows update options.*

- *Override Windows Update Site URL.* Provides another Web location to which you want to point your users.

Settings in the APPSINI.ADM Template

A new addition to Windows 98 Second Edition, this template provides you with a method of installing "user-approved" applications and utilities from a network location. This choice adds a Network Install tab to the Add\Remove Network Install tab found in Control Panel.

Computer \ Network Install \ Use APPS.INI for Network Install

- Enable Add \Remove Programs, Network Install tab. See Figure 12-7.

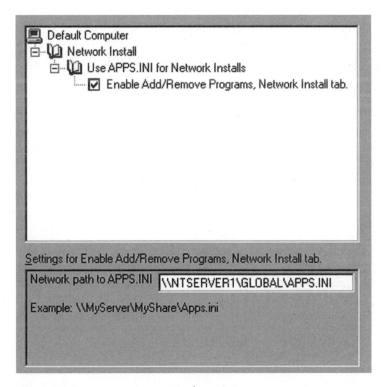

Figure 12-7 Network Install tab options.

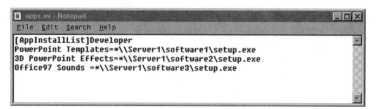

Figure 12-8 APPS.INI created with Notepad.

By using Notepad and creating an INI file called APPS.INI, you can specify the installation script for any software you desire your users to have control of installing or reinstalling. See Figure 12-8.

The Network install tab is now added to the user's Add / Remove options in the Control Panel. See Figure 12-9.

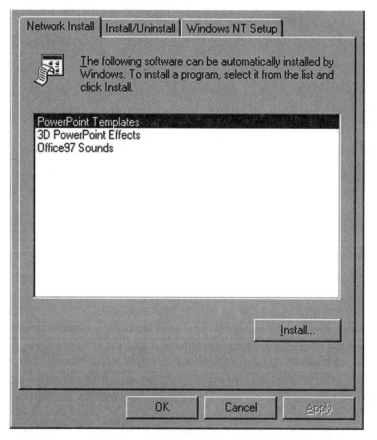

Figure 12-9 Add/ Remove options with NETAPPS.INI enabled.

13

System Policies
for Office 2000

This chapter provides you with the system policy settings for all the modules of Microsoft
Office 2000. With the release of Office 2000,
the choices for software and system policies
increase. The system policy changes are quite
broadminded when compared to Office 97. The
software applications that are now considered
Office 2000 worthy are: Word, PowerPoint,
Excel, Access, and Outlook plus Publisher,
Front Page, and Clip Art Gallery. Most of the
system policy settings you can deploy are for
the user and groups of users. There is a
plethora of toggle on/off settings where you are
prompted to Check to enforce
setting on; uncheck to force setting off.

The first template we will dissect is OFFICE9.ADM, the master template for Office 2000. The majority of settings are for the user, with only a few specifically designed for computer settings. Settings are for both Windows 98 and NT 4.0. Settings that need explanations are provided; otherwise, you can rightly assume that the settings are toggle settings, either deployed or disabled.

The OFFICE9.ADM Template: User Policies

User \ Microsoft Office 2000 \ Tools | Customize | Options

A lot of the choices in this section are toggle settings with the description as follows: Check to enforce setting on; uncheck to force setting off. Details are provided when there are other choices to select.

- Menus; show recently used command first

- Show full menus after a short delay

- Large icons

- List font names in their fonts

- Show ScreenTips on toolbars

- Show shortcut keys in ScreenTips

- *Menu animations.* Choices are random if enabled or none if disabled.

Microsoft Office 2000 \ AutoCorrect (Excel, Powerpoint, and Access)

- Correct TWo INitial CApitals

- Capitalize first letter of sentence

- Capitalize names of days

- Correct accidental use of cAPS LOCK key

- Replace text as you type

See Figure 13-1.

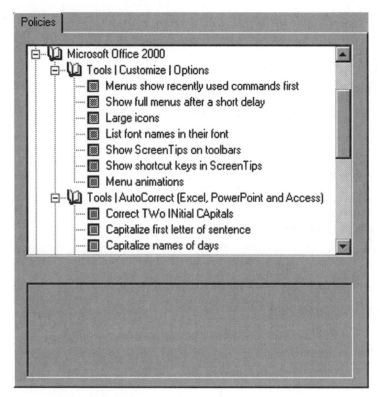

Figure 13-1 *Office 2000 user settings.*

Microsoft Office 2000 | Tools | Options | General | Web Options \ General

- *Rely on CSS for font formatting.* Checked CSS is used for font formatting. You can also apply this CSS setting if you are using Word as an email editor.

Microsoft Office 2000 | Tools | Options | General | Web Options \ Files

- Organize supporting files in a folder
- Use long filenames whenever possible
- Update links on save
- Check if Office is the default editor for Web pages created in Office

- *Download Office Web Components.* Specifies the UNC path for office Web components on your network or Internet location.

Microsoft Office 2000 | Tools | Options | General | Web Options \ Pictures

- Rely on VML for displaying graphics in a browser
- Allow PNG as an output format
- *Target Monitor.* Sets the monitor's resolution and pixels per inch.

Microsoft Office 2000 | Tools | Options | General | Web Options \ Encoding

- *Default or specific encoding.* Specifies the alphabet in which to save the document. The default is the Western alphabet.

Microsoft Office 2000 \ Help | Office on the Web

- *Office on the Web URL.* Specifies the help location for this help menu option.

Microsoft Office 2000 \ Shared Paths

Use these paths to centralize your company's storage of templates, themes, user templates, and Web queries.

- User templates path
- Shared templates path
- Shared themes path
- Web queries path

See Figure 13-2.

Microsoft Office 2000 \ Assistant \ General

- *Choose Assistant file.* Chooses from several assistant choices.
- *Tip timeout.* How long in seconds from 1 to 9999 will the tip bulb stay on?

Microsoft Office 2000 \ Assistant \ Options Tab

- Use Office Assistant

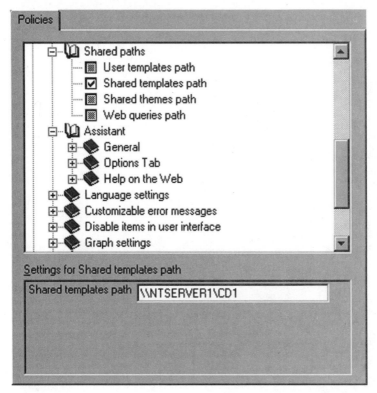

Figure 13-2 *Shared UNC paths for Office 2000 support files.*

- Use F1 key
- Help with wizards
- Display alerts
- Search for both product and programming help
- Move when in the way
- Guess help topics
- Make sounds
- Using features more effectively
- Using the mouse more effectively
- Keyboard shortcuts
- Only show high priority tips
- Show the tip of the day at startup

Microsoft Office 2000 \ Assistant \ Help on the Web

- *Feedback button label.* Replaces the button on the Assistant label with a custom message.

- *Feedback dialog text.* Customizes the Web help button.

- *Feedback URL.* Redirects feedback to a specific URL.

Microsoft Office 2000 \ Language settings

- User Interface

- *Display menus and dialog boxes in.* Chooses the language for Office 97 menu and dialog boxes.

- *Display help in.* Chooses the language for Office 97 help.

See Figure 13-3.

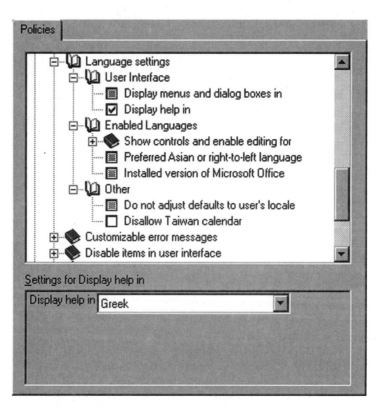

Figure 13-3 *Office 2000 language settings.*

Microsoft Office 2000 \ Language settings \ Enabled languages

These settings show Microsoft's attempts to woo the huge software market worldwide.

- *Show Controls and enable editing for...*Chooses from 94 languages.

- *Preferred Asian or right-to-left language.* Chooses from 9 right-to-left languages.

- *Installed Version of Microsoft Office.* Checks off one of 13 versions of Office 2000.

Microsoft Office 2000 \ Language settings \ Other

- Do not adjust default settings to user's locale

- Disallow Taiwan Calendar

Microsoft Office 2000 \ Customizable error messages

- Base URL

- Default Button text

- List of error messages to customize

- Default save prompt text

Microsoft Office 2000 \ Disable items in User Interface

We can finally customize the message to the end user when features have been disabled.

- *Tool tip for disabled toolbar buttons and menu items.* Chooses the message to let users know a feature has been enabled. See Figure 13-4.

Microsoft Office 2000 \ Graph Settings

- Graph gallery path

- List of error messages to customize

- Custom Answer wizard database path

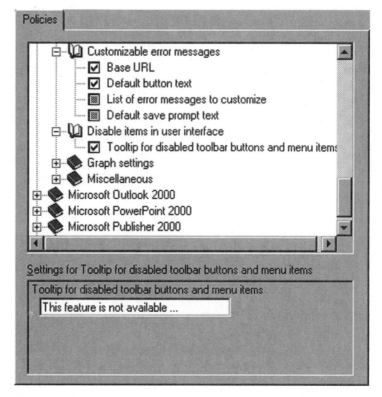

Figure 13-4 *Customize the tool tip for communicating with users.*

Microsoft Office 2000 \ Miscellaneous

- Provide feedback with sound

- Use system font instead of Tahoma

- Do not track document-editing time

- Disable Clipboard Toolbar triggers

- Do not replace tabs with spaces in HTML

- Do not upload Media files

The CLIPGAL5.ADM Template: User Policies for CLIPART 5.0

Clip Gallery 5.0 is now part of Office 2000. We have a choice of one with this template, enabling or disabling clip art from the Internet.

Microsoft Clip Gallery 5.0

- Disable Clips Online access from Clip Gallery

The EXCEL9.ADM Template: User Policies for Excel 2000

Excel is also heavily Web enabled. Settings are provided for the user and groups that have system policies defined.

Microsoft Excel 2000 \ Tools | Options \ View

- Show Formula bar in Normal View
- Show Status bar in Normal View
- Show Formula bar in Full View
- Show Status bar in Full View
- Windows in Taskbar
- Comments

Microsoft Excel 2000 \ Tools | Options \ Edit

- Edit directly in cell
- Allow cell drag and drop
- Alert before overwriting cells
- Move selection after Enter
- Move selection after Enter direction
- Fixed decimal to 2 places
- Cut, copy, and sort objects with cells
- Ask to update automatic links
- Provide feedback with Animation
- Enable AutoComplete for cell values
- Extend list formats and formulas
- Enable automatic percent entry

See Figure 13-5.

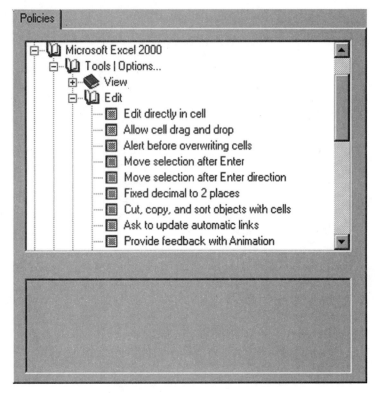

Figure 13-5 *Excel Edit options for Office 2000.*

Microsoft Excel 2000 \ Tools | Options \ General

- R1C1 reference style
- Ignore other applications
- Recently used file list
- Prompt for workbook properties
- Zoom on roll with Intellimouse
- Default Sheets
- Fonts
- Default file location
- Alternate startup location

Microsoft Excel 2000 \ Web Options...General

- Save any additional data necessary to maintain formulas
- Load pictures from Web pages not created in Excel

Microsoft Excel 2000 \Transition

- *Save Excel files as.* Chooses from all previous versions of Excel or as a Web page (HTML format).
- *Microsoft Excel menu or Help key.* Chooses the key to start help; also chooses Excel or Lotus help.
- Transition navigation keys

Microsoft Excel 2000 \Chart

- Show names
- Show values

Microsoft Excel 2000 \Right-to-left

- *Default direction.* Left to right or right to left movement.
- *Cursor movement.* Logical or visual movement.
- Show control characters

Microsoft Excel 2000 \Tools | Macro \ Record New Macro...

- Store macro in Personal Macro Workbook by default
- Customizable error messages

Microsoft Excel 2000 \ Security

- *Security Level.* High, medium, or low security levels linked to Internet Explorer security levels.
- Trust all installed add-ins and templates

Microsoft Excel 2000 \ Customizable error messages

- List of error messages to customize

Microsoft Excel 2000 \ Disable items in user interface \ Predefined

This section allows an extra level of file and Web security at the application level. Word and PowerPoint have the same basic list of menu items that can be disabled. See Figure 13-6.

● Disable command bar buttons and menu items

⇒ Files | Open.. | Tools | Find...
⇒ File | Save as Web Page
⇒ File | Web Page Preview
⇒ File | Send To | Mail Recipient
⇒ Insert | Hyperlink...
⇒ Tools | Protection
⇒ Tools | Protection | Protect Sheet
⇒ Tools | Protection | Protect Workbook
⇒ Tools | Protection | Protect and Share Workbook

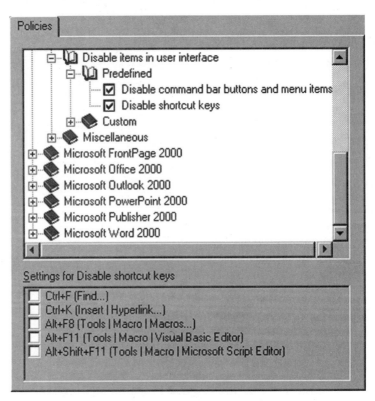

Figure 13-6 *Disable command bar items and menu items.*

⇒ Tools | Online Collaboration

⇒ Tools | Macro |

⇒ Tools | Macro | Macros...

⇒ Tools | Macro | Record New Macro

⇒ Tools | Macro | Security

⇒ Tools | Macro | Visual Basic Editor

⇒ Tools | Macro | Microsoft Script Editor

⇒ Tools | Add-Ins

⇒ Tools | Customize

⇒ Tools | Options

⇒ Help | Office on the Web

⇒ Help | Detect and Repair

⇒ Web | Refresh Current Page

⇒ Web | Start Page

⇒ Web | Search the Web

⇒ Web | Favorites

⇒ Web | Go

⇒ Web | Address

- Disable shortcut keys

⇒ Ctrl + F (Find...)

⇒ Ctrl + K (Insert | Hyperlink...)

⇒ Alt + F8 (Tools | Macro | Macros...)

⇒ Alt + F11 (Tools | Macro | Visual Basic Editor)

⇒ Alt + Shift + F11 (Tools | Macro | Microsoft Script Editor)

Microsoft Excel 2000 \ Custom

We can also disable any command bar, menu item, or shortcut key by entering its defined ID. These are defined in the Office 2000 Resource Kit.

- Disable command bar buttons and menu items

- Disable shortcut keys

Microsoft Excel 2000 \ Miscellaneous

- Chart Gallery Path

- Chart Answer Wizard database path

- *Enable four-digit year display.* Allows a four-digit display of the date for any Y2K needs.

The FRONTPG4.ADM Template: User Policies for Front Page 2000

In this era of Internet awareness, Microsoft assumes that everyone who purchases this product has an active Internet connection. Front Page 2000 is now either an added feature/bonus or unneeded software, depending on your ties to the Net.

Microsoft Front Page 2000 \ Predefined

- Disable items in user interface
    - ⇒ File | Open
    - ⇒ View | Toolbars | Customize
    - ⇒ Format | Style
    - ⇒ Format | Style Sheet Links...
    - ⇒ Format | Position
    - ⇒ Insert | Advanced | Active X Control
    - ⇒ Insert | Component | Office Spreadsheet
    - ⇒ Insert | Component | Office Pivot Table
    - ⇒ Insert | Component | Office Chart
    - ⇒ Insert | Advanced | Java Applet...
    - ⇒ Insert | Component | Banner Ad Manager...
    - ⇒ Insert | Component | Hover Button...
    - ⇒ Insert | Component | Hit Counter...
    - ⇒ Insert | Component | Search Form...
    - ⇒ Insert | Component | Confirmation Field...
    - ⇒ Insert | Component | Marquee...
    - ⇒ Insert | Picture | Video...
    - ⇒ Insert | Advanced | Design-Time Control
    - ⇒ Insert | Advanced | PlugIn
    - ⇒ Insert | Advanced | Show Design-Time Controls
    - ⇒ Insert | Database | Results...
    - ⇒ Insert | Database | Column Value
    - ⇒ Format | Dynamic HTML Effects
    - ⇒ Format | Page Transition
    - ⇒ Format | Theme
    - ⇒ Format | Shared Borders
    - ⇒ Tools | Security | Permissions
    - ⇒ Tools | Security | Change Password

⇒ Tools | Add-Ins...

⇒ Tools | Customize

⇒ Tools | Web Settings...

⇒ Tools | Macros | Macros...

⇒ Tools | Macros | Visual Basic Editor

⇒ Tools | Macros | Microsoft Script Editor

⇒ Tools | Options

⇒ Help | Office on the Web

⇒ Help | Detect and Repair

Microsoft Front Page 2000 \ Custom

- *Disable command bar buttons and menu items.* We can also disable any command bar, menu item, or shortcut key by entering its defined ID. These are defined in the Office 2000 Resource Kit, available at *www.microsoft.com/ork.*

The OUTLK9.ADM Template: Computer and User Options for Outlook 2000

This template provides settings to preset for Outlook 2000. A lot of these settings will be of interest if your company is deploying Outlook 2000 across your organization as the front end for email and document management. Both computer and user/group settings are provided. If you are using roaming user profiles, remember that the system policy gets applied to the roaming user profile as well.

Users that share a computer may also be affected by the computer settings if your system policy contains only a `Default Computer` icon and not defined computer icons. See Figure 13-7.

Computer \ Microsoft Outlook 2000

- Outlook Mail Configuration

- Using Schedule+ as Outlook Calendar

- Prevent users from changing primary calendar application

- *S/MIME password settings.* The settings for S/MIME passwords are where you can define the default and maximum password time in minutes.

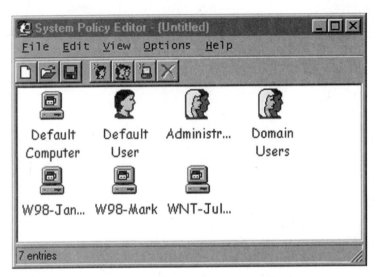

Figure 13-7 *Computer profiles in a system policy.*

User \ Microsoft Outlook 2000 \ Tools | Options \ Preferences \ E-mail Options

- *Message Handling.* Defines the action of Office 2000 after a message is deleted or moved. Choices are: open the previous or next item in the list or return to the Inbox. Options are also present for the following:

  1. Close the original message when replied to or forwarded
  2. Save copies of messages in the Sent Items folder
  3. Display a notification message when new mail arrives

User \ Microsoft Outlook 2000 \ Tools | Options \ Preferences \ E-mail Options \ Advanced E-mail options

- *Save Messages.* Saves all unsent items in: Drafts, Inbox, Outbox, or Sent Items. Also set the seconds until Autosave backs up unsent email messages.

- *More save messages.* In all folders other than the Inbox you can save replies and forwarded messages with original message.

- *When new items arrive.* Plays a defined sound or changes the mouse cursor briefly.

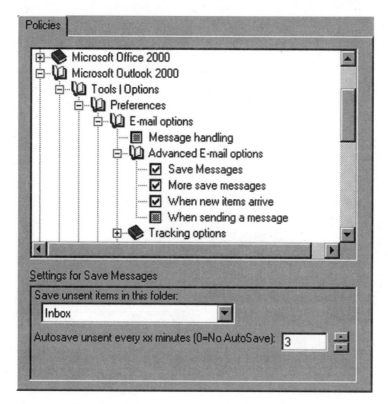

Figure 13-8 *Advanced email options for Outlook 2000.*

- *When sending a message.* Sets the importance of the message (Low, Normal, or High) and the sensitivity (Confidential, Normal, Personal, or Private). Choices are also available for:

  1. Allowing commas as address separator
  2. Automatic name checking before sending
  3. Deleting meeting request from Inbox when responding to email

See Figure 13-8.

User \ Microsoft Outlook 2000 \ Tools | Options \ Preferences \ E-mail Options \ Tracking Options \ Options

- Process requests and response on arrival
- Process receipts on arrival

- After processing, move receipts

- Delete blank voting and meeting response after processing

- Request a read receipt for all messages a user sends

- Request delivery rcpt for all msg. a user sends (Exchange only)

- When Outlook is asked to respond to a read receipt request:
  ⇒ Always send a response
  ⇒ Ask before sending a response
  ⇒ Never send a response

- *On replies and forwards.* When replying to or when forwarding a message, the choices for the preceding options are:

  1. Attach original message
  2. Do not include original message
  3. Prefix each line of the original message
  4. Include original message text
  5. Include and indent original message text

- *Prefix each line with.* Chooses the character to prefix each line of your email when the default is >.

- *Allow user's comments to be marked.* Marks user's comments with a phrase or heading.

Microsoft Outlook 2000 Tools | Options \ Preferences \ Calendar Options

These preferences set the options for groups of users on their electronic calendar. Options are setting calendar items lengths and how long in minutes reminders should be, as well as setting the workweek length and starting day of the workweek, the start of the year, and the working hours. Finally choose the numbering of the calendar weeks and whether to use iCalendar to send meeting requests.

- Reminders on Calendar items

- Calendar item defaults

- Work week

- First day of the week

- Working hours

- Calendar week numbers

- Meeting Requests using iCalendar

- Free / Busy Options

  1. Options Months of Free / Busy information published
  2. Free / Busy updated on the server every xxx seconds
  3. Internet Free / Busy Options
  4. Publish or search at this URL: free promotional materials for your company that you would attach to email

User \ Microsoft Outlook 2000 \ Tools | Options \ Preferences \ E-mail Options \ Task Options

- *Color options.* Sets the default colors for overdue and complete outlook 2000 tasks.

- *Task reminder options.* Sets a default reminder time for when tasks are due.

User \ Microsoft Outlook 2000 \ Tools | Options \ Preferences \ E-mail Options \ Contact Options

- Select the default setting for how to file new contacts Default Full Name [First (Middle) Last] and File As (Last, First) order

User \ Microsoft Outlook 2000 \ Tools | Options \ Preferences \ E-mail Options \ Journal Options

These options set the journaling to Outlook 2000 or all of Microsoft 2000 and define the applets to be journaled.

- Level of journaling

- Disable journaling of these Outlook items

- Automatically journal these items

- Automatically journal files from these applications

- Journal entry options

User \ Microsoft Outlook 2000 \ Tools | Options \ Preferences \ E-mail Options \ Notes Options

- *Notes appearance.* Sets the size and color of notes.

User \ Microsoft Outlook 2000 \ Tools | Options \ Mail Services (Corporate or Workgroup Configuration)

- *Synchronize*. Defines when to synchronize outlook folders when you are both online and offline. If you use remote access (RAS) or other means to check your email, this may be an important bandwidth option.

- *Profile prompt*. Be prompted for the user profile to use.

User \ Microsoft Outlook 2000 \ Tools | Options \ Mail Delivery (Internet Only Configuration)

- *Mail account options*. Forces sending of messages immediately and when to check for new messages in minutes.

- *Dial-up options* (see Figure 13-9)

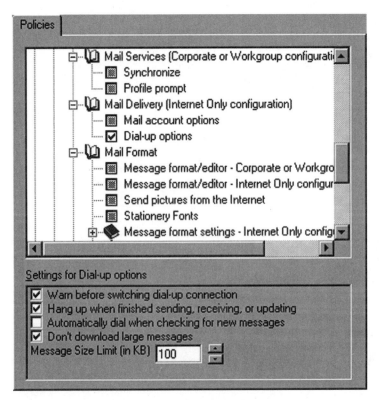

Figure 13-9 *Dial-up options for Outlook 2000.*

1. Warn before switching dial-up connection
2. Hang up when finished sending, receiving, or updating
3. Automatically dial when checking for new messages
4. Don't download large messages
5. Set message size limit in KB

User \ Microsoft Outlook 2000 \ Tools | Options \ Mail Format

Choose from plain text, outlook rich text, or HTML using Outlook or Microsoft Word for the message format and editor.

- Message format / editor—Corporate or Workgroup

- Message format / editor—Internet Only Configuration

- *Send pictures from the Internet.* When using HTML format, includes pictures.

- *Stationary Fonts.* Specifies the type of font used as stationary; the user's font or the font specified in stationary options.

User \ Microsoft Outlook 2000 \ Tools | Options \ Spelling / General

1. Always suggest replacements for misspelled words

2. Always check spelling before sending

3. Ignore words in UPPERCASE

4. Ignore words with numbers

5. Ignore original message text in reply or forward

User \ Microsoft Outlook 2000 \ Tools | Options \ Security

- *Required Certificate Authority.* Deploys X.59 issue DN specs for certificate levels.

- *Minimum encryption settings.* Sets the minimum key size in bits.

- *S/MIME interoperability with external clients.* Handles security externally or internally.

- *Outlook Rich Text in S/MIME messages.* Specifies to read outlook rich text in S/MIME messages.

User \ Microsoft Outlook 2000 \ Tools | Options \ Other

- Empty Deleted Items Folder
- AutoArchive
    1. Turn on AutoArchive
    2. Number of days between AutoArchiving
    3. Prompt before AutoArchiving
    4. Delete expired items when AutoArchiving email
- Preview Pane
    1. Mark message as read
    2. Mark item as read when selection changes
    3. Single key reading using spacebar

User \ Microsoft Outlook 2000 \ Tools | Options \ Advanced

- *General.* When selecting text automatically selects entire word.
- *More Options.* Warns before permanently deleting items.
- *Appearance options—Notes.* When viewing Notes, shows the time and date.
- *Appearance options—Tasks.* Tasks working hours per day and per week, in minutes.

User \ Microsoft Outlook 2000 \ Tools | Options \ Reminder Options

- Reminders
    1. Display the reminder
    2. Play reminder sound
- More reminders
    `Path` and `.wav` file to play for reminder
- Advanced Tasks
    1. Set reminders on tasks with due dates
    2. Keep updated copies of assigned tasks on user's task list
    3. Send status reports when assigned tasks are completed

User \ Microsoft Outlook 2000 \ Tools | Options \ Right-to-left

- Layout Options

1. Set layout direction
2. Set global text direction
3. Set primary language
4. Use secondary calendar
5. Set secondary calendar language

User \ Microsoft Outlook 2000 \ Customizable error messages

- List of error messages to customize

User \ Microsoft Outlook 2000 \ Disable items in user interface

- Predefined
  ⇒ Disable command bar buttons and menu items
  ⇒ All folders and items: Help | Detect and Repair
  ⇒ All folders: Favorite menu
  ⇒ All folders: Go menu
  ⇒ All folders: File | Open in default browser
  ⇒ All folders: File | New | Outlook Bar shortcut to Web pages
  ⇒ All folders: Go | Internet Call
  ⇒ Inbox: Tools | Services
  ⇒ Mail item: View | Bcc Field
  ⇒ Mail item: View | From Field
  ⇒ Contact item: Actions | Display Map of Address
  ⇒ Web toolbar: Refresh Current Page
  ⇒ Web toolbar: Start Page
  ⇒ Web toolbar: Search the Web
  ⇒ Web toolbar: Addresses

- *Disable shortcut keys.* There is but one option: CTRL-ENTER (Send in a Mail item).

User \ Microsoft Outlook 2000 \ Disable items in user interface \ Custom

We can also disable any command bar, menu item, or shortcut key by entering its defined ID. These are defined in the Office 2000 Resource Kit. See Figure 13-10.

- Disable command bar buttons and menu items

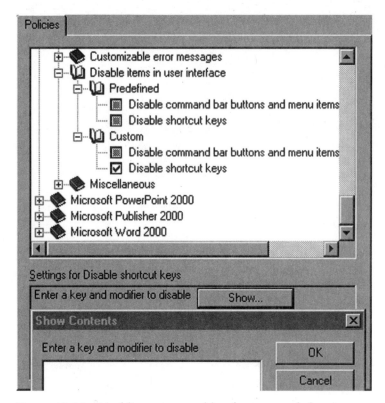

Figure 13-10 *Disabling command bar buttons and shortcut keys.*

- Disable shortcut keys

User \ Microsoft Outlook 2000 \ Miscellaneous

- *Resource scheduling.* Allows a user's hours to be scheduled in blocks.

- *NetMeeting.* Disables or enables NetMeeting.

- *Categories.* Defines your user's master category list of folders in Outlook.

- Date format for importing cc:Mail (DB8 only)

- *Junk e-mail filtering.* Turns on Junk email filters.

- *Auto-repair of MAPI32.DLL.* Specifies that when Outlook starts up that the correct version of MAPI32.DLL is available and loaded.

- *Net Folders.* Net folder is available or not available.

User \ Microsoft Outlook 2000 \ Miscellaneous \ Exchange settings

- *Exchange view information.* Defines the publish rights of exchange view information in either public and/or personal folders.

- *Folder size display.* Displays the size of the entire folder in properties.

- *OST Creation.* Defines or disables OST.

- *Personal distribution lists (Exchange only).* Forces validation of all personal distribution lists when using exchange.

User \ Microsoft Outlook 2000 \ Miscellaneous \ Outlook Today settings

- *Outlook Today availability.* Allows or restricts Outlook Today.

- *URL for custom Outlook Today.* Defines the URL for Outlook Today.

- *Folders in the Messages section of Outlook Today.* Defines the folders that will appear in the messages section of Outlook Today. A total of 10 folders can be defined.

User \ Microsoft Outlook 2000 \ Miscellaneous \ Folder Home Pages for Outlook \ Special folders

- Disable Folder Home Pages
- Folder Home Page Security
- Inbox Folder Home Page
- Calendar Folder Home
- Contacts Folder Home Page
- Deleted Items Folder Home Page
- Drafts Folder Home Page
- Journal Folder Home Page
- Notes Folder Home Page
- Outbox Folder Home Page

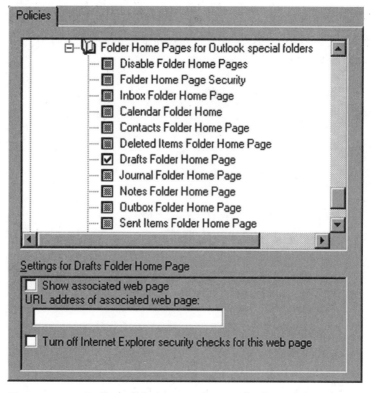

Figure 13-11 *Define global URLs for Outlook 2000 home pages.*

- Sent Items Folder Home Page
- Tasks Folder Home Page

See Figure 13-11.

The WMP. ADM Template: Computer and User Policies for Media Player

The Windows Media Player is now part of Office 2000. This isn't a surprise, since streaming video content and Internet radio are becoming a big part of the delivery of video services.

Windows Media Player \ Computer \ Favorites

- *Windows Media Player Favorites*. Does not install the Windows Media Player Favorites in Media.

- *Favorites \ Radio toolbar settings.* Radio toolbar settings provide three choices:

  1. Disable Radio toolbar (may require a reboot)
  2. Disable menu for finding new Radio Stations
  3. URL for finding new Radio Stations

User \ Customizations

- Customize the Windows Media Player

  1. Prevent automatic codec download
  2. Title bar of the Windows Media Player
  3. Button name on Windows Media Player navigation bar
  4. URL for button on Windows Media Player navigation bar

- Customize Network Settings

  ⇒ Default number of milliseconds to buffer data:
  ⇒ Enable HTTP protocol
  ⇒ Enable Multicast
  ⇒ Enable TCP protocol
  ⇒ Enable UDP protocol
  ⇒ Use Proxy
  ⇒ Use custom proxy settings (do not detect)

        Proxy Hostname:
        Proxy host port:

The PUB9.ADM Template: User Policies for Publisher

Microsoft Publisher has been granted membership in Office 2000 so it should come as no surprise that it has its system policy settings for users and groups.

User \ Microsoft Publisher 2000 \ Default
File Locations

- *Publication location.* Defines the URL for Microsoft Publisher publication location.

- *Picture location.* Defines the URL for Microsoft Publisher picture location.

**User \ Microsoft Publisher 2000 \ Tools | Options...
\ General**

- Preview fonts in font list

- Use Catalog at startup

- Show rectangle for text in Web graphic region

**User \ Microsoft Publisher 2000 \ Tools | Options...
\ Edit**

- Drag-and-drop text editing

- When selecting, automatically select entire word

- When formatting, automatically format entire word

- Automatically hyphenate in new text frames

- Use single-click object creation

**User \ Microsoft Publisher 2000 \ Tools | Options...
\ User Assistance**

- Preview Web site with Preview Troubleshooter

- Use Quick Publication wizard for blank publications

- Step through wizard questions

- Update personal information when saving

- Show tippages

- Remind to save publication

- Minutes between save reminders

- Use helpful mouse pointers

See Figure 13-12.

**User \ Microsoft Publisher 2000 \ Tools | Options...
\ Print**

- Automatically display Print Troubleshooter

**User \ Microsoft Publisher 2000 \ Tools | Options...
\ Spelling**

- Check spelling as you type

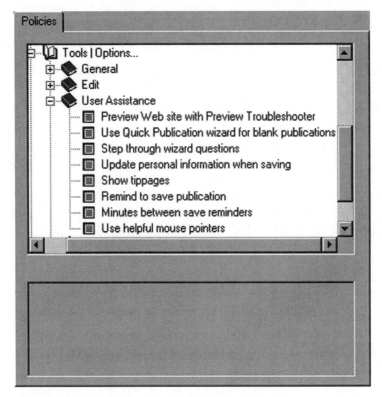

Figure 13-12 *Publisher settings for User Assistance.*

- Ignore words in UPPERCASE

- Show repeated words

The PPOINT9.ADM **Template for PowerPoint 2000**

Like Excel 2000, PowerPoint is heavily oriented toward the Internet. Options for users and groups are provided for system policy control.

User \ Microsoft PowerPoint 2000 \ Tools | Options...\ View

- Startup dialog

- New slide dialog

- Status bar

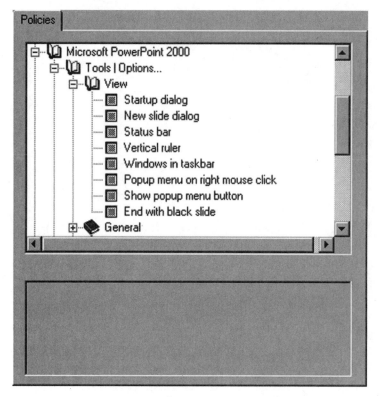

Figure 13-13 *View settings for PowerPoint 2000.*

- Vertical ruler
- Windows in taskbar
- Popup menu on right mouse click
- Show popup menu button
- End with black slide

See Figure 13-13.

User \ Microsoft PowerPoint 2000 \ Tools | Options...\ General

- *Recently used file list*. Enables the recently used file list and specifies the size.
- *Link Sounds File Size*. Links sounds with file size greater than (KB): default 100.

User \ Microsoft PowerPoint 2000 \ Tools | Options...\ Web Options...

- *Slide navigation.* Adds slide navigation controls and color choices of white text on black or black text on white.
- Show slide animation while browsing
- Resize graphics to fit browser window

User \ Microsoft PowerPoint 2000 \ Tools | Options...\ Edit

- Replace straight quotes with smart quotes
- Drag-and-drop text editing
- When selecting, automatically select entire word
- Use smart cut and paste
- New charts take on PowerPoint font
- Auto-fit text to text placeholder
- AutoFormat as you type
- Maximum number of undos

User \ Microsoft PowerPoint 2000 \ Tools | Options...\ Print

- Background printing
- Print TrueType fonts as graphics
- Print inserted objects at printer resolution

User \ Microsoft PowerPoint 2000 \ Tools | Options...\ Save

- Allow fast saves
- Prompt for file properties
- Save AutoRecover info
- Enable save AutoRecover info
- AutoRecover save frequency (minutes)
- Convert charts when saving as previous version

- Save PowerPoint files as:

  ⇒ PowerPoint Presentation (*.ppt)

  ⇒ Web Page (*.htm; *.html)

  ⇒ PowerPoint 95 (*.ppt)

  ⇒ PowerPoint 97-2000 & 95 (*.ppt)

  ⇒ PowerPoint 4.0 (*.ppt)

  ⇒ PowerPoint 4.0 FE (*.ppt)

- *Default file location.* Specifies the default local or network location to save slideshows.

User \ Microsoft PowerPoint 2000 \ Tools | Options...\ Spelling and Style

- Check spelling as you type

- Always suggest corrections

- Ignore words in UPPERCASE

- Ignore words with numbers

- Check style

User \ Microsoft PowerPoint 2000 \ Tools | Options...\ Spelling and Style \ Style Options...\ Case and End Punctuation

- *Check slide title case.* Title Case or UPPERCASE.

- *Check body text case.* Sentence case or lower case.

- *Check slide title punctuation.* Other than a period.

- *Check body punctuation.* Paragraphs have punctuation, Paragraphs do not have punctuation.

- Slide title end punctuation other than period

- Body text end punctuation other than period

See Figure 13-14.

User \ Microsoft PowerPoint 2000 \ Tools | Options...\ Visual Clarity

- *Check number of fonts.* Number of fonts should not exceed 3.

- *Check title text size.* Title text should be at least 36.

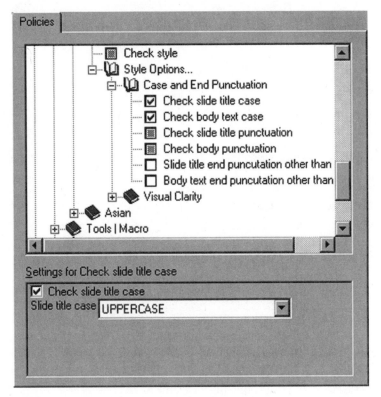

Figure 13-14 *Defining case and ending punctuation.*

- *Check body text size*. Body text should be at least 20.

- *Check number of bullets*. Number of bullets should not exceed 6.

- *Check number of lines per title*. Number of lines per title should not exceed 2.

- *Check number of lines per bullet*. Number of lines per bullet should not exceed 2.

User \ Microsoft PowerPoint 2000 \ Tools | Options...\ Asian

- True inline conversion for Japanese IME

- Convert font-associated text

  1028   Chinese (Traditional)

  1042   Korean

2052   Chinese (Simplified)

• Allow font subnetting

User \ Microsoft PowerPoint 2000 \ Tools | Options...\ Tools | Macro \ Security

• Security Level
  Medium or Low

• Trust all installed add-ins and templates

Slide Show | Online Broadcast | Set Up and Schedule...\ Broadcast Settings

• Send audio

• Send video

• Camera/microphone is connected to another computer

• *Recording*. Records the broadcast and saves it in the following defined location.

User \ Microsoft PowerPoint 2000 \ Slide Show | Online Broadcast ... Other Broadcast Settings
  Use this section to define the URLs for global broadcast settings.

• Chat server URL

• Chat file CAB

• Override default chat client

• Media Player ActiveX download

• Transfer Control Active X download

• Media Player non ActiveX download

• Event URL

• Mail to

• Help page URL

• Video / audio test page URL

User \ Microsoft PowerPoint 2000 \ Slide Show | Online Broadcast ...Server Options

• Shared file location

- Local NetShow server on this LAN
- The server will access presentation files from

**User \ Microsoft PowerPoint 2000 \ Slide Show |
Online Broadcast ...Server Options \ Other
NetShow Settings**

- ConnectTimeout
- FECRedundancyRatio
- Netshow Server high bandwith
- Netshow Server low bandwith
- Multicast TTL
- Unicast rollover
- Location of audio ASD file
- Location of video ASD file
- Contact address
- Contact phone number
- Copyright
- Multicast address
- Read/write admin URL
- Read only admin URL
- Drop dead time

**User \ Microsoft PowerPoint 2000 \
...Customizable error messages**

- List of error messages to customize

**User \ Microsoft PowerPoint 2000 \ ...Disable
items in user interface \ Predefined**

⇒ File | Open... | Tools | Find...

⇒ File | Save as Web Page...

⇒ File | Web Page Preview

⇒ File | Send To | Mail Recipient

⇒ Insert | Hyperlink...

⇒ Tools | Online Collaboration

⇒ Tools | Macro

⇒ Tools | Macro | Macros...

⇒ Tools | Macro | Record New Macro...

⇒ Tools | Macro | Security...

⇒ Tools | Macro | Visual Basic Editor

⇒ Tools | Macro | Microsoft Script Editor

⇒ Tools | Add-Ins...

⇒ Tools | Customize...

⇒ Help | Office on the Web

⇒ Help | Detect and Repair...

⇒ Web | Refresh Current Page

⇒ Web | Start Page

⇒ Web | Search the Web

⇒ Web | Favorites

⇒ Web | Go

⇒ Web | Address

User \ Microsoft PowerPoint 2000 \ ...Custom

• Disable command bar buttons and menu items

• Disable shortcut keys

User \ Microsoft PowerPoint 2000 \ ...Miscellaneous

• Custom Answer Wizard database path

The WORD9.ADM Template for Word 2000

Microsoft Word 2000 is Internet ready, as Microsoft assumes that you will do your Internet work with this applet.

User \ Microsoft Word 2000 \ Tools | Options...\ View \ Show

- Highlight
- Bookmarks
- Status bar
- ScreenTips
- Animated tips
- Horizontal scroll bar
- Vertical scroll bar
- Picture placeholders
- Field codes
- Field shading
- *Left scroll bar*. This policy also sets right ruler (print view only).

User \ Microsoft Word 2000 \ Tools | Options...\ View \ Formatting marks

- Tab characters
- Spaces
- Paragraph marks
- Optional hyphens
- Hidden text
- Optional hyphens
- Optional breaks
- All

See Figure 13-15.

User \ Microsoft Word 2000 \ Tools | Options...\ View \ Print and Web Layout options

- Drawings
- Object anchors

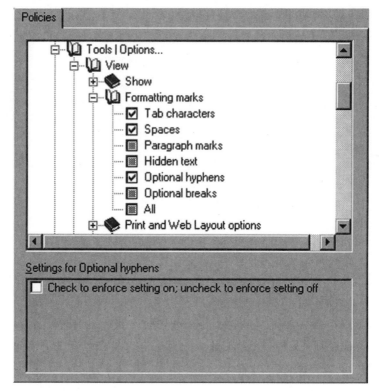

Figure 13-15 *Formatting marks for Word 2000.*

- Text boundaries
- Vertical ruler (print view only)

User \ Microsoft Word 2000 \ Tools | Options...\ View \ Outline and Normal options

- Wrap to window
- Draft font
- *Style area width.* Sets the style options from 0 inches through 0.25, 0.5, 0.75, 1, 1.25, 1.5, 1.75, 2, 2.25, and 2.5.

User \ Microsoft Word 2000 \ Tools | Options...\ General

- Blue background, white text
- Provide feedback with animation

- Confirm conversion at Open

- Update automatic links at Open

- Mail as attachment

- Recently used file list

- Help for WordPerfect users

- Navigation keys for WordPerfect users

- Asian fonts also apply to Latin text

- Contain Asian text (Open normally, Autodetect Asian text)

- Measurement units

- Show pixels for HTML features

- Use character units

- English Word 6.0/95 documents

User \ Microsoft Word 2000 \ Tools | Options...\ Web Options... \ General

- *Disable features not supported by browser.* Disables any features of Internet Explorer 5.0, Internet Explorer 4.0, and Navigator 4.0.

User \ Microsoft Word 2000 \ Tools | Options...\ Web Options \ Files

- Check if Word is the default editor for all other Web pages

User \ Microsoft Word 2000 \ Tools | Options...\ Edit

- Typing replaces selection

- Drag-and-drop text editing

- When selecting, automatically select entire word

- Picture editor (Microsoft Word, Microsoft Photo Editor 3.0, Microsoft Draw 98 Drawing)

- Use the INS key for paste

- Tabs and backspace set left indent

- Use smart cut and paste

- Allow accented uppercase in French
- Enable click and type
- IME Control Active
- IME TrueInLine

User \ Microsoft Word 2000 \ Tools | Options...\ Print \ Printing options

- Draft output
- Update fields
- Update links
- Allow A4/Letter paper resizing
- Background printing
- Reverse print order

User \ Microsoft Word 2000 \ Tools | Options...\ Print \ Include with document

- Document properties
- Field codes
- Comments
- Hidden text
- Drawing objects

User \ Microsoft Word 2000 \ Tools | Options...\ Print \ Options for Duplex Printing

- Front of sheet
- Back of the sheet

User \ Microsoft Word 2000 \ Tools | Options...\ \ Save

- Always create backup copy
- Allow fast saves
- Prompt for document properties
- Prompt to save Normal template

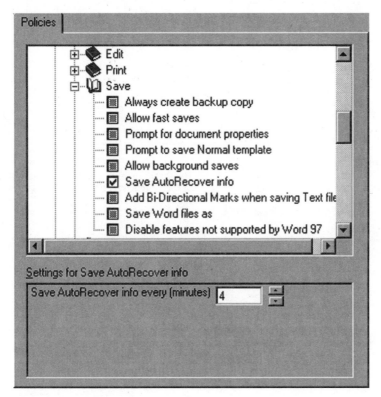

Figure 13-16 *Word 2000 save options.*

- Allow background saves
- Save AutoRecover info
- Add Bi-Directional Marks when saving Text files
- Save Word files as
- Disable features not supported by Word 97

See Figure 13-16.

User \ Microsoft Word 2000 \ Tools | Options...\ Spelling & Grammar

- Check spelling as you type
- Always suggest corrections
- Suggest from main dictionary only

- Ignore words in UPPERCASE
- Ignore words with numbers
- Ignore Internet and file addresses
- Use German post reform rules
- Combine aux. verb/adj.
- Use auto-change list
- Process compound nouns
- Hebrew (Full, Partial, Mixed, Mixed authorized)
- Arabic modes (None, Strict initial alef hamza, Strict final yaa, Both strict)
- Check grammar as you type
- Check grammar with spelling
- Show readability statistics
- Writing style (Casual, Standard, Formal, Technical, Custom)

User \ Microsoft Word 2000 \ Tools | Options... \ File Locations

- Documents
- Clipart pictures
- AutoRecover files
- Tools
- Startup

User \ Microsoft Word 2000 \ Tools | Options...\ Hangul Hanja Conversion

- Fast conversion
- Display recently used items
- Ignore Hangul ending
- Multiple words conversion (Hangul to Hanja or Hanja to Hangul)

User \ Microsoft Word 2000 \ Tools | Options...\ Right-to-left

- Document view (Right-to-left or Left-to-right)
- Add control characters in Cut and Copy
- Add double quote for Hebrew alphabet numbering
- Numeral
- Movement
- Visual selection
- WBlock Block
- Control characters
- Diacritics
- Different color for diacritics
- Month names

User \ Microsoft Word 2000 \ Tools | AutoCorrect...

- Correct TWo INitial CApitals
- Capitalize first letter of sentence
- Capitalize names of days
- Correct accidental use of cAPS LOCK key
- Replace text as you type

See Figure 13-17.

User \ Microsoft Word 2000 \ Tools | Options...\ Print \ AutoFormat as you type \ Apply as you type

- Headings
- Borders
- Tables
- Dates
- Automatic bulleted lists
- Automatic numbered lists

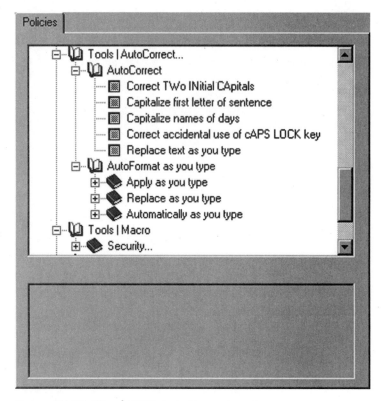

Figure 13-17 *Word 2000 AutoCorrect options.*

- First line indent
- Closings

User \ Microsoft Word 2000 \ Tools | AutoCorrect \ Replace as you type

- Straight quotes with smart quotes
- Ordinals (1st) with superscript
- Fractions (1/2) with fraction character
- Symbol characters (—) with symbols
- *Bold* and _italic_ with real formatting
- Internet and network paths with hyperlinks
- Match parentheses

- Auto space
- Dash-like characters

User \ Microsoft Word 2000 \ Tools | AutoCorrect \ Automatically as you type

- Format beginning of list item like the one before it
- Define styles based on your formatting

User \ Microsoft 2000 \ Tools | Macro \ Security

- Security Level (High, Medium, Low)
- Trust all installed add-ins and templates

User \ Microsoft 2000 \ Tools | Language \ Set Language...

- Detect language automatically

User \ Microsoft 2000 \ Tools | Language \Chinese Translation...

- Translation direction (Traditional Chinese to Simplified Chinese or Simplified Chinese to Traditional Chinese)
- Use Taiwan, Hong Kong, and Macao character variants
- Translate common terms

User \ Microsoft 2000 \ Tools | Customizable error messages

- *List of error messages to customize.* Enters error ID for Value Name and custom button text for Value.

User \ Microsoft 2000 \ Disable items in user interface \ Predefined

- Disable command bar items and menu items
  ⇒ File | Open... | Tools | Find...
  ⇒ File | Save as Web Page...
  ⇒ File | Web Page Preview
  ⇒ File | Send To | Mail Recipient

⇒ Insert | Hyperlink...

⇒ Tools | Protect Document...

⇒ Tools | Online Collaboration

⇒ Tools | Macro

⇒ Tools | Macro | Macros...

⇒ Tools | Macro | Record New Macro...

⇒ Tools | Macro | Security...

⇒ Tools | Macro | Visual Basic Editor

⇒ Tools | Macro | Microsoft Script Editor

⇒ Tools | Templates and Add-Ins...

⇒ Tools | Customize...

⇒ Help | Office on the Web

⇒ Help | Detect and Repair...

⇒ Web | Refresh Current Page

⇒ Web | Start Page

⇒ Web | Search the Web

⇒ Web | Favorites

⇒ Web | Go

⇒ Web | Address

- Disable shortcut keys

⇒ Ctrl+F (Find)

⇒ Ctrl+K (Insert | Hyperlink...)

⇒ Alt+F8 (Tools | Macro | Macros...)

⇒ Alt+F11 (Tools | Macro Visual Basic Editor)

⇒ Alt+Shift+F11 (Tools | Macro | Microsoft Script Editor)

User \ Microsoft 2000 \ Disable items in user interface \ Custom

- *Disable command bar buttons and menu items*
- *Disable shortcut keys.* Enters a command bar ID to disable command bar buttons, menu items, and/or shortcut keys. The Resource Kit for Office 2000 has these details.

User \ Microsoft 2000 \ Miscellaneous

- Volume Preferences

1. Use Drive letter or UNC as entered

2. Convert Drive letter to UNC
3. Convert UNC to Drive letter

- Custom Answer Wizard database path

- Alternate revision bar position in printed document

- Disable MRU list in font dropdown

System Policies for Terminal Server

This chapter introduces you to a new service offered by Microsoft, namely Terminal Server. You will learn:

- The basics of Terminal Server
- System policy settings to consider for Terminal Server
- ZAK: The Zero Administration Kit for Terminal Server
- Setup and performance tips

Terminal Server for NT 4.0

A new offering from Microsoft that you should be aware of (and perhaps you already are) is included in a new flavor of NT 4.0 called *Windows NT Terminal Server*. As you learn about this product over the next few pages, you may pause and think "Don't I know about this product but under a different name?" If so, you're probably thinking of a product developed and marketed by Citrix, called *WinFrame*.

It was and still is a very popular "thin client," but Microsoft has somewhat upstaged Citrix's initial offering. In the last few years, Microsoft entered into a partnership with Citrix to license the technology. It is now offered for NT 4.0 Terminal Server and is also an integral network service of Windows 2000.

As part of the agreement, Citrix is limited to offering thin-client solutions for Windows 3.X users; once Windows 2000 is released, it will perhaps be allowed to target Windows 4.0. For now, however, Microsoft has taken over and controls the newer Windows version.

In a nutshell, Terminal Server allows us to deliver Windows NT Desktops using so-called thin-client technology to local and remote clients using hardware and software platforms you may not have considered viable in today's corporate computing world. The term *thin-client* means the clients needs are small by today's standards—usually less than 8 MB—but for certain applications and conditions, the thin client can be just as powerful as a full NT workstation client. See Figure 14-1.

What all of this means is that you can successfully use 486-based machines running older versions of Windows to deliver a newer NT software environment that includes any 32-bit Windows application written for NT.

Figure 14-1 *Terminal Server 4.0 splash screen.*

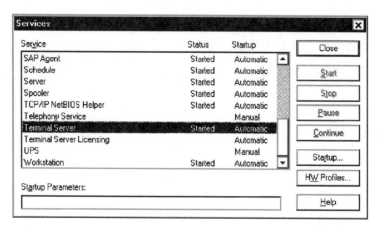

Figure 14-2 *The new terminal service has been added to NT.*

A real-world example would be a user that has an older computer system such as a 486 with 16 MB of RAM running Windows 3.11. The user needs access to Office 97/Microsoft Word and Outlook Express on a limited basis and also to a custom application written in C++. Accessing the NT Terminal Server world allows the legacy user a doorway into the current NT Windows-based application software world at a fraction of the hardware cost.

Windows NT Terminal Server 4.0 has been written to be able to run multiple NT desktops running on the server simultaneously. All of the user's processing needs occur at the server; only the selected desktop is sent to the user. In effect, a new service has been added to the network services to support this new feature. See Figure 14-2.

At the user's end, the terminal server client's duty is to send back the user's interface, mouse, and keyboard changes to the server, in effect remotely controlling their desktop running on the server. Utilizing thin-client protocols designed to perform well under low-bandwidth conditions provides an acceptable means of network communication. The current thin-client protocols used in the Windows world are RDP (Remote Desktop Protocol) written by Microsoft for Terminal Server or ICP (Independent Computer Architecture) written by Citrix for its WinFrame environment.

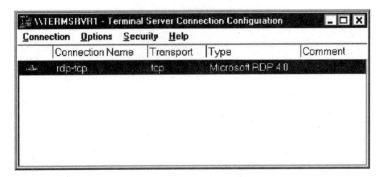

Figure 14-3 *The Terminal Server protocol RDP and TCP/IP.*

RDP can run on Windows for Workgroups, Windows 95, 98, and Windows CE; however, all platforms using RDP must be using TCP/IP. In the Microsoft world, TCP/IP also means the ability to connect through RAS, PPP, or PPTP. By comparison, ICP can run on all versions of Windows as well as many versions of UNIX; and Macintosh, using many common network protocols using Frame Relay, ISDN, TCP/IP, IPX/SPX or NetBEUI. See Figure 14-3.

Both Remote Desktop Protocol (RDP) and Independent Computer Architecture (ICP) have the following features:

- Full-screen text and graphic presentation

- Encryption and compression hooks for secure communications

- Print redirection

- The ability to cut and paste across Terminal Server sessions

- Full local device support for floppy and hard drive, printer, and com port mapping

Terminal Server Advantages

- *Administrative Control.* Since you are probably an administrator, you'll be pleased to know the main advantage of the Terminal Server environment is administrative control: All software installations and user maintenance are performed at the server, which means Terminal Server clients can't mess up their own PCs. Full session administration is provided with a set of Terminal Server tools in the Administrative Tools (Common)

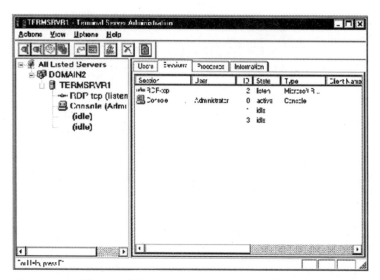

Figure 14-4 *Terminal Server Administration of users and sessions.*

Group, including the utility Terminal Server Administration. See Figure 14-4.

- *Runs Native 32-bit NT Client Applications.* Any application written for the Win32 world will execute under Terminal Server. Terminal Server supports any software application written utilizing Microsoft's WIN32 API. In fact, any DOS or Windows 3.X (WIN 16 API) designed application is also supported, although the older applications require more bandwidth.

- *Small Client Footprint.* An average RAM footprint for running Win32 applications on Terminal Server is 16 MB of RAM. Documentation from many sources indicates 8 MB of RAM is sufficient—in the real world, plan for double the suggested amount.

- *Standard and Reliable.* The groundwork for Terminal Server has been tested and refined with Citrix and WinFrame over the last 6 years. But keep in mind the label "standard and reliable" is meant to apply to the remote protocols; a badly functioning application in the Windows world is not a pretty sight, period. Reliability and performance can be monitored through new Terminal Server counters added to `Performance Monitor`. See Figure 14-5.

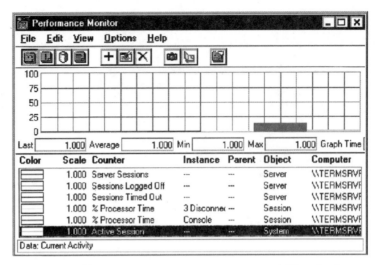

Figure 14-5 *Using* `Performance Monitor` *to track Terminal Server clients.*

- *Built in to Windows 2000.* Included in Windows 2000 Professional Server as a network server, this will allow you to designate the users that you want to connect as terminal server domain clients and those you want to connect as regular "full service" domain clients. See Figure 14-6.

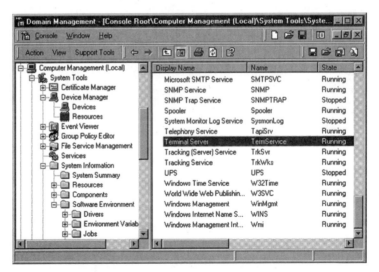

Figure 14-6 *Windows 2000 and Terminal Server.*

User Profiles and Terminal Server

Terminal Server takes advantage of the NT requirement that each user has his or her own user profile. When you log into the NT domain, you can choose to use a locally cached user profile stored in `WINNT\PROFILES\Username` on your local PC; in fact, this is the normal scenario for user profile operation. Your user profile is stored and retrieved locally and executed in the local PC RAM space working alongside the system portion of the Registry that is found in local location `WINNT\SYSTEM32\CONFIG`. Software applications are installed in most cases on the local PC.

Here's a quick summary of the integral software pieces that a regular NT session requires and uses:

- The local user profile (the user's own registry *and* user profile)
- The local system registry
- Locally installed software applications (.EXEs and .DLLs)

Terminal Server moves all of the three local options to the file server. We can run anything we want logged in and sitting at the NT server, right? Now we can do the same thing, but remotely. Defining user profile paths is through User Manager for Domains at the Terminal Server console. See Figure 14-7.

Terminal Server offers the choice of two user profile paths that can both be defined for controlling the user settings you wish your users to use when they log on to the network: a `User Profile` path and a `Terminal Server Profile` path.

Always enter all network paths in the UNC format `\\Server\Profiles\%username%`, making sure that any network location for user profiles has been shared so that users can access their user profile from the Terminal Server.

The three options for logging onto a Terminal Server are:

1. The "usual" logon from a computer system running Windows client software

2. Log on to the Terminal Server at the server console

3. Log on using the Terminal Server client software

If only the `User Profile` path is specified in the user's profile

Figure 14-7 *Defining user profile paths for Terminal Server clients.*

settings in User Manager for Domains, the user will receive the user profile in that location every time he or she logs on to the server.

If only the `Terminal Server Profile` path is specified in the user's profile settings in User Manager for Domains, when the user logs in from any system configured as a Terminal Server client, the user will receive the user profile in that location.

However, if both a `User Profile` path and a `Terminal Server Profile` path are specified, the user will use the defined `User Profile` path if the user logs on with a Windows 98 or Windows NT Workstation computer (that is, by not using the Terminal Server client); but when using the Terminal Server client or logging into the Terminal Server itself, the `Terminal Server Profile` path will be used.

Also note that, for logon purposes, the Terminal Server console is considered the same as a remote Terminal Server client session.

So, if you specify a `Terminal Server Profile` path in your domain and the user logs on to the domain from any Terminal Server console, she or he will use the `Terminal Server Profile` path.

However, the profile will be cached in the `WINNT\PROFILES\ USERNAME` user profile location when the user logs on locally at the server. And when a user logs on using the Terminal Server client, that user's profile is always cached on the Terminal Server where the user is connecting (as that is where the user profile is actually executing). If your users need different user profiles, just specify a different profile path for `User Profile` path and for `Terminal Server Profile` path.

If deployed, multiple user profiles can also be different types; that is, one could be mandatory and the other nonmandatory.

> An interesting point to note is that with Terminal Server, user profile types can be mixed and matched. If a user has two defined user profile paths, one user profile can be mandatory and the other local or roaming; however, this can also produce undesired results. If users log on to different domains in which they have different profile types defined (for example mandatory or non-mandatory), the user's profile will not work as you may have expected. The mandatory user profile path in one domain may not be defined as mandatory in the other domain, resulting in unrestricted user settings being downloaded. The reverse is also true, as nonmandatory user profiles may also not be used if the user has a locally cached user profile. This situation can also be produced if a user to begin with has a `User Profile` path to a mandatory profile and subsequently the user is given a non-mandatory `Terminal Server Profile` path.

Note

Tips for Success Deploying Terminal Server

A successful deployment of terminal server and terminal server clients is made much easier by following some simple guidelines.

- *Don't skimp on server hardware.* Plan on allocating 10 to 25 users per installed processor on your Terminal Server. It almost goes without saying that the CPUs should be as fast as you can buy. For RAM allocation, 256 MB RAM plus 20 MB RAM per user is a good starting point. Finally, designate 10 to 15 MB hard drive space on the Terminal Server for each user's profile as well.

- *Pick or check your hardware from the HCL.* The hardware compatibility list (HCL) is your Terminal Server's bible. Check out the latest version at *www.microsoft.com/hwtest/hcl/*.

- *Get your third-party drivers from the Web.* Make sure that your network interface adapter, video adapter, and your SCSI hardware drivers are up to date. I can almost guarantee that the drivers that arrived with your new hardware are months old. Try *www.paperbits.com* or *www.windrivers.com* for up-to-date driver locations on the Web.

- *Test your Terminal Server hardware.* Prior to installing Terminal Server, test and benchmark your hardware. If you need software testing tools, head to *www.zdnet.com/* and search for stress-testing software for your NT server.

- *Use NTFS for your Terminal Server partition.* NTFS is a must for the file system partition for proper setup of directory and file restrictions. The Terminal Server installation applies a special default level of file security that is not applied if your file system is FAT.

- *RAID 2 or RAID 5.* Your hard drive subsystem is so important—it holds all user software, user profiles, and shared virtual memory. At the very least, choose hardware duplexing, which is two hard drive controllers feeding two hard drive platters. The best solution is RAID 5, where your valuable data and software are striped in a data-parity mix across multiple hard drive platters. Money, money, money, I know; but remember in the Terminal Server world, all processing is performed at the server using its resources.

- *Dedicated Terminal Server.* The Terminal Server you deploy should be focused on serving Terminal Server clients only. Don't bog your server down with unnecessary tasks.

System Policy Choices for Terminal Server Clients

The design and layout of a terminal server client can severely hinder performance if the desktop is cluttered and full of graphics.

- *Clean and simple desktops.* Probably the most important point to agree on before deploying Terminal Server is the need to have clean and simple desktops. Transferring graphically intensive background designs and tons of shortcuts across the network can waste network bandwidth. Start with (no pun intended) the Start button and add only the icons that the user needs to effectively do his or her work. Make sure that there is no wild and graphic wallpaper, and any screen saver should be blank.

- *Terminal design means terminal access.* If your users have the required shortcuts and icons to do their job, removing access to the command prompt, the Run command, and any other operating system access point should be carried out with a system policy as well.

- *Available drive letters are the server's drive letters.* The default drive letters available to a Terminal Server client are the actual drive letters on the actual Terminal Server. No drive letters should be made available—only the user's shared folders should be given access on the server.

ZAK and Terminal Server

The Zero Administration Kit (ZAK) for Windows NT 4.0 Terminal Server is a set of administrative tools designed to help administrators with deploying NT workstations from a central location on the network. Besides the fancy name, the reality is that ZAK will be deployed in bits and pieces through Windows 2000, for NT 4.0 if you used Office 97, and IE4 on NT Workstations exclusively, then there are also some ZAK pieces that may already be deployed.

With ZAK, two options are provided for configuring your workstations:

1. *Taskstation mode* is for users that run only one dedicated application period. Microsoft's suggestion is to use Internet Explorer; it becomes the application and shell all in one. An intranet workstation would be one example, but it should be pointed out that this and any scenario you may think of is quite limiting.

2. *Appstation mode* is the other selection: the idea is that your users will have a concise set of Microsoft applications (32-bit applications) that they run. This mode can be used to install both NT workstation and the required applications from a central distribution server. Other application software choices other than Office 97 and IE require extensive scripts created using SysDiff, another Microsoft deployment tool. Network bandwidth hovering in the 10-MB range and no clear corporate rules as to what Microsoft software the user must use make this choice limiting as well.

Since Terminal Server now allows us to run our clients in a terminal environment, ZAK for Terminal Server is a much smaller feature set. Relevant features to consider are:

- Terminal Server login script commands `ACLS.CMD`, `HIDE.CMD`, and `UNHIDE.CMD`

- System Policies settings

ZAK Script Files

When installing Terminal Server, NTFS must be used as the file partition type in order to be able to protect the common set of system files all users are sharing on the server. The pieces for ZAK are contained in a self-extracting file called `ZAKWTSB2.EXE`. ZAK for Terminal Server is installed at the command prompt by running `ZAKINSTALL.CMD`, which is executed automatically by `ZAKWTSB2.EXE`. You must be logged on as Administrator before installing ZAK.

The ZAK install steps are as follows: First `ZAKINSTALL.CMD` is executed, which in turn copies the group of ZAK script files from the compressed archive file to `C:\WNTSRV\ZAK\SCRIPTS`.

Next `ZAKBLWRK.CMD` is called and executed. It first checks the file location \ALL USERS\STARTUP and cleans up any files that may have been left after the Office 97 installation. Next, it then calls and executes the script file ACLS.CMD, which sets read-only permissions and other file security levels on NT and Office 97 directories for proper operation for all users. Finally it calls HIDE.CMD, which hides much of the local file system for every user that does not have administrative rights. The ACLS.CMD and HIDE.CMD are fully documented and can be edited with Notepad if you want to make any further changes. UNHIDE.CMD is also included; this allows the administrator to reverse the HIDE.CMD's actions of hiding all files.

Running the ACLS.CMD results in the following security levels being set for all nonadministrators.

- Boot files are available only to administrators

- Read-only permissions are set on the PROGRAM FILES directory

- Change permissions are granted in the OFFICE and OFFICE\ TEMPLATE folder

- Permissions to the TEMP directory, but no rights to delete

- WNTSRV and subdirectories set to Read-Only

- Access is denied to EXE, INF, and HLP files in the system folder

- Locks users from the ZAK folder

- Permits read access to OFFICE 97 files

- Accessories are hidden from users

HIDE.CMD Listing

The following listing shows with comments how HIDE.CMD is deployed through ZAK for Terminal Server.

```
REM This is used to hide the files on the system
REM
attrib +h /s %SystemDrive%\*.*
For /R %SystemDrive%\ %%i in (.) do attrib +h "%%i"
attrib -h /s %SystemRoot%\profiles\*.*
For /R %SystemRoot%\profiles %%i in (.) do attrib -h "%%i"
REM
REM Some directories and files don't get the right permissions because
REM they have already been marked as system. We cover them specially
  here
```

```
REM

attrib +h +s %SystemRoot%\fonts
attrib +h +s %SystemRoot%\tasks
attrib +h +s %SystemRoot%\wintrust.hlp
attrib +h +s %SystemDrive%\boot.ini

REM unhide the zak\scripts directory files, otherwise we won't be able
  to
REM continue
attrib -h %SystemRoot%\zak\scripts\*.*

REM
REM unhide the exchange.prf file in the c:\temp directory. this is in
  case it
REM got left behind
REM

attrib -h %SystemDrive%\%temp%\exchange.prf
REM
REM unhide Power Point template (.pot) files, as per ZAK release notes
REM
attrib -h "%systemdrive%\Program Files\Microsoft Office\templates\
  *.pot" /s
rem attrib -h "%systemdrive%\Program Files\Microsoft Office\
  templates\presentations\*.pot"

rem
rem the office compatibility script will want to set these read only.
  we'll hide them
rem and set them read only here.
rem
If Exist "%SystemDrive%\Program Files\Microsoft Office\Templates\
  Presentations\AutoContent Wizard.Pwz" Attrib + H +R "%SystemDrive%\
  Program Files\Microsoft Office\Templates\Presentations\AutoContent
  Wizard.Pwz"
If Exist "%SystemDrive%\Program Files\Microsoft Office\Office\
  Ppt2html.ppa" Attrib + H +R "%SystemDrive%\Program Files\Microsoft
Office\Office\Ppt2html.ppa"
If Exist "%SystemDrive%\Program Files\Microsoft Office\Office\
  bshppt97.ppa" Attrib + H +R "%SystemDrive%\Program Files\Microsoft
  Office\Office\bshppt97.ppa"
If Exist "%SystemDrive%\Program Files\Microsoft Office\Office\
  geniwiz.ppa" Attrib + H +R "%SystemDrive%\Program Files\Microsoft
  Office\Office\geniwiz.ppa"
If Exist "%SystemDrive%\Program Files\Microsoft Office\Office\
  ppttools.ppa" Attrib +R "%SystemDrive%\Program Files\Microsoft
  Office\Office\ppttools.ppa"
```

```
rem
rem office compatibility logon script for Office needs to see these
  files
rem
if Exist "%SystemDrive%\Program Files\Microsoft Office\Office\ShortCut
  Bar" attrib -h "%SystemDrive%\Program Files\Microsoft Office\Office\
  ShortCut Bar"
if Exist "%SystemRoot%\forms" attrib -h "%SystemRoot%\forms"
if Exist "%SystemRoot%\artgalry.cag" attrib -h "%SystemRoot%\
  artgalry.cag"
if Exist "%SystemDrive%\Program Files\Microsoft Office\Office\
  custom.dic" attrib -h "%SystemDrive%\Program Files\Microsoft
  Office\Office\custom.dic"
if Exist "%SystemDrive%\Program Files\Microsoft Office\Office\ShortCut
  Bar" attrib -h "%SystemDrive%\Program Files\Microsoft Office\Office\
  ShortCut Bar\*.*" /s
if Exist "%SystemRoot%\forms" attrib -h "%SystemRoot%\forms\*.*" /s
```

Several system policy settings should be applied to the default user as to apply to all users, administrators included. The following are specific restrictions to consider for Terminal Server clients. The template choices are found in WINNT.ADM and COMMON.ADM on Terminal Server.

> The most up to date Terminal Server settings for system policies
> are found when deploying the Terminal Server Service Pack 4. This
> is a different service pack than NT service pack for NT 4.0, so be
> careful that you deploy the right service pack for the right version
> of the operation system.   **Note**

1. *Disable the use of Registry editing.* Registry editing using Regedt32 and Regedit are editing the Terminal Server's registry, not the client's. All editing should be performed only at the server itself. See Figure 14-8.

2. *Restrict the use of the Control Panel Display Applet.* The display options should be tightly controlled to ensure that the desktop remains clean and devoid of graphic backgrounds and screen savers. See Figure 14-9.

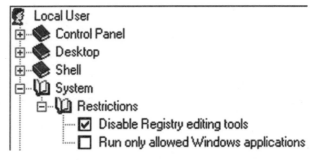

Figure 14-8 *Disable Regedt32, Regedit, and TWEAKUI with this option enabled.*

Figure 14-9 *Display restrictions.*

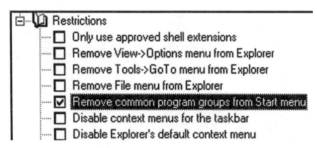

Figure 14-10 *Common administrative software tools.*

3. *Restrict common shortcuts.* The common options are administrative options on Terminal Server for administrative control. See Figure 14-10.

4. *Hide all unneeded desktop shortcuts.* This includes shortcuts such as Accessories and Internet Explorer. See Figure 14-11.

5. *Make the application the shell upon boot-up.* If you have the need for a single application when accessing Terminal Server, then that application can be the shell. See Figure 14-12.

6. *Security options to consider deploying.* See Figure 14-13.

   - *Run logon scripts synchronously.* Force the login script to finish completely before the desktop is loaded.
   - *Don't display last user name.* An extra level of security is not saving and displaying the last user to log on Terminal Server.
   - *Logon banner.* This can be handy to alert users that they are starting a Terminal Server session.

Figure 14-11 *Restrict access to common accessories.*

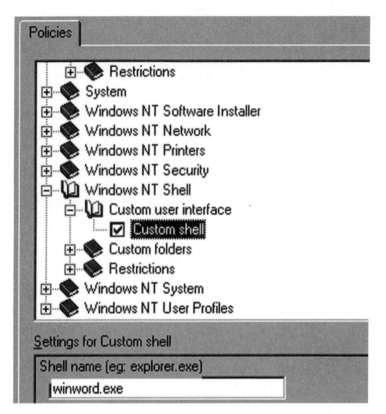

Figure 14-12 *Defining Microsoft Word as the shell.*

7. *Restrict the user profile loading process.* Specify roaming or local user profile use. See Figure 14-14.

8. *Restrict the user profile size.* If this option is enabled, the system will prompt users when their user profile has exceeded the mandated size. Note that you can also define what folders are included with the user profile. See Figure 14-15.

9. *Remote update.* Set the location for your Terminal Server system policy files. If you have different system policy needs for different users you can specify the manual location of the system policy POL file. The path must be UNC (\\) and the POL file must be included in the path. See Figure 14-16.

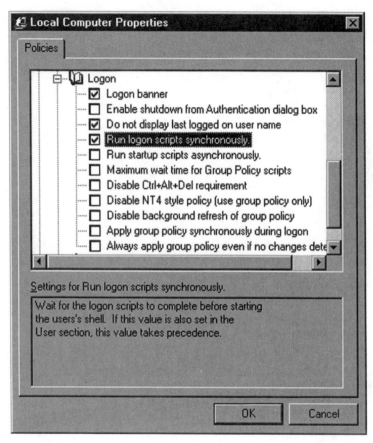

Figure 14-13 *Security options to consider deploying.*

10. *Desktop color.* Perhaps mandate a background color to define Terminal Server sessions, Windows NT sessions, and Windows 98 sessions. See Figure 14-17.

11. *Shell restrictions.* A collection of Explorer shell restrictions to streamline your Terminal Server sessions. See Figure 14-18.

12. *NT shell restrictions.* Explorer shell security options for NT clients accessing Terminal Server. See Figure 14-19.

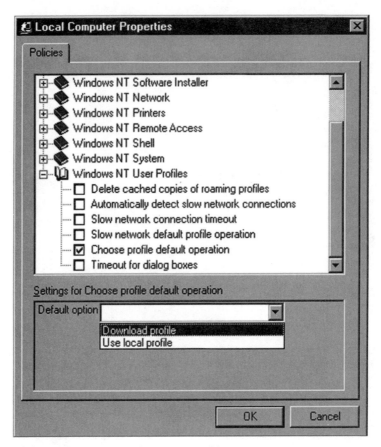

Figure 14-14 *Define what user profile to activate.*

Software Running as a Terminal Server Application

An application that executes well on Terminal Server must adhere to the following rules:

- Application bits and pieces must go in the installed location and machine registry settings must go in the HKEY_LOCAL_MACHINE (HKLM) hive in the registry.

- User settings can be stored as files or as registry settings. Files will go in the user's profile, specifically under the \PROFILES\USERNAME\APPLICATION DATA folder. The user-specific

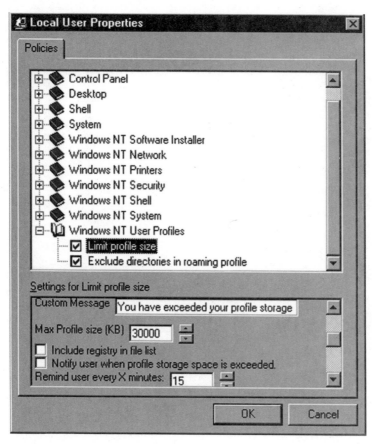

Figure 14-15 *Settings for user profiles.*

registry settings must go in the HKEY_CURRENT_USER (HKCU) hive in the registry.

- The paths must be defined so there are no hard-coded path names in the registry. A Terminal Server application must be able to keep track of other network locations where the requested file(s) may be found. As an example, Office 2000 includes the Microsoft Installer. It is kept aware of these locations and keeps track of the installed file's location instead of requiring the administrator/installer to hard-code them into the registry. The reasoning for this new path requirement is due to Windows 2000's eventual support for clustering of NT Servers.

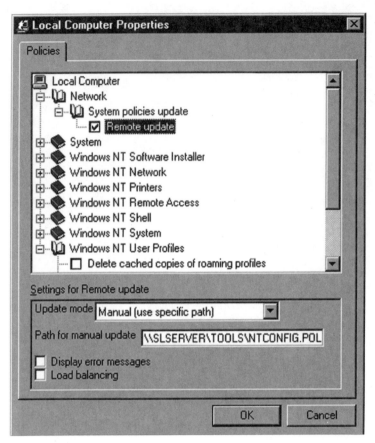

Figure 14-16 *Defining manual download.*

If the default Terminal Server were unavailable, the system will be smart enough to point the software request to the next available server.

- Use NT environment variables wherever possible. These environment variables are handy for pointing a path to a different server storage location. %Username% is the most widely used environment variable and needs to be expanded for each individual user. This allows setting of the environment variables to detect the next clustered storage location.

- Use the My Documents folder as the default for user data storage. Terminal Server stores data centrally, where My Documents provides a central built-in network location.

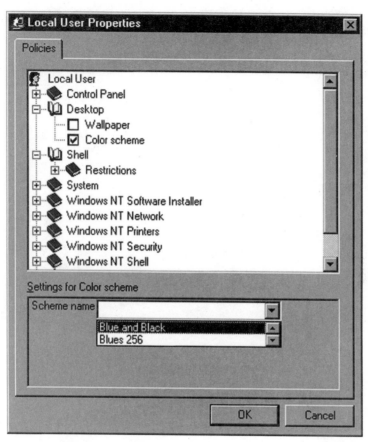

Figure 14-17 *Pick your favorite color.*

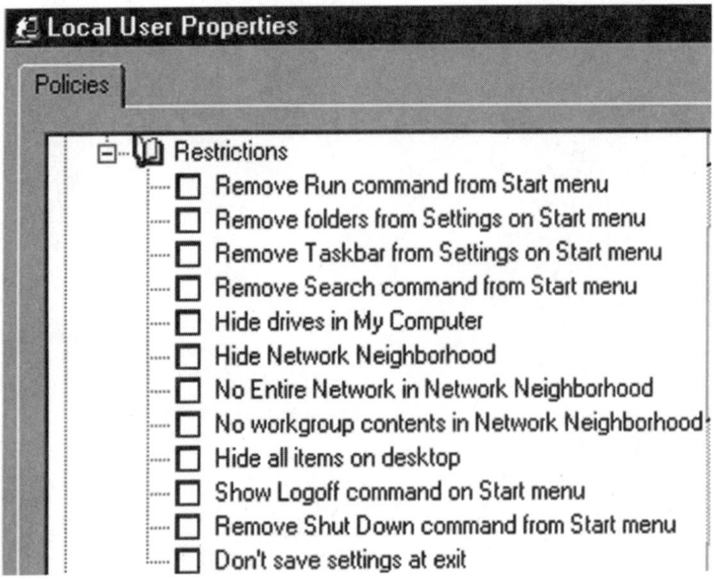

Figure 14-18 *Explorer shell restrictions.*

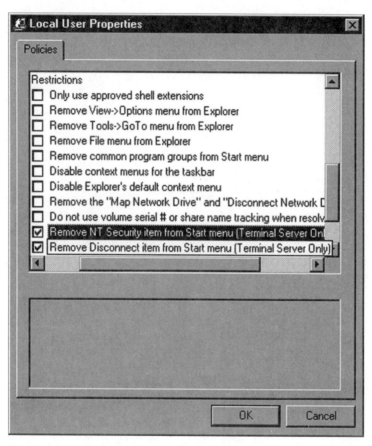

Figure 14-19 *Security options for NT clients.*

Mixed NetWare
and NT Environments

This chapter introduces you to how NetWare is coping with NT's taking a large chunk of its networking market. You will learn:

- How NetWare 5.0 embraces NT with system policy, user profile, and Registry support through the NDS Tree

- What system policy settings are available for the IntranetWare Client for Windows NT and Windows 98

- What Microsoft system policy settings are available for Windows 98 clients in the Net-Ware world

Certainly the main corporate file servers in use today are Net-
Ware and NT Server. With NetWare at version 5.0 the end result is
that it doesn't really matter what server type you are now using as
both NetWare 5.0 and NT 4.0 have the following shared features

- *Support for the IP protocol.* However, if your company wants
  to continue to run IPX, NetWare 5 supports both IP and IPX,
  so you can use IP, IPX, or both.

- Support for DNS and DHCP Services

- *System Polices.* Using the features of Zero Effort Networking,
  you can now deploy and control system policy settings through
  the NDS tree.

- *User Profiles.* Both roaming and mandatory user profiles can
  be activated and controlled through the NDS tree for Windows
  95/98 and NT 4.0 clients through the Novell Workstation
  Manager.

- *REG file Administration.* The use of Registry settings in REG file
  format is now supported through the NDS tree.

- *Management of workstations from a central location.* This centralized management includes creating Windows policies,
  scheduling workstation changes, configuring Novell client software, creating Windows NT user accounts, and delivering
  applications when users need them.

Netware 5.0 and Policy Packages

System policy templates can be deployed through the NDS tree by
creating a policy package that takes advantage of the ADM template files for Windows 95/98 and NT Workstation users. The
policy packages can also be made mandatory, so users cannot
change the defined settings. You can also use a workstation policy
package to run certain applications on a workstation, regardless
of which user is using the workstation.

Creating a Policy Package Object

You can use the 32-bit version of the NWADMIN utility to create
a Policy Package object in NDS.

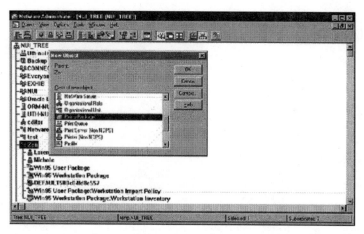

Figure 15-1 *Policy package objects created with NWADMIN.*

To create a `Policy Package` object for a Windows NT workstation, you complete the following steps:

1. Start by launching the 32-bit version of the NWADMIN utility. Next select the container object in which you want to create a `Policy Package` object, selecting the `Create` option from the `Object` menu. The `New Object` menu will then appear. See Figure 15-1.

2. Selecting the `Policy Package` option then allows you to select the workstation policy package for the workstation you are supporting: either Windows 3.1, Windows 95/98, or Windows NT.

3. Next you must provide a name for the `Policy Package` object.

4. Select the `Define Additional Properties` option and click the `Create` button. The `Workstation Package` page for the client you are creating then appears.

5. Next click the `Computer Systems Policy` button.

6. Check the desired options that you will connect with this `Policy Package` object. As an example, you could predefine a process to run every time this user logs onto the NDS tree. See Figure 15-2.

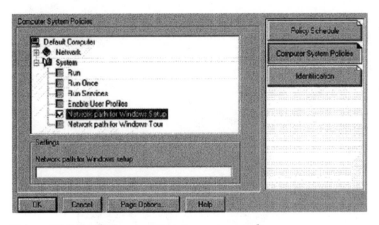

Figure 15-2 *Defining a computer system policy.*

7. Finally, by clicking the Associate button you select either the
   container object or the individual Workstation object.

Support for NT Users

When a user logs in to the network using the Z.E.N. client for
NT, Z.E.N. works to authenticate this user both to NDS and to
the Windows NT workstation. NetWare and Z.E.N. now fully
support local, roaming, and mandatory user profiles stored and
maintained through the NDS tree. The user account is also
defined in the Z.E.N. world as either volatile or nonvolatile. A
volatile user account is removed from the workstation's SAM
once the user logs out of the network.

A *nonvolatile user account* is a user profile that remains in the
workstation's SAM after the user logs out of the network. A user
could then access the local workstation resources if the network
were unavailable.

System Policy Support for NetWare 3.X and 4.X

All of the system policy settings contained in this book are available to NetWare 3.X and 4.X networks with one important dis-

tinction. NetWare groups are not global groups, so they are not supported through system policies. Individual users and computers, however, are fully supported. The workaround is to use the Default User in your system policy, effectively controlling all NetWare users as one large group of users. Remember to add all individual users that perform Administrator functions, or users that you do not wish to be controlled by the Default User settings.

NetWare is also included in the default properties of where the Microsoft Windows 98 or NT 4.0 Workstation Client expects to find the system policy POL file. POL storage defaults are either NTCONFIG.POL for NT 4.0 clients or CONFIG.POL for Windows 95/98 clients. The NetWare location for the POL files will be a familiar one: SYS:PUBLIC\"POLICYFILE.POL".

NetWare-Supplied Templates for System Policies

NetWare provides supporting templates for system policies for their network clients for Windows 98 and Windows NT. The choices are:

- IntranetWare Client for Windows 98
- IntranetWare Client for Windows NT

Each client comes with a system policy template: for Windows 98 users the template is CLIENT32.ADM; NT clients using the IntranetWare client can deploy NWNT.ADM.

The IntranetWare Client for NT

This client provides a seamless login to NT servers, NetWare bindery, and NDS environments. It also interfaces with NetWare and the Workgroup Manager, allowing the following choices:

1. User profile storage in user's home directory

2. Roaming profile storage location

3. System policy file storage location

See Figure 15-3.

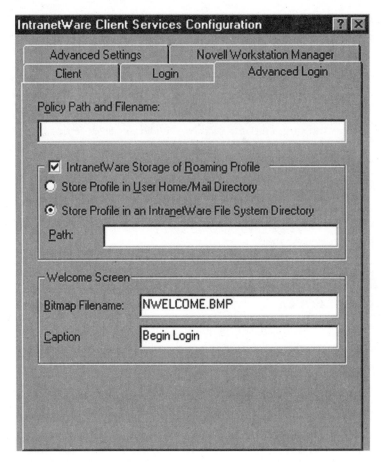

Figure 15-3 *Logon options for NT clients using the Intranet-Ware Client.*

NWNT Template Settings for NetWare and NT Networks

The templates provided by NetWare are for the system portion of the Registry, that is, the default or defined computer icon. Keep this in mind when enabling these settings on computers that are shared by more than one user. A summary of the type of settings available is easy: we are predefining the settings found in `Control Panel | Network` icon and properties of the IntranetWare Client services, and when we log on using the IntranetWare client.

Computer \ Novell NetWare Client for Windows NT \ Client

- Preferred server

- Preferred Tree

- *Name and Default Name Context Pairs.* Up to five tree and context options can be defined for NetWare users.

Computer \ Novell NetWare Client for Windows NT \ Login

Login options are the choices the user can select when logging into the network. See Figure 15-4.

- *Display Connection Page.* See Figure 15-5.

  1. Login to tree
  2. Login to server
  3. Bindery connection
  4. Clear current connections

- *Display Script Page.* Login script and user profile choices can be mandated with these settings. The next three options set the login script options for the client.

  1. Display script results window
  2. Close script results automatically
  3. Run login scripts

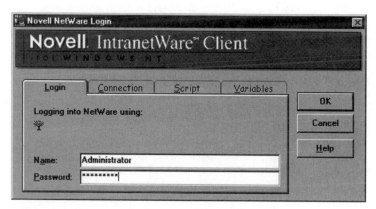

Figure 15-4 *Properties of the IntranetWare Login.*

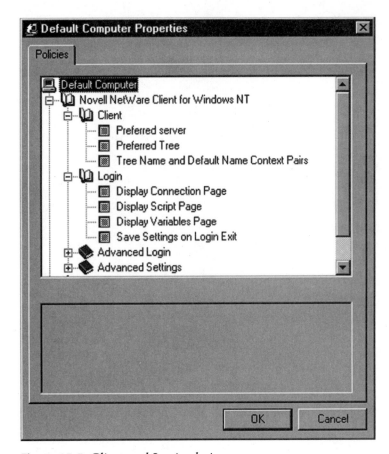

Figure 15-5 *Client and Login choices.*

- *Display Variables Page.* Up to four login script variables can be defined.

- Save Settings on Login Exit

Computer \ Novell NetWare Client for Windows NT \ Advanced Login

These options are the choices on the Advanced Login tab for the IntranetWare client.

- Policy Path and Filename

- NetWare Storage of Roaming Profile

- Store Profile on User Home/Mail Directory

- Store Profile on a NetWare File System Directory

- Bitmap Filename in the local workstation NT directory

- Caption

Computer \ Novell NetWare Client for Windows NT \ Advanced Settings \ Environment, NETX Compatibility

If you are using software that requires compatibility with the older NETX NetWare Client and NET.CFG settings these choices provide compatibility. See Figure 15-6.

- *Receive Broadcast Message.* The workstation can be set to accept messages only from the server or messages from all workstation and server nodes.

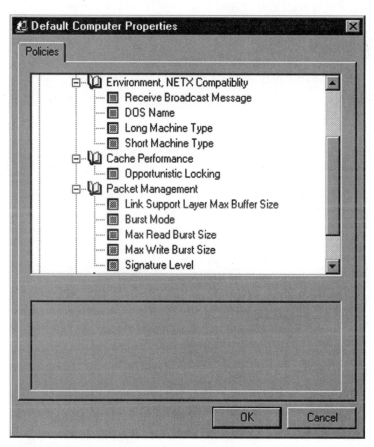

Figure 15-6 *NET.CFG compatibility settings.*

- *DOS Name.* This is the operating system name used by the %OS environment parameter with login scripts.

- *Long Machine Type.* This is the workstation type used by the %MACHINE environment parameter with login scripts.

- *Short Machine Type.* This type determines what overlay file is used when older 3.X NetWare utilities such as SYSCON or FILER are put to use.

Computer \ Novell NetWare Client for Windows NT \ Advanced Settings \Cache Performance

- *Opportunistic Locking.* This setting can be used to allow the operating system to cache files. This can be a setting that can actually hurt performance, as your software might also cache files for performance, setting up a fight between NetWare and the application for the right to cache files. The end result is no performance. Lotus Notes does not like this setting turned on, but some applications written in Betrieve do. Testing applications is required before deploying this setting in a production environment.

Computer \ Novell NetWare Client for Windows NT \ Advanced Settings \ Packet Management

- *Link Support Layer Max Buffer Size.* Defines the maximum packet size that is supported. Token Ring LANs can take advantage of this setting, as the default packet size is 576 bytes.

- *Burst Mode.* If you are using packet burst on your NetWare Servers, then burst mode turns on packet burst on the workstation.

- Read Burst Size

- *Max Read Burst Size.* This setting defines the maximum number of bytes per packet read while packet burst is enabled. The read window size will change dynamically as network conditions improve or slow down.

- *Max Write Burst Size.* This setting defines the maximum number of bytes per packet written while packet burst is enabled.

- *Signature Level.* NetWare provides four levels of packet signing. We can improve security but decrease performance, as each packet has to be verified by the server before it is accepted.

  Level 0—No packet signatures
  Level 1—Perform packet signatures if the workstation requires them
  Level 2—Perform packet signatures if the workstation has been set up to use them
  Level 3—Always require packet signatures

Computer \ Novell NetWare Client for Windows NT \ Advanced Settings \ WAN

- *Large Internet Packets.* The packet size used on the local network will also be used across routers and bridges connecting other subnets.

- *Large Internet Packet Start Size.* You can define the largest packet size to be used in your network to shorten the negotiation time for packet size.

- *Minimum Time To Net.* Set your timeout rate for slow network links.

See Figure 15-7.

Computer \ Novell NetWare Client for Windows NT \ NetWare/IP \ Parameters

- Custom Configuration

  NetWare IP / Domain Name
  Retries to DSS during startup
  Number of seconds between retries
  Broadcast SAP nearest server queries to network
  NetWare/IP 1.1 compatibility

Computer \ Novell NetWare Client for Windows NT \ NetWare/IP \ Servers

- Nearest NetWare/IP Servers
- Preferred Domain SAP/RIP Servers

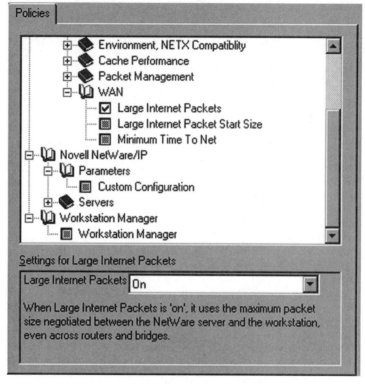

Figure 15-7 *System policy settings for NetWare / WAN environments.*

Computer \ Novell NetWare Client for Windows NT \ NetWare/IP \ Workstation Manager

- *Trusted Trees.* Defines the NDS trees that the users on this computer will have access to. Enter the trees in a comma-delimited format.

Windows 98 and IntranetWare

For Windows 98 users (and for Windows 95 clients, for that matter) that deploy the IntranetWare Client for Windows 98, we have template settings for the computer side of system policies. The template is CLIENT32.ADM. Quite a few settings are for controlling the protocol, IPX and SPX settings, and IntranetWare Client defaults that could be manually set through the Network icon in the Control Panel. CLIENT32.ADM settings are shown below.

Computer \ Novell NetWare Client 32 \ Client 32

- Preferred Server
- Preferred Tree
- *Name and Default Name Context Pairs.* Up to five tree and context options can be defined for NetWare users.

Computer \ Novell NetWare Client 32 \ Login

`Logon` options are the choices the user can select when logging into the network.

- Display Connection Page
    1. Login to Tree
    2. Login to Server
    3. Bindery Connection
    4. Clear Current Connections

- *Display Script Page.* Login script and user profile choices can be mandated with these settings. The next three options set the login script options for the client.
    1. Display Script Results Window
    2. Close Script Results Automatically
    3. Run Login Scripts

- *Display Variables Page.* Up to four login script variables can be defined.

- Save Settings on Login Exit

Computer \ Novell NetWare Client 32 \ Advanced Settings \ Connections

- Auto Reconnect Level
- NetWare Protocol

Computer \ Novell NetWare Client 32 \ Advanced Settings \ Environment, NETX compatibility

These settings are for older hardware and software environments where Windows 3.X and DOS software may still exist.

- *Cache NetWare Password.* Holds current password in RAM for auto-logon when the server goes down and is brought back up.

- *DOS Name.* The %OS% parameter used in login scripts.

- *Environment Pad.* Adds RAM space for SET commands.

- Force First Network Drive

- *Hold Files.* Any software that uses file control blocks for I/O should have this option turned on.

- *Long Machine Type.* The %Machine% parameter used in login scripts.

- *Max Current Dir Length.* Makes the DOS prompt longer.

- *Search Dirs First.* If on, directories will be shown before files are listed.

- *Search Mode.* Sets options from 1 to 5 for search mode level.

- *Set Station Time.* Synchronizes workstation to NetWare file server.

- *Short Machine Type.* Default is IBM; matches overlay files needed for 3.X utilities.

- *Show Dots.* NetWare does not show . and .. options for sub-directories.

- Use Video BIOS

See Figure 15-8.

Computer \ Novell NetWare Client 32 \ Advanced Settings \ File System

The first two options are used to modify default values for software that uses the MSDOS SHARE utility:

- Lock Delay

- Lock Retries

- *Read Only Compatibility.* Some applications require this to be on. It allows a file with a read-only attribute to be opened with a read/write access call.

Computer \ Novell NetWare Client 32 \ Advanced Settings \ Checksum

- Large Internet Packets

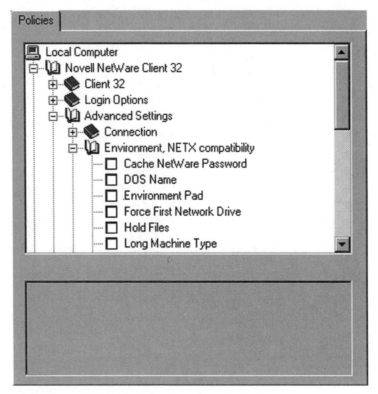

Figure 15-8 *NETX options for Windows 98 clients.*

- *Max Link Support Layer Buffer Size.* Defines the maximum packet size that is supported. Token Ring LANs can take advantage of this setting, as the default packet size is 576 bytes.

- *Packet Burst Buffers.* If you are using packet burst on your NetWare Servers, then burst mode turns on packet burst on the workstation.

- *Packet Burst Read Window Size.* This setting defines the maximum number of bytes per packet read while packet burst is enabled. The read window size will change dynamically as network conditions improve or slow down.

- *Packet Burst Write Window Size.* This setting defines the maximum number of bytes per packet written while packet burst is enabled.

- *Signature Level.* NetWare provides four levels of packet signing. We can improve security but decrease performance, as each packet has to be verified by the server before it is accepted.

  Level 0—No packet signatures
  Level 1—Perform packet signatures if the workstation requires them
  Level 2—Perform packet signatures if the workstation has been set up to use them
  Level 3—Always require packet signatures

Computer \ Novell NetWare Client 32 \ Advanced Settings \ Cache Performance

- *Cache Writes.* Sets a write cache for improved file performance.

- *Close Behind Ticks.* Sets the time limit data, which are held in cache before being written to disk (there are 10 ticks per second).

- *Delay Writes.* Works with the "close behind ticks" setting for caching files that are opened and closed frequently.

- *File Cache Level.* Sets the file cache level from 0 to 4 on the workstation. The higher the number, the better the performance.

- *Max Cache Size.* Specifies the maximum cache size to be used.

- *Opportunistic Locking.* This setting can be used to allow the operating system to cache files. This can be a setting that can actually hurt performance, as your software might also cache files for performance, setting up a fight between NetWare and the application for the right to cache files.

- *True Commit.* Enable this value if you want a data integrity check performed for every file read and write.

See Figure 15-9.

Computer \ Novell NetWare Client 32 \ Advanced Settings \ Printing

- *Network Printers.* Defines the number of logical LPT ports up to a total of nine for local printing needs.

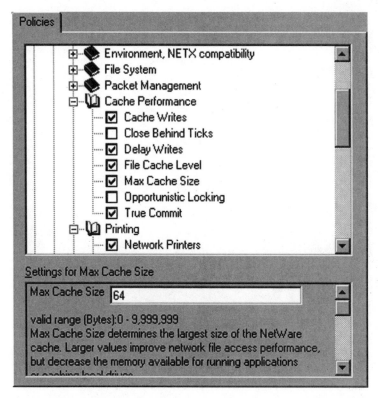

Figure 15-9 *Setting cache performance for the local NetWare client.*

- *Print Header.* If you have a postscript printer define a print header of 255 bytes; this is used for postscript information on the current print job that is sent before the actual print job.

- *Print Tail.* Also used for postscript printers, a print tail of 64 bytes allows a reset printer command to reset the printer at the end of the print job.

See Figure 15-10.

Computer \ Novell NetWare Client 32 \ Advanced Settings \ TroubleShooting

- *Alert Beep.* Forces a beep when a popup message is displayed by NetWare.

- *Handle Net Errors.* If your software used INT24 for error handling (read old software), then this should be enabled.

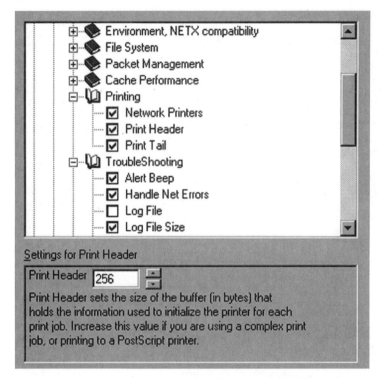

Figure 15-10 *Postscript printing options.*

- *Log File.* Specifies the location of the log file that can be created to assist in NetWare client troubleshooting.

- *Log File Size.* Sets the log file size.

- *Net Status Busy Timeout.* Sets your IPX timeouts to a larger number if you have a slow network. After the number of defined IPX timeouts has been reached, the error message `Error connecting` will be displayed.

- *Net Status Timeout.* Sets the number of seconds an application will wait for a response from the server before displaying an error message.

Computer \ Novell NetWare Client 32 \ Advanced Settings \ WAN

- *LIP Start Size.* Defines the size of large Internet packets, if used.

- *Minimum Time To Net*. Sets your timeout rate for slow network links.

- *NCP Max Timeout*. Sets the time limit for retrying a network connection.

Computer \ Novell NetWare Client 32 \ Network Provider

- *Enable Send Message Utility*. If your users use the 25th line message utility, you can enable it here.

Computer \ IPX 32-Bit Protocol for Novell NetWare Client 32 \ IPX

- *IPX Retry Count*. Defines the number of IPX retries when using the IPX/SPX protocol.

- Allow IPX access through interrupt 7AH

- Allow IPX access through interrupt 64H

- IPX Diagnostics Enabled

- Preallocate VGNMA memory

- Source Routing

Computer \ IPX 32-Bit Protocol for Novell NetWare Client 32 \ SPX

- *SPX Connections*. Defines the number of SPX connections.

- *SPX Verify Timeout*. Sets the time limit in clock ticks for waiting for verification from the SPX session.

- *SPX Listen Timeout*. Sets the time limit for waiting for a response time from an SPX session.

- *SPX Abort Timeout*. Sets the abort time for the SPX session

- Allow Connection Watchdogging

Computer \ IPX 32-Bit Protocol for Novell NetWare Client 32 \ IPX Advanced

- *Primary Logical Board*. Your primary logical network adapter can be one of many accepted protocols. Some of the many examples are shown below.

ETHERNET_802.2
ETHERNET_802.3
ETHERNET_SNAP
ETHERNET_II
TOKEN-RING
TOKEN-RING_SNAP
FDDI_802.2
FDDI_SNAP
ISDN

Computer \ Novell NetWare/IP \ Parameters

• Custom Configuration

NetWare/IP Domain Name
NWIP Domain
Retries to DSS during startup
Number of seconds between retries
Broadcast SAP nearest server queries to network
NetWare/IP 1.1 compatibility
Verbose

See Figure 15-11.

Computer \ Novell NetWare/IP \ Servers

• Nearest NetWare/IP Servers

• Preferred Domain SAP/RIP Servers

Computer \ Novell SNMP Agent \ SNMP

If you are using SNMP services, you can define your community settings here.

• Enable Monitor Community

• Monitor Community

• Enable Control Community

• Control Community

• System Name

• System Location

• System Contact

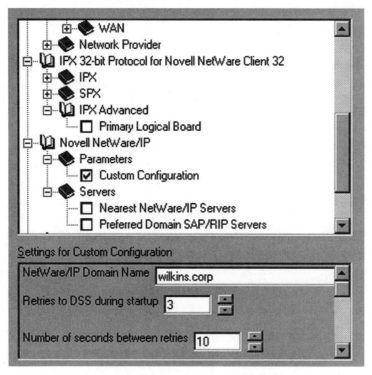

Figure 15-11 *Setting IP parameters for NetWare IP.*

- Enable Authentication Traps

Computer \ Host Resource MIB for Novell Client 32 \ Printers and Modems

These settings are used if you are collecting inventory with ManageWise.

- Local Printers
- Local Modems

Computer \ Host Resource MIB for Novell Client 32 \ Tape Drives

These settings are used if you are collecting inventory with ManageWise.

- Local Tape Drives

Computer \ Host Resource MIB for Novell Client 32 \ Software Search

You can define the level of directory level access on the file server as well as additional search paths.

- Directory levels to search from root

- Additional Search Paths

Computer \ Novell Target Service Agent for Windows 95

These settings are used if you are using NetWare's install on demand features and/or NAL (NetWare Application Launcher).

- User name:

- Password:

- Server name:

- Auto register:

- Show icon on task bar

- Include Drives

Computer \ File/Folder Shell Extensions

These settings define whether or not the client has the listed advanced file rights for changing trustees, changing compression, and showing property tabs on registered file types

- Allow Users to add/remove/change Trustees

- Allow Users to change Compression

- Show NetWare Rights property page

- Allow Users to change Extended Properties

- Network Provider

- Enable Send Message Utility

System Policy Settings for the Microsoft Client for NetWare

Windows 98 supports the full NetWare bindery and NDS environment by providing the IPX/SPX protocol and the Microsoft Client for NetWare. The system policy template WINDOWS.ADM has some NetWare relevant settings that you should be aware of. They are computer-based system policy settings, so these settings will affect all users that share a computer system.

Computer \ Windows 98 Network \ Access Control

- *User-level access control.* If you are using file and print services for Windows 98, access control can help streamline password deployment with local node shares. Either NetWare or NT can be chosen as the security provider to authenticate users for file and print sharing. The authenticator types are: NetWare 3.x or 4.x, Windows NT Server or Workstation, or Windows NT Domain. See Figure 15-12.

Windows 98 Network \ Logon

Defines a logon banner and text that must be acknowledged by the client.

- Logon Banner

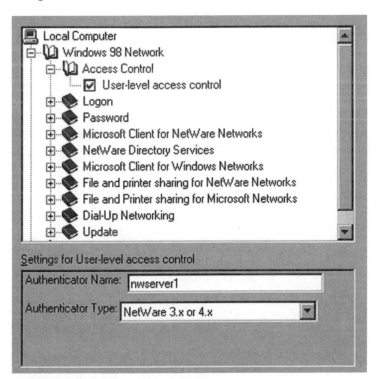

Figure 15-12 *Setting user-level access control.*

- *Require validation from network for Windows access.* When enabled, this setting forces the user to log on to the NT domain or NetWare server before Windows 98 will load.

- *Don't show last user at logon.* An obvious security setting to deploy.

Windows 98 Network \ Password

Disabling the caching of passwords is also recommended. The scenario: Your server is taken down for maintenance while your Windows 98 clients are working on the network. Assume that no server access is attempted until your server comes back online. The caching of passwords allows the Windows 98 PC to autolog onto the server once it is up again. It's a good idea to force users to enter their logon name and password every time they need network access.

- Disable password caching

Windows 98 Network \ Microsoft Client for NetWare Networks

The following settings are for the NetWare Client supplied by Microsoft in Windows 98.

- Preferred server
- Support long file names
- Support long file names on:

    NetWare 3.12 and above
    All NetWare servers that support LFNs

- *Disable automatic NetWare login.* Again caching username and passwords is a security problem.

Windows 98 Network \ NetWare Directory Services

- Preferred Tree

    Tree Name:

- Load NetWare DLLs at startup
- Disable automatic tree login
- Enable login confirmation

- Don't show advanced login button
- Default type of NetWare login

  Log in to server in bindery mode
  Log in to NDS tree

- Don't show servers that aren't NDS objects
- Don't show peer workgroups
- Don't show server objects
- Don't show container objects
- Don't show printer objects
- Don't show print queue objects
- Don't show volume objects

See Figure 15-13.

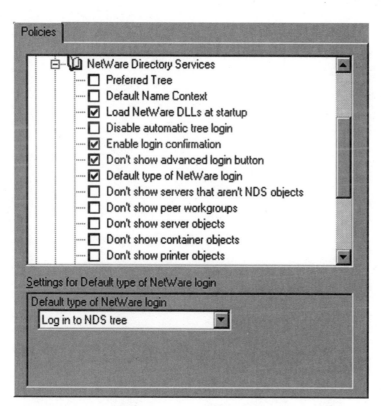

Figure 15-13 *Setting NDS options for the Microsoft client.*

Rolling Out
Zero Administration

This chapter introduces you to a concept of centralized computing called Zero Administration. You will learn:

- What the term *Zero Administration* means
- How to deploy the Zero Administration Kit for Windows NT 4.0 Workstation Clients
- How to deploy the Zero Administration Kit for Windows 98 Clients
- Customization techniques for Zero Administration system policy templates
- ZAK software utilities and scripts and how they are used

In 1997 Microsoft made the bold announcement that it had developed new software tools to aid in administering a large network—the Zero Administration Kit (ZAK).

At first people were excited about Microsoft's "new" features, but then they realized that ZAK was not that new at all. And now...the rest of the ZAK story.

In the Beginning...Before ZAK

When NT Server 3.5 was first released, it included a few new features—namely, the Registry, user profiles, and a choice to automate the NT installation through files, called *answer files*, that held the answers to the questions posed by the installation.

In 1995 when Windows 95 was first released, it featured three "new" system components that at the time were not initially seen to be huge changes. These features were the Registry and Regedit, user profiles, and system policies.

When NT 4.0 was released, it also included Windows 95-type user profiles, Regedit, and system policies, as well as a choice to automate the NT installation through those files called "answer files," and a tool called *Sysdiff* that allowed you to clone all or part of the NT workstation plus the application software mix.

This recounting of Windows history from 1994 up to now hopefully shows you that we are living and working in the Microsoft "laboratory" full time. Features that started out in Windows 95 were refined and then appear in NT and, after being refined a bit more, are migrated to Windows 98...and so on, back and forth we go.

The current platforms of Windows 98 Second Edition and Windows NT 4.0 may be merged into one final product some day in the future. That actual day is anyone's guess, but it's a safe bet that the current home and business computer market drives the speed of merging of all Microsoft Windows platforms into one.

This brings us to the featured software tool offered to us by Microsoft for network administration and user support, called the *Zero Administration Kit* or ZAK, which aims to stop the cost of lost productivity by reducing the desktop and software choices that the user can make. Guess what? That's what system policies are! So again, from the Microsoft laboratory, a seemingly new product is created from the following already available software tools plus a few new features. The components of ZAK are:

- User profiles
- New ZAK system policy settings
- Sysdiff and answer files
- Regedit and the Registry
- Network installs of Office 97

ZAK is available for Windows 95, Windows 98, Windows NT 4.0, and Windows 4.0 Terminal Server products. It will not be available for Windows 2000 because (you guessed!) it's built in as a software feature called *Install on Demand*. With Windows 2000, the full working version of ZAK will include the Microsoft applications we all use (Office 2000, Internet Explorer 5.0) and links to BackOffice 4.5, which includes Site Server and Systems Management Server, Exchange, and SQL. Also, with the inclusion of Terminal Server as a network service in Windows 2000, there will not be a need for ZAK as a separate product.

The reality is that Microsoft provides enough features in ZAK hopefully to get us hooked and wanting more so that we rush to upgrade to BackOffice 4.5 and Windows 2000.

Benefits of ZAK

The main benefits of deploying ZAK for the NT 4.0 and Windows 98 environment are the capacity to:

1. Centrally store a copy of Windows NT and the current Service Pack, or Windows 98 that would be installed with a custom answer file.

2. Centrally configure and store Office 97 just once, and then distribute Office 97 to users' local PCs. Users would not participate in the installation. (This would be the Sysdiff and Registry components.)

3. Customize the users' desktop from a central network location to govern their access to menu options and commands. (This would be the system policy component.)

4. Secure the users' local computer surroundings by removing access to the local hard drive. [This would be the new ZAK system policy template(s).]

ZAK Modes: AppStation and TaskStation

The two modes of the Zero Administration Kit are called `AppStation` and `TaskStation`. Both modes introduce the familiar Explorer shell that is effectively a dumb terminal mode that can run selected Windows-based application software.

One of these modes could fit a particular cross section of workers in your company, especially ones that use a minimum set of applications, or new computer users that were moving from an actual terminal mode to either Windows 98 or NT. Restrictions of what they could access would be quite helpful to them and to the help desk and desktop support personnel. However, even Microsoft has acknowledged that ZAK will not be (and is not meant to be) installed on every client's PC.

The Task-Based Worker: Task Station Mode

The `TaskStation` mode is for new users that need access to one software program, such as travel agents, bank tellers, or public intranet workstations. All other desktop programs are removed, including the standard user interface and file system elements. The user will not even have access to the `Start` button or the task manager. If NT Workstations are used, NTFS security will be applied to the local files to prevent ZAK users from changing or deleting them. See Figure 16-1.

The Application-Based Mode: App Station Mode

The `AppStation` mode is for the new user that needs access to a limited suite of software. Most of my users need a word processor

Figure 16-1 *ZAK and* `TaskStation` *mode.*

and maybe a spreadsheet plus email/Internet access. The `Start` menu is created with shortcuts to all of the necessary programs. The software is installed on a file server but, due to the typical bandwidth of most networks, a local install might be necessary. See Figure 16-2.

Note

Even the choices ZAK allows can present problems. Some of the help files might have commands that will allow the user to access parts of the operating system that were assumed to be locked out. Examples of this are the Printer Troubleshooter and the Network Troubleshooter.

Installing the Zero Administration Kit for NT

The `ZAKSetup.exe` setup program defines the central location for installing ZAK files, Windows NT Workstation, or Windows 98. If you decide to use the `AppStation` mode, you must also define the following server locations where your application(s) are to be installed.

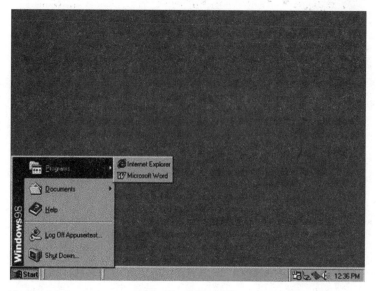

Figure 16-2 AppStation *mode and ZAK.*

- *Distribution Server.* This server provides the location for installing, configuring, and distributing ZAK and Windows files to client computers.

- *Primary Domain Controller.* The primary domain controller is required for storing and configuring system policy files and logon scripts.

- *Applications Server.* This server is used for storing the network-installed programs that AppStation users will run. The applications server can be the same server as the distribution server or the primary domain controller.

User and Group Accounts for ZAK Clients

ZAK uses Windows NT global groups to manage AppStation and TaskStation user accounts and resources. The AppStation or TaskStation users are grouped using global groups to co-ordinate ZAK user accounts.

Printer Support for ZAK Clients

You can initially configure only a single printer for a user during the ZAK setup. In order to add multiple printers, the user's login script is used in conjunction with the CON2PRT command supplied with ZAK. For example, if you specified Printer-HP1 located on PrintServer1 during the ZAK Setup process, the CON2PRT command would appear as follows:

```
CON2PRT /F /F \\PrintServer1\Printer-HP1
```

/F   deletes all existing printer connections

/C   adds a printer connection

To add a printer named Printer-HP2 located on PrintServer2, you would configure the CON2PRT command as follows:

```
CON2PRT /C \\PrintServer2\Printer-HP2
```

File Server Organization for ZAK Clients

Assuming that you accepted the default file locations during ZAK setup, the following folder/directory structure will be found. The ZAKADMIN path holds all of the needed files for administration, including login scripts, system policy files, and policy templates. A ZAKAppDist is created for AppStation and a ZAKTaskDisk folder is created for TaskStation. These folders contain Windows OS files, Service Pack files, batch files, and ZAK tools used during the installation. See Figure 16-3.

For AppStation only, ZAK also creates a NETAPPS folder on the network applications server for storing all of the Microsoft Office 98/97 related files, including the MSApps, MSOffice, and remote Start Menu folders. See Figure 16-4.

ZAK System Policy Templates

The AppStation and TaskStation templates contain the required policies for operating system and program settings. See Figure 16-5.

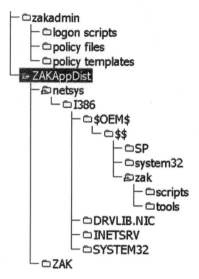

```
├─ ⌂zakadmin
│   ├─ ⌂logon scripts
│   ├─ ⌂policy files
│   └─ ⌂policy templates
├─ ▰ ZAKAppDist
│   ├─ ▱netsys
│   │   └─ ⌂I386
│   │       ├─ ⌂$OEM$
│   │       │   └─ ⌂$$
│   │       │       ├─ ⌂SP
│   │       │       ├─ ⌂system32
│   │       │       └─ ▱zak
│   │       │           ├─ ⌂scripts
│   │       │           └─ ⌂tools
│   │       ├─ ⌂DRVLIB.NIC
│   │       ├─ ⌂INETSRV
│   │       └─ ⌂SYSTEM32
└─ ⌂ZAK
```

Figure 16-3 *ZAK folder structure.*

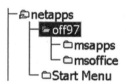

```
├─ ▱netapps
│   ├─ ▰ off97
│   │   ├─ ⌂msapps
│   │   └─ ⌂msoffice
│   └─ ⌂Start Menu
```

Figure 16-4 *The NETAPPS folder on the server.*

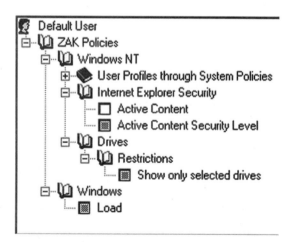

Figure 16-5 *ZAK system policy templates for NT clients.*

Minimum NT Server Requirements for ZAK Clients

- A Primary Domain Controller (PDC) with 1 GB free hard drive space
- At least 128 MB RAM
- Windows NT Server version 4.0
- The file system should be NTFS
- TCP/IP must be installed as the network protocol

Minimum NT Workstation Requirements for ZAK Clients

- Pentium 100 or higher
- 32 MB RAM or higher
- Clean hard drive with at least 400 MB of free space
- MS-DOS network boot disk

Your client hardware configurations should be as similar as possible. Network cards must also be designed as "unattendable." Refer to the Windows NT Deployment Guide, "Automating Windows NT Setup," found in the Zero Administration Kit, for a list of unattendable network cards. If your network card is not supported, ZAK will not work.

Other Software Requirements

- Zero Administration Kit CD
- Service Pack 3 or later for Windows NT Server version 4.0
- Windows NT Workstation version 4.0
- Microsoft Office 97 (for AppStation only)
- Microsoft Windows NT Workstation Deployment Guide, "Automating Windows NT Setup" (found on the ZAK CD)

ZAK Setup for NT creates either a TaskStation or AppStation distribution point on your server. These distribution points can

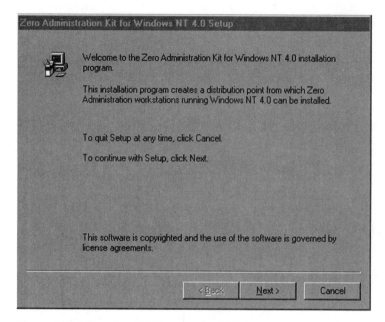

Figure 16-6 *Starting ZAK setup for NT.*

then be used for the unattended installations of ZAK NT Workstation clients. To start the ZAK installation for NT, the command to execute the ZAK setup from the ZAK CD is
ZAKSETUP.EXE. The Zero Administration Kit for Windows NT 4.0
Setup dialog box will then be displayed. See Figure 16-6.

After accepting the license agreement, you will be prompted to
which client you wish to install, Intel or Alpha. See Figure 16-7.

You are now prompted to choose the type of ZAK client
install, either AppStation or TaskStation. See Figure 16-8.

Next specify the root of the distribution point on a selected
server in the domain. The drive selected should be NTFS so that
proper file and folder security can be applied. The default location selected by the install is ZAKAppDist. See Figure 16-9.

Now you must tell ZAK where your network applications will
reside on the distribution server in these dialog boxes:

- *Network Application Directory.* Type the complete path to the
  folder in which you are installing applications that clients can
  run from the server.

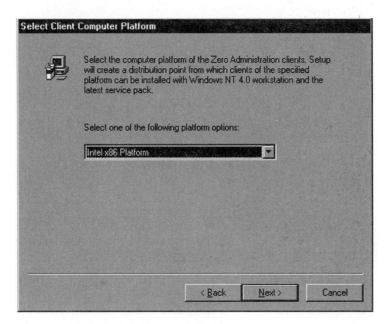

Figure 16-7 *Selecting the ZAK client.*

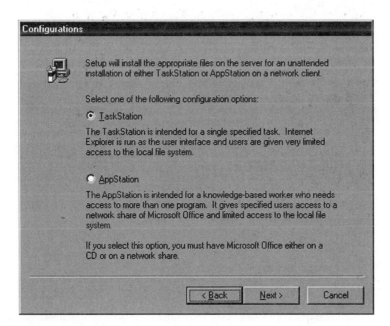

Figure 16-8 AppStation *or* TaskStation *modes.*

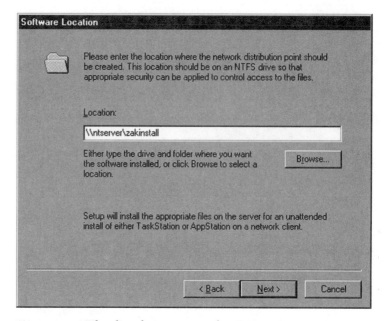

Figure 16-9 *The distribution point for ZAK.*

- *Network Applications Server Name.* Type the name of the
  server that will host the `AppStation` software.

- *Network Applications Share Name.* Type the share name you
  want to use for application installations.

See Figure 16-10.

   You are then asked to enter a drive letter that `AppStation`
clients can use to connect to the network application share.
Choose `Drive O:`. See Figure 16-11.

   At this point in the ZAK install, the `Install Microsoft
Office as Network Application Suite` dialog box is displayed.
If you are planning to install Microsoft Office, click `OK`. If you
are not installing Office, clear the checkbox. ZAK now will
prompt you for the network location to copy its administrative
files. ZAK Setup then creates the system folder and three subfolders: `Logon Scripts`, `Policy Files`, and `Policy Templates`.
See Figure 16-12.

   The `Domain Administrator Information` dialog box is now displayed. The installation needs a domain administrator to be able

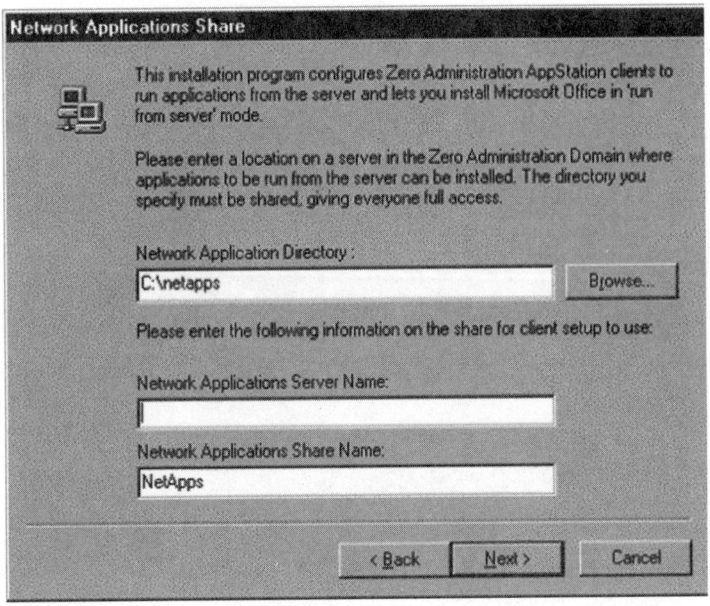

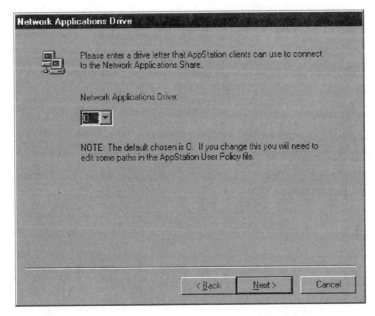

Figure 16-10 *Network locations for application software.*

Figure 16-11 *Enter the network share drive letter for ZAK clients.*

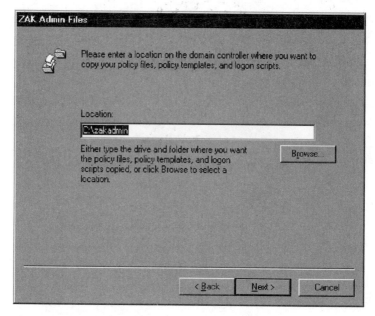

Figure 16-12 *Define the network location for ZAK system files.*

to access the distribution server to perform the unattended install of the ZAK client. See Figure 16-13.

The domain information you must enter is as follows:

- *Domain Name.* Enter the name of the domain clients will log onto.

- *Username.* Enter the user account name.

- *Password.* Enter the user's password.

- *Confirm Password.* Enter the same password you typed in the preceding `Password` field.

Next choose a network printer that you would like your ZAK clients to use. See Figure 16-14.

- *Printer Server.* The print server name.
- *Printer Share.* The share name of a printer.

If you are using Exchange Server, you are then prompted to enter the name of the exchange server.

ZAK Setup now starts copying its files to the server. You will

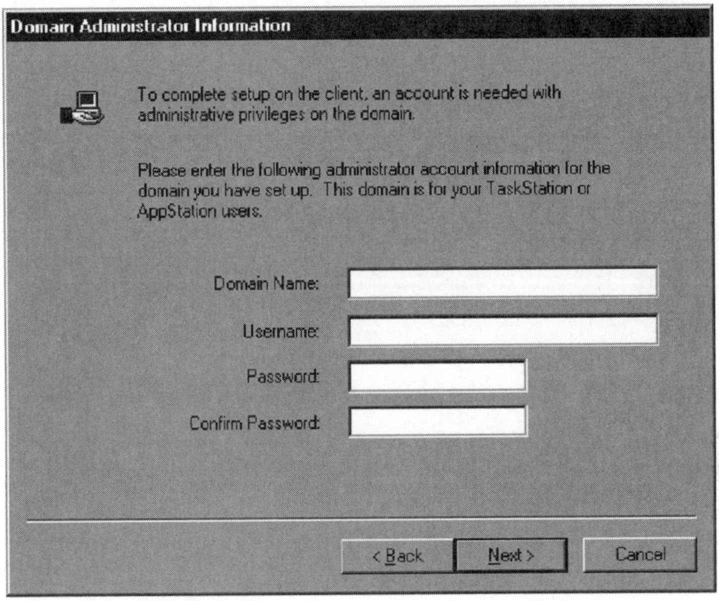

Figure 16-13 *Enter Domain Administrator Information.*

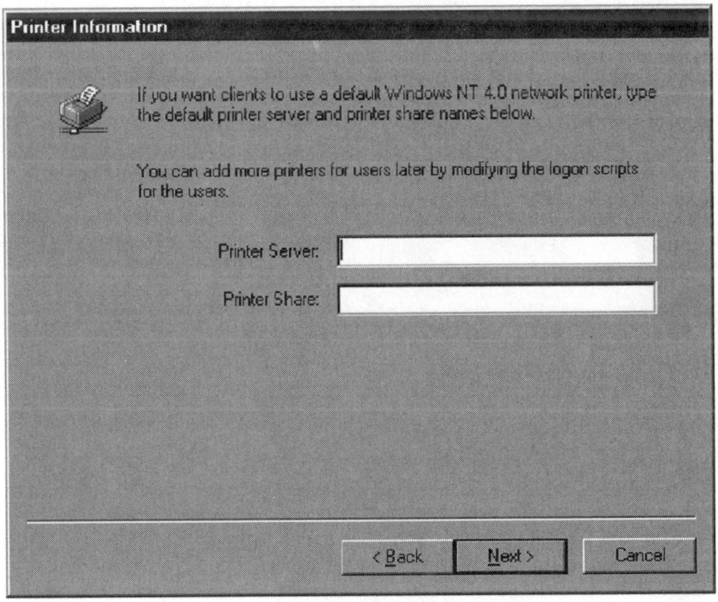

Figure 16-14 *Choose your print server for ZAK clients.*

then be prompted for the ZAK CD. Then you will be prompted for the location of the NT Workstation CD. Enter the path to WINNT\i386, and then click OK. Finally, you will be prompted for the location of Service Pack 3 or later. Enter the path for service pack X\i386, and then click OK.

If you chose earlier to install Microsoft Office 97, you are now prompted for the location of the Office files. Type the complete path to the location of the Microsoft Office 97 files; for example, F:\Office97 and then click OK. ZAK Setup then will start the Microsoft Office 97 Setup. The Office 97 Admin Setup requires information related to choices made during the setup of the network applications share.

The information you enter will be provided in a reminder slash screen to assist with your setup of Office 97 in run-from-server mode. See Figure 16-15.

Note   Write down the location of the Destination folder and the MSAPPS folder, and the Path and Drive indicated in the Office Setup Instructions dialog box—you will need this information later during Office Setup.

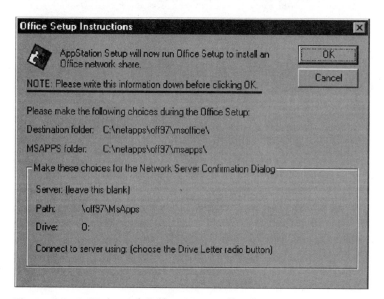

Figure 16-15 *Essential Office 97 install information.*

The automated portion of ZAK Setup for the `AppStation` distribution point is now complete. There are several manual steps that you must perform to finish the full ZAK setup.

Manual Steps to Complete the ZAK Installation for NT Clients

Once the automated ZAK setup has finished, you can first verify your installation by editing the `ZAKB1WRK.CMD` found in the following location on the server: `NETSYS\I386\$OEM$\$$\ZAK\SCRIPTS`.

ZAK Setup stores the choices that you made during setup in this file. Recheck the net use and net user commands listed, making sure the listed parameters (server names, shares, account names, and passwords) are all exact.

> To view a `.CMD` file, right-click the desired file and click `Edit`.   **Note**

The following manual steps must be completed to finish the setup of ZAK:

1. Create global groups

2. Create ZAK user accounts

3. Define ZAK user profiles

4. Define a reference ZAK client for new users

5. Create the `Start Menu` on the Network

Creating Global Groups

1. Go to `Administrative Tools` and open `User Manager for Domains`.

2. Select the `User` menu and then `New Global Group`.

3. Enter `Appusers` for the group name in the `Group Name` text box. Don't allow any other users in this global group.

4. Click `OK` to add the group.

Next create another group called `Taskusers` by repeating steps 2 through 4. (These names must be used, as they are the global groups that are defined in `ZAKCONFIG.POL`.)

Creating ZAK User Accounts

Using `User Manager for Domains`, you next create user accounts of the new ZAK client user accounts to be added to the `Appusers` or `Taskusers` global groups.

1. On the `User` menu in `User Manager for Domains`, click `New User`.

2. Enter the information as required in the `New User` dialog box.

Creating ZAK User Profiles

1. Click `Profile` to open the selected users profile. For `Logon Script Name`, enter `APPLOGON.CMD` for `Appstation` clients and `TSKLOGON.CMD` for `Taskstation` clients.

2. In `Connect`, select the drive letter `U:`.

3. In `To`, type the path to the folder (for example, `\\<SERVER-NAME>\HOME\%USERNAME%`) and click `OK`.

4. In the `New User` dialog box select either the `Appusers` or `Taskusers` in `Not Member of`, and then click `Add` to add the user to the group you just created.

5. Click `OK`.

6. Select `Add` to add the new user to the domain.

To add multiple users repeat steps 1 through 6. See Figure 16-16.

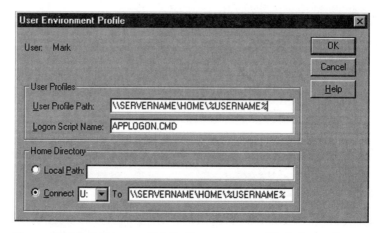

Figure 16-16 *Setting up ZAK clients user profile information.*

> A network share must also be created on the server in order for the home directory to be used as the user's home folder on the network. To create the user's share, first create a folder called, for example, `\\SERVERNAME\HOME\ZAKUSERS` on the server. Then share this folder giving the global group `Everyone` Full Control permissions.

Note

Finalizing the Distribution Server

The ZAK files and folders must now be set up on the server. If you accepted all of the default file locations during setup, ZAK has placed a set of folders on the root of your server hard drive. For the `AppStation` installation, the `NETAPPS` folder is used to store Office 97-related files and folder information including the `MSApps`, `MSOffice`, and remote `Start menu` folders.

The `ZAKADMIN` folder is the location for logon scripts, policy files, and policy templates. The installation you chose (`ZAKAppDist` is created for `AppStations` and a `ZAKTaskDisk` folder is created for `TaskStations`) will determine whether `ZAKAppDist` or `ZAKTaskDist` is the location where the Windows NT Workstation files, the service pack files, the ZAK custom batch files, as well as miscellaneous tools used during the installation process, such as Shutdown and Sysdiff, are found. Assuming that you accepted the setup defaults, a logon scripts folder was created in `ZAKADMIN\LOGON` scripts.

ZAK Files and Shares on the Server

If you have one domain controller or multiple domain controllers, the file locations for the ZAK system files will be different.

- *One Domain Controller.* Copy all of the files that `Zakadmin\logon` contains to the `NETLOGON` share of the PDC (`%SystemRoot%\system32\Repl\import\scripts`).

- *Multiple Domain Controllers.* Copy all of the files that `Zakadmin\logon` contains to the `NETLOGON` share of the PDC (`%SystemRoot%\system32\Repl\import\scripts`). Next set up directory replication to the `NETLOGON` share on all other domain controllers.

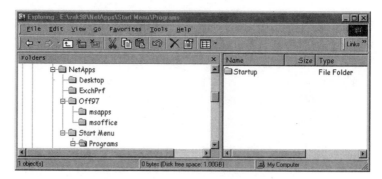

Figure 16-17 *ZAK folder structure in the server.*

Now create the `NETAPPS` and `NETSYS` shares on the server. (If you installed `TaskStation Mode` you do not have to create the `NETAPPS` share.) See Figure 16-17.

1. Share the `NETAPPS` folder assigning the global group `Everyone` Full Control on the share.

2. Initiate `NTFS Security` to the `NETAPPS` folder and all subfolders assigning the global group `Everyone` Read permission and the global group `Domain Admins` Full Control.

3. Assign the global group `Everyone` Change permission on the `NETAPPS\OFF97\MSOFFICE\WORKDIR` folder.

4. Share the `NETSYS` folder, giving the global group `Domain Admins` Read permission and remove the global group `Everyone` from the permissions list.

5. Initiate `NTFS Security` to this folder and all subfolders giving `Domain Admins` Full Control. Remove the global group `Everyone` from the `Directory Permissions` list.

Enabling ZAK System Policies

ZAK system policy settings found in `ZAKWINNT.ADM` will be additions to the existing `WINNT.ADM` and `COMM.ADM` system policy settings, creating a "master template."

1. Open the system policy editor.

2. Click `Options`, and then click `Policy Template`.

3. Click `Add` to add all the template files that were installed by

ZAK Setup. The template files are located in the `ZAKADMIN\POLICY Templates` folder.

4. Open the `ZAKCONFIG.POL` file in system policy editor located in the `ZAKADMIN\POLICY Files` folder.

5. Double-click on the `Appusers` policy.

6. In the `Appusers Properties` window, click on `Zak Policies`, `Windows NT`, `Drives`, `Restrictions`.

7. Verify that `Show only selected drives` is checked.

8. Select `Show only selected drives` and choose `Only O:`.

9. Click `OK` to close the `Appusers Properties` window.

10. If your test network has only one domain controller, save `ZAKCONFIG.POL` to the `NETLOGON` share of your PDC as `NTCONFIG.POL`.

Creating the Start Menu on the Network

Log on with the administrator account for the local computer with the password that you supplied during ZAK setup.

1. Open Explorer and on the `View` menu, click `Folder Options`, selecting `Show all files`.

2. Copy all of the `.lnk` files in `%SYSTEMROOT%\PROFILES\ALL USERS\START MENU` to the `NETAPPS\START MENU` folder located on the server.

3. Copy the `.lnk` files in `%SYSTEMROOT%\PROFILES\ALL USERS\START MENU\PROGRAMS` to the `NETAPPS\START MENU\PROGRAMS` folder located on the server.

See Figure 16-18.

Creating the New ZAK Client

The first task is to create a boot disk that contains a custom `Unattend.txt` file for each client. Another name for the `Unattend.txt` file is an *answer file*. It provides ZAK with answers to questions required by Setup, enabling you to perform unattended installations of programs. This file contains client-specific information, such as the computer name and user name; and network information, such as domain name and domain administrator

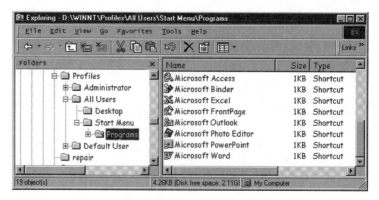

Figure 16-18 *Start menu items to copy to the server.*

account and password. Figure 16-19 defines what settings must
be set for all computers and all users.

Modify the sample `Unattend.txt` file found on the ZAK CD in
the `I386 \SCRIPTS` folder. You must add the appropriate domain,
administrative account, and password for that domain. There are
text notes provided inside the file itself to help you, as well as
ZAK notes on full creation of the `Unattend.txt` file found on the
ZAK CD.

In this Group Section	Sample Parameter	With
[UserData]	OrgName	Company name
[UserData]	ProductID	CD KEY
[GuiUnattended]	TimeZone	Your time zone
[Network]	JoinDomain	Domain
[Network]	CreateComputerAccount	Domain Administrator
[UserData]	FullName	The ZAK User name
[UserData]	Computer Name	Computer name

Figure 16-19 `Unattend.txt` *settings to change.*

```
[unattended]
OemPreinstall = yes
; NoWaitAfterTextMode = 0
NoWaitAfterGuiMode = 1
FileSystem = ConvertNTFS
targetpath = Winnt

[UserData]
FullName = "NetPC User"
OrgName = " "
ComputerName = "************** CHANGE THIS LINE ************"
ProductID = "111-1111111"

[GuiUnattended]
OemSkipWelcome = 1
OemBlankAdminPassword = 1
TimeZone = "(GMT-08:00) Pacific Time (US & Canada); Tijuana"

[OEM_Ads]
Banner = "Windows NT 4.0 ZAK CLIENT SETUP"
[Network]
DetectAdapters = DetectParams
InstallProtocols = ProtocolsSection
; ********** CHANGE THE FOLLOWING LINES**********************
; Change the "NetPC Domain" to the domain ZAK clients will be joining.
; On the CreateComputerAccount change the NetPCAdmin to an
  administrative
; account that lets the computer create a computer account in the
  domain
; you will be joining, in the NetPCAdminPassword give the account
  password
; ********** CHANGE THE FOLLOWING LINES**********************
JoinDomain = "NetPC Domain"
CreateComputerAccount = NetPCAdmin,NetPCAdminPassword

[DetectParams]
DetectAdapters = ""
DetectCount = 1

[ProtocolsSection]
TC = TCPIPParams

[TCPIPParams]
DHCP = yes

[Display]
BitsPerPel = 8
XResolution = 800
```

```
YResolution = 600
VRefresh = 60
AutoConfirm = 1
```

Next, start your new ZAK client with an MS-DOS network boot disk created from the Network Client Administrator utility found on any PDC `Administrative Tools` menu, and connect to the shared `NETSYS` folder on the distribution server. From the `Run` box execute the following command line:

```
F:\i386\winnt /u:a:\unattend.txt /s:x:\i386
<drive letter>:\<path to winnt.exe>\winnt.exe
/u:<drive letter>:\<path to unattend.txt>\unattend.txt
/s:<drive letter>:\<path to Windows NT install files>
```

You have now completed the ZAK setup. The next step is to use the DOS network client boot disk to install the `TaskStation` or `AppStation` mode on your clients' PCs.

Windows NT TaskStation Restrictions

The following user interface policies are in effect for the ZAK TaskStation client:

- Remove the Run command.
- Remove folders from settings on the Start menu.
- Remove taskbar from settings on the Start menu.
- Remove the Find command.
- Hide drives in My Computer.
- Hide Network Neighborhood.
- Hide all items on desktop.
- Disable the Shut Down command.
- Don't save settings at exit.
- Enable Custom Shell by running: `runapp c:\program files\plus!\microsoft internet explorer\iexplorer.exe -k`
- Remove File menu from Windows NT Explorer.
- Remove Common program groups from Start menu.

- Disable context menus for the taskbar.
- Disable default context menu from Explorer.
- Remove Map Network Drive and Disconnect Network Drive from the Tools menu in Explorer.
- Disable link file tracking from Explorer.
- Disable Task Manager.
- Disable show welcome tips at logon.
- Show only selected drives.

Windows NT AppStation Restrictions

The following user interface system policy restrictions are in effect for the ZAK AppStation client:

- Remove the Run command.
- Remove folders from Settings on the Start menu.
- Remove taskbar from Settings on the Start menu.
- Remove the Find command.
- Hide drives in My Computer.
- Hide Entire Network in Network Neighborhood.
- Hide workgroup contents in Network Neighborhood.
- Hide all items on the desktop.
- Disable the Shut Down command.
- Don't save settings on exit.
- Windows 98 TaskStation System Policies.
- Remove the Run command.
- Remove folders from settings on the Start Menu.
- Remove taskbar from settings on the Start Menu.
- Remove the Find command.
- Hide drives in My Computer.
- Hide Network Neighborhood.

- No 'Entire Network' in Network Neighborhood.
- No workgroup contents in Network Neighborhood.
- Hide all items on desktop.
- Don't save settings at exit.

ZAK Software Utilities

Several software utilities are bundled with ZAK on the ZAK CD-ROM. These are used by the ZAK automated setup during installation. If you so choose, you can manually install ZAK using these utilities.

CACLS

This utility is used to change the state of the access control lists, also called *permissions*, on files.

During the installation of the two modes of ZAK—TaskStation and AppStation—Cacls.exe is used at length in the ZAK custom batch file ACLS.CMD, to place strict security on the server file system.

Syntax:	CACLS filename [/T] [/E] [/C] [/G user:perm] [/R user [...]] [/P user:perm [...]] [/D user [...]]
/T	Changes the ACLs of specified files in the current directory and all subdirectories.
/E	Edits the ACL instead of replacing it.
/C	Continues on any access-denied errors.
G user:perm	Grants specified user access rights. Permission can be: R, read; C, change, (write); or F, full control.
/R user	Revokes specified user's access rights (valid only with /E).
/P user:perm	Replaces specified user's access rights. Permission can be: N, none; R, read; C, change (write); or F, full control.
/D user	Denies specified user access.

FIXPRF

During installation of ZAK you are prompted as to whether your users use Exchange. If you answered Yes, this utility will be used during the Client install of ZAK using the user name of the logged-on user, creating the profile automatically.

Syntax: FIXPRF <Fully Qualified Path to .PRF file>
            <MailboxName> <ProfileName>
            <ExchangeServerName>

FLOPPYLOCK

FloppyLock uses *Discretionary Access Control Lists* (DACLs) to control the access to ZAK client's floppy disk drive(s). These DACLs continue to exist, even when users log off and log back on. Members of the Administrators and Power Users groups can access the floppy drives when the service is started on Windows NT Workstation. Only members of the Administrators group can access the floppy drives when the service is started on NT Server.

Floplock.exe must be installed as a service on every NT computer where you want to lock the floppy drives. Then use Control Panel and the Services icon to arrange for this service to start automatically.

INSTSRV

The utility INSTSRV both installs and removes system services from NT computer systems.

Syntax: INSTSRV <service name> (<exe location> |
            REMOVE) [-a <Account Name>] [-p <Account
            Password>]

CON2PRT

The CON2PRT utility is used to add multiple printers to ZAK clients through login scripts.

Syntax: CON2PRT [/? | /h | /f | [/c
            \\printserver\share | /cd \\printserver\share]+]
/?   Displays usage.
/h   Displays usage.
/f   Deletes all existing printer connections.

/c	Connects to \\printserver\share printer.
/cd	Connects to \\printserver\share printer and sets it as the default printer.

RUNAPP

This executable is used in `TaskStation` mode to start the dedicated user interface software application. `RunApp` syntax is but a single piece of information: The name of the `.exe` to automatically start.

SHUTDOWN

ZAK Setup uses the `Shutdown` command to restart the client computer in between the Windows NT, Service Pack installation, and the Office 97 installation.

ZAK System Policy Choices for Windows NT Clients

ZAK choices for system policy settings are all for the ZAK user or group of users.

User \ ZAK Policies \ Windows NT \ Profiles Through System Policies

- AppData Folder
- Favorites Folder
- NetHood Folder
- PrintHood Folder
- Recent Folder
- SendTo Folder

These paths are where the ZAK clients network location is for their user profile folders. See Figure 16-20.

User \ ZAK Policies \ Windows NT \ Internet Explorer Security

- *Active Content*

    Allow downloading of ActiveX content

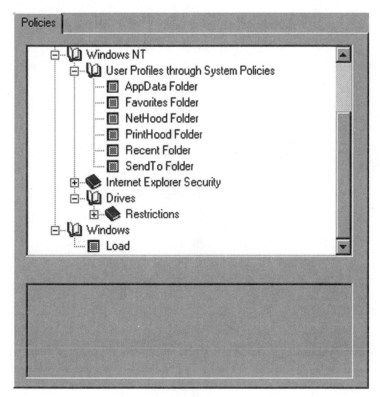

Figure 16-20 *ZAK system policy choices.*

Enable ActiveX Controls and Plug-ins
Run ActiveX Scripts
Enable Java Programs

- *Active Content Security Level.* Select the security level of Internet Explorer to as security level of High, Medium, or No Security. If No Security is selected, Active Content will be downloaded without prompting the user.

User \ ZAK Policies \ Windows NT \ Drives \ Restrictions

- *Show only selected drives.* See Figure 16-21.

  Don't show any drives, Only C:, Only U:
  Both C: and U:
  Both C: O: and U:

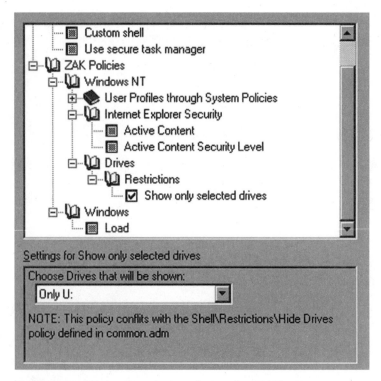

Figure 16-21 *Drive Restriction choices for ZAK.*

This policy will show only the selected drive letters on the ZAK client's computer. This setting uses a decimal number, which converts to a 26-bit binary string, with each bit representing a drive letter from A to Z. So the first binary digit is A, the second is B, and so on. It's really a drive letter mask with 26 toggle positions.

11111111111111111111111111

ZYXWVUTSRQPONMLKJIHGFEDCBA

This configuration converts to 67108863 decimal and will hide all local drive letters from A to Z. If you wanted to hide the C: drive, you would change the third lowest bit to a binary 0 and then convert the binary string to a decimal number.

There are several presets for this system policy setting; if you want this policy setting to show a different combination of available drive letters, simply create the desired binary string and convert it to decimal. Check out Chapter 8 on creating custom ADM scripts to see how it is done in detail.

User \ ZAK Policies \ Windows NT \ Windows

• *Load.* Enter the Program to be run on Startup.

ZAK for Windows 98 Clients

Before starting the ZAK setup for Windows 98, make sure you have a network Administrator account on the domain where ZAK is to be installed. Also make sure that you have write access to the NETLOGON share, as this is where ZAK stores system policy information and login scripts.

Needed 98/98 Software and Operating System Files

• The Zero Administration Kit for Windows 98 CD
• Complete packaged product version of Windows 98 (not the upgrade version)
• Microsoft Office 97 CD

Needed Software and Operating System Files

• Zero Administration Kit compact disc
• Microsoft Windows 98
• Microsoft Office 97

ZAK Installation for Windows 98 Clients

To start the ZAK installation for Windows 98, the command to run from the ZAK CD is ZAKSETUP.EXE. The Zero Administration Kit for Windows 98 Setup dialog box will then be displayed. See Figure 16-22.

The ZAK client install for Windows 98 installs all files for both AppStation and TaskStation. Next, specify the root of the distribution point on a selected NT server in the domain. The drive selected should be NTFS so that proper file and folder security can be applied.

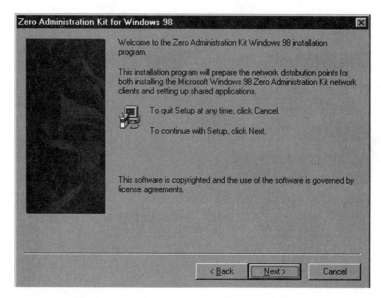

Figure 16-22 *Starting ZAK setup for Windows 98.*

You are then asked if you would like to create an Office 97
component share from which AppStation clients can run Office
97 applications.

If you answered Yes to creating an Office 97 share, you are
now prompted for the network location where Office 97 can be
installed. You need a minimum of 500 MB of free space. See Figure 16-23.

You are now given the option to create a Client boot disk for
use when ZAK is installed for new Windows 98 clients. This is an
MS-DOS network boot disk that will allow you to attach to the
distribution server to install ZAK on a new Windows 98 Client.
See Figure 16-24.

Installation Tasks

1. The domain that your Windows 98 TaskStation and AppStation users will log on to must now be entered.

2. Next, the workgroup that your Windows 98 TaskStation and
   AppStation users will log on to must now be entered.

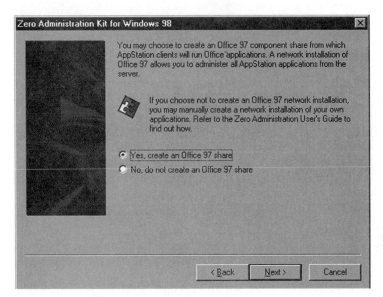

Figure 16-23 *Office 97 installation for* `AppStation` *clients.*

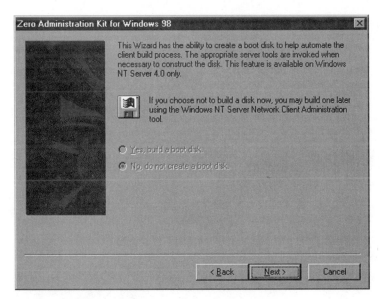

Figure 16-24 *The option to create a DOS boot disk.*

3. If they log on to a domain rather than a workgroup, then reenter the name of the logon domain.

4. The passthrough validation agent for your network must now be entered. Again, this is your logon domain.

5. Now you must tell ZAK what network location you want to use to store your policy files, login scripts, and system policy templates.

6. Next choose a network printer that you would like your ZAK clients to use.

7. Next enter the directory name on the client machine where Windows 98 will be installed.

Setup now starts copying its files to the server. You will then be prompted for the ZAK CD. ZAK will then copy the Windows 98 system files to the server. You are prompted as to what network location to use. See Figure 16-25.

ZAK Setup then starts Microsoft Office 97 Setup. The Office 97 Admin Setup requires information related to choices made during the setup of the `Network Applications` share. The information you entered is provided in a reminder slash screen to assist with your setup of Office 97 in run-from-server mode. See Figure 16-26.

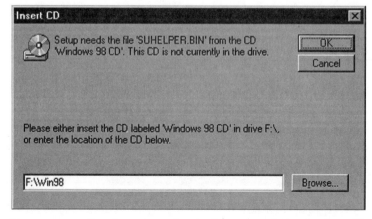

Figure 16-25 *Setup prompts for the location of Windows 98 files.*

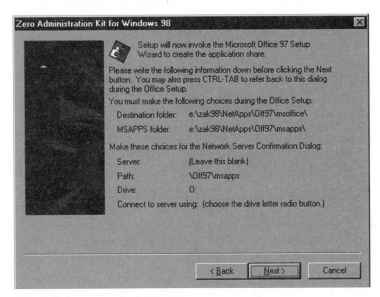

Figure 16-26 *Essential Office 97 information.*

Write down the location of the Destination folder and the
MSAPPS folder, and the Path and Drive indicated in the Office
Setup Instructions dialog box—you will need this information
later during Office Setup.

Note

The automated portion of ZAK Setup for the AppStation distribution point is now complete. There are several manual steps
that you must perform to finish the full ZAK setup.

Completing ZAK for Windows 98 Clients

There are three primary tasks you must complete to set up
Microsoft Windows 98 Zero Administration Kit clients:

1. Prepare the distribution server.

2. Set up Windows 98 with an automated setup script.

3. Administer the Windows 98 Zero Administration Kit clients.

Prepare the Distribution Server

ZAK will copy all source files for your preferred client to the server. For the Zero Administration Kit `TaskStation` and `AppStation` deployments, this includes Windows 98, the Zero Administration Kit client system files, and Office 97. By default, the directories are created in a single `ZAK98` directory, then organized in two sets of directories. See Figure 16-27.

The following list is a summary of the tasks you must complete to finish the ZAK install:

1. Create a setup script (`MSBATCH.INF`) to automate the setup process.

2. Create an MS-DOS network boot disk to connect to the distribution server.

3. Format the Zero Administration Kit client computer hard drive.

4. Run `Setup` with the automated setup script.

5. Administer the Windows 98 Zero Administration Kit clients.

6. Create user accounts and global groups for the users you wish to include in the Zero Administration Kit implementation.

7. Create `Windows 98 System Policies` to manage user settings.

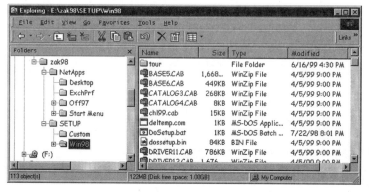

Figure 16-27 *File locations for Windows 98 ZAK clients.*

Creating Global Groups for Windows 98 ZAK Clients

1. Go to `Administrative Tools` and open `User Manager for Domains`.

2. Select the `User` menu and then `New Global Group`.

3. Enter `Appusers` for the group name in the `Group Name` text box. Don't allow any other users in this global group.

4. Click `OK` to add the group.

Next create another group called `Taskusers` by repeating steps 2 through 4. (These names must be used as they are the global groups that are defined in the `ZAKCONFIG.POL`.)

Creating ZAK User Accounts

Using `User Manager for Domains`, you next create user accounts of the new ZAK client user accounts to be added to the `Appusers` or `Taskusers` global groups.

1. On the `User` menu in `User Manager for Domains`, click `New User`.

2. Create a `ZAKSETUP` user account, assign `ZAKSETUP.BAT` as login script, and add `ZAKSETUP` to `Domain Admins` global group.

3. Create user accounts and assign the `APPLOGON.BAT` login script for `AppUser` accounts, and then add them to either the `TaskUser` or `AppUser` group.

Creating ZAK User Profiles

1. Click `Profile`, in `Logon Script Name`, and enter `APPLOGON.CMD` for `AppStation` clients.

2. In `Connect`, select the drive letter `S:`.

3. In `To`, type the path to the folder (for example, `\\<SERVER-NAME>\HOME\%USERNAME%`) and click `OK`.

4. In the `New User` dialog box select either the `Appusers` or `Taskusers` in `Not Member of`, and then click `Add` to add the user to the group you just created.

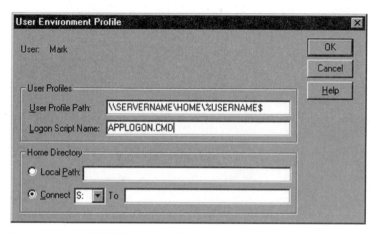

Figure 16-28 *ZAK client profile settings.*

5. Click OK.

6. Select Add to add the new user to the domain.

To add multiple users repeat steps 1 through 6. See Figure 16-28.

Note

> A user share must also be created on the server to be used as the user's home folder on the network. To create the user's share:
> 1. Create a folder called Users on the server.
> 2. Share this folder giving Everyone Full Control permission.

Organizing ZAK Files and Shares on the Server

If you have one domain controller or multiple domain controllers, the file locations for the ZAK system files will be different.

- *One domain controller.* Copy all of the files that Zakadmin\logon contains to the NETLOGON share of the PDC (%SystemRoot%\system32\Repl\import\scripts).

- *Multiple domain controllers.* Copy all of the files that Zakadmin\logon contains to the NETLOGON share of the PDC (%SystemRoot%\system32\Repl\import\scripts). Next, set up directory replication to the NETLOGON share on all other domain controllers.

1. Now create the NETAPPS and NETSYS shares on the server. If you installed TaskStation Mode, you do not have to create the NETAPPS share.

2. Share the NETAPPS folder assigning the global group Everyone Full Control on the share.

3. Initiate NTFS Security to the NETAPPS folder and all subfolders assigning the global group Everyone Read permission and the global group Domain Admins Full Control.

4. Assign the global group Everyone Change permission on the NETAPPS\OFF97\MSOFFICE\WORKDIR folder.

5. Share the NETSYS folder, giving the global group Domain Admins Read permission and remove the global group Everyone from the directory permissions list.

6. Initiate NTFS Security to this folder and all subfolders giving Domain Admins Full Control. Remove the global group Everyone from the directory permissions list.

Create the Start Menu on the Network

1. Log on with the administrator account for the local computer with the password that you supplied during ZAK setup.

2. Open Windows Explorer.

3. On the View menu, click Folder Options, selecting Show all files.

4. Copy all of the .lnk files in %SYSTEMROOT%\PROFILES\ALL USERS\START MENU to the NETAPPS\START MENU folder located on the server.

5. Copy the .lnk files in %SYSTEMROOT%\PROFILES\ALL USERS\START MENU\PROGRAMS to the NETAPPS\START MENU\PROGRAMS folder located on the server.

Creating a Windows 98 Autoinstall with

MSBATCH.INF

Windows 98 installs with the help of a script file called MSBATCH.INF. The MSBATCH.INF is located in the \SETUP\WIN98

directory of your distribution network share. Open the
MSBATCH.INF using Notepad and replace 00000-00000-00000-
00000-00000 with the Product Key for your site, which is
printed on either the Windows 98 CD or your Certificate of
Authenticity.

You will also want to change the Name, Org, and Client
Computer values in MSBATCH.INF. Default values are provided. The
[Setup], [NameAndOrg], and [Network] sections of the MSBATCH.INF
are listed here:

```
[Setup]
Express=1
InstallDir="C:\Windows"
InstallType=3
ProductKey="00000-00000-00000-00000-00000"
EBD=0
ShowEula=0
ChangeDir=0
OptionalComponents=1
Network=1
System=0
CCP=0
CleanBoot=0
Display=0
DevicePath=0
NoDirWarn=1
Uninstall=0
NoPrompt2Boot=1

[NameAndOrg]
Name="ZAK Users"
Org="Microsoft"
Display=0

[Network]
ComputerName="ZAKComputer"
Workgroup="MyDomain"
Display=0
PrimaryLogon=VREDIR
Clients=VREDIR
Protocols=MSTCP
Services=VSERVER
Security=DOMAIN
PassThroughAgent="MyDomain"
```

Final Steps for Starting ZAK Setup for Windows 98 Clients

To set up ZAK for a new Windows 98 Client, first log on to the NT Server with ZAKSETUP.BAT. The ZAKSETUP.BAT logon script batch file will run when you log on with the ZAKSETUP account.

Setup requires that you log in to the network several times throughout the process. Make sure you log in using the ZAKSETUP account so that Windows runs the ZAKSETUP.BAT logon script, which correctly maps the drives.

Using Notepad or another text editor, edit APPLOGON.BAT that was copied to the NETLOGON share of your PDC by the Zero Administration Kit Installation. You must check and replace the \\<office application server>\<netapps share> and the \\<dist-server>\<user share> values with the correct server and share names, respectively, that you entered during the ZAK install. For example, if the server name of your PDC is NTSERVER and the share name you assigned the \NETAPPS directory is NETAPPS, the values could be:

```
net use O: \\NTSEVER\NETAPPS
net use U: \\NTSERVER\USERS
```

Using Notepad, edit ZAKSETUP.BAT. You must change the \\<office application server>\<netapps share> as well as the \\<dist-server>\<setup share> values with the correct server and share names, respectively.

Active Zero Administration Settings for Windows 98 Clients

The following Windows 98 Zero Administration system policy settings are in effect for the TaskStation:

- Custom Shell: c:\program files\internet explorer\ iexplore.exe -k
- Use Secure Task Manager: Yes
- Disable Registry editing tools.

- Only run allowed Windows applications (with no applications in the list).

- Disable MS-DOS prompt.

- Disable single-mode MS-DOS applications.

Windows 98 AppStation System Policies

The following user shell restrictions are in effect for the AppStation:

- Remove the Run command.

- Remove folders from Settings on the Start Menu.

- Remove taskbar from Settings on the Start Menu.

- Remove the Find command.

- Hide drives in My Computer.

- No workgroup contents in Network Neighborhood.

- Hide all items on the desktop.

- Don't save settings on exit.

- Disable Registry editing tools.

- Disable MS-DOS prompt.

- Disable single-mode MS-DOS applications.

ZAK System Policy Choices for Windows 98 Clients

There are two ZAK system policy settings for Windows 98 clients. See Figure 16-29.

User \ Zero-Administration Settings

- *Custom shell*. A custom shell can be entered—for example, `iexplorer.exe`—for `TaskStation` clients.

- *Use secure task manager*. When enabled, this setting stops the use of Task Manager until the client has logged into the network.

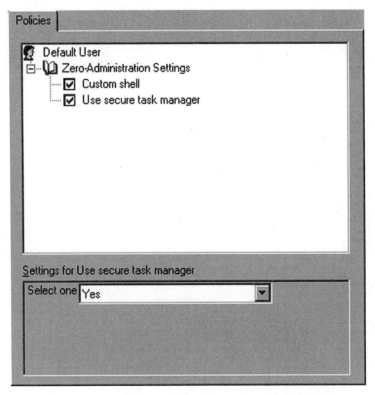

Figure 16-29 *ZAK system policy choices for Windows 98 clients.*

Index

About the Author

Mark Wilkins is a course director and technical instructor for Data Tech Institute, which provides technical seminars and video-based training materials to Fortune 500 companies around the world. He has taught numerous seminars for supporting and troubleshooting NT and Windows and has also contributed and/or co-authored *Bulletproofing NetWare* (McGraw-Hill, 1996) and *Windows 95 Registry for Dummies* (IDG).